W9-AZY-676

How to Live
Separately Together:
A Guide for
Working Couples

How to Live Separately Together: A Guide for Working Couples

Dick Irish

ANCHOR PRESS/DOUBLEDAY
GARDEN CITY, NEW YORK
1981

Brief excerpts from this book appeared in an entirely altered form in Glamour magazine, Association Management, and The Washington Post.

ISBN: 0-385-14650-7
Library of Congress Catalog Card Number 78-22637

Copyright © 1981 by Richard Irish

To all working couples hanging tough and taking pleasure in love and work:

> "Get on your knees and thank God
> You're on your feet."
>   (Old Irish Blessing)

QUESTION: "What should a normal person be able to do well?"
ANSWER: "Lieben und arbeiten."
(To love and work)

SIGMUND FREUD

Contents

Acknowledgments

Now is the time to praise famous men and women.

Thanks go to Rebecca Dembs Tinker for typing the first draft of the manuscript, Gloria Carter the second, and the Middleburg Secretarial Services the third. One of my employers, TransCentury Corporation, provided the paper and the paper clips and Warren Wiggins supplied inspiration; his thoughts on "circumferential mobility" provided a peg on which to hang some of my ideas (See *Ethics, Work and Worth*).

Peter Ognibene, no slouch as a writer himself, gave me the concept for the book for which he has earned my thanks and a free lunch at a place of *my* choosing. Don Cutler, my agent, placed the book with Loretta Barrett, my editor: thanks to both.

Ruth Farwell read over the manuscript in its final form and made important suggestions. And the entire staff of TransCentury Corporation offered many suggestions on which I imperfectly acted. That goes for the hundreds of people "living together," "married," and "remarried," I interviewed as part of my regular work.

Finally, thanks above all to my wife, Sally, who read and commented on the manuscript and provided invaluable advice. However, I wish she would knock off the cue cards, "On page 234, you say husbands should . . ." Well, you get the idea. But that's a fact of life for any writer about marriage who commits pen to paper!

Marshall, Virginia
September 10, 1980

Author, a Memorandum from the

TO: The Reader
SUBJECT: What this book is about, who should read it, how to use it, and why I wrote it.

This book can be read in a five-hour airline flight. It's a book to dip into anywhere—read backwards or forwards—organized like a glossary. Readers can find any subject in a few seconds and read everything I say about it in a few minutes. This book is much like a river: You can never step in the same river twice; it's the same and different. And a marriage is much like this book: No matter what angle you look at it, it's the same—and different. Thus, the last chapter could easily be the first. But if you want a narrative line, yes, by all means, start with the first chapter and then follow the thread of my thinking through the book.

A note on definitions:

Tough love means married love.

Responsibility means to yourself, not other people.

Money marriage means having the power to pursue happiness.

Happiness is feeling free.

Feeling free is becoming separate.

Becoming separate is quintessential to love and work.

To love and work is hanging tough and taking pleasure in both.

Hanging tough is saying "yes" to living when life says "no."

Taking pleasure is in the company of someone you love.

To keep you awake and me on my toes, short self-assessment statements precede each chapter. The point is to fit the shoe to your foot to see if it fits; if the shoe pinches, well, pain as well as pleasure is part of reality. Besides, I would rather challenge than please and if I do both, we both get a bonus.

The statements are simple declarations made by people talking about marriage. And I've thought many of the same things. The book is organized on the basis of these statements into a series of subjects (money, sex, time, housekeeping). Each statement is followed by what I think.

By the way, my messages are repeated in sometimes clumsy, sometimes cunning disguise throughout the book. I've learned I don't remember anything I read only once. That's why in the Navy every order is repeated three times so we won't miss the ship. So every idea is repeated different times in different ways in different places. My point has been made when you feel *impaled* on it!

For example, how many times have you heard people say, "There are *no* happy marriages"? My aim is to take this simple-minded statement by the nape of the neck, shake it hard, and separate out the sense from the nonsense. My aim is to jar you into thinking about love and work.

My tone is insufferably breezy and occasionally prickly. No apologies. It's, cross my heart and hope to die, my "defensive mechanism." I laugh about the business of marriage; otherwise I couldn't write about it. The *un*importance of being earnest is a major theme of this book.

This book is about money marriages—two-paycheck couples. But it's also for:

> Single types looking forward to marriage or a "relationship," as they say in California.
>
> Harried marrieds in midstream, swimming in rough water in opposite directions.
>
> People "living together."
>
> Those belly-up (the formerly married who want to try again).
>
> People exiting from displeasing marriages.
>
> Younger marrieds appalled by the divorce epidemic infecting their best married friends.

Finally, it's for traditional marrieds ("He works, she runs the home") who are considering a change. Oh, by the way, it's not true she doesn't *work!* Any wife with three kids, who is an effective home manager, and President of the PTA . . . works!

A few items to clear up but which will be mentioned again:

If yours is a money marriage, don't expect it to be glamorous. Don't be surprised if "other people" think your marriage *is* glamorous.

Don't be suckered into believing working parents are less effective parents. This could be true but it's not necessarily because each parent is working.

Don't give in to despair because you *can* buy real estate, draw up a trust and buy out a company, but *can't* make it with your husband, get it up with your wife or get along with your children. Everybody has trouble.

Forget the "We-ism" philosophy of marriage so popular in the fifties: The togetherness thing won't work. Also, the "helping others" syndrome—the mark of the sixties—is passé: People who help others and can't help themselves are burned-out Roman candles. As for the seventies, eschew at all costs "Me-ism"—Looking Out for Number 1: Narcissus pined away looking at his own image. For the eighties, forget *we* and *they* and *me* but focus instead on "I" and then "Thou." That's the perennial philosophy.

For those of you in money marriages caught up in a nostalgia kick to be single again: Pull yourself together! Single people spend most of their down-time trying to get something going; married folk already have something going. Working couples think they give up their freedom when they marry; to be free is to be single. The syndrome is sometimes called the "Seven-Year Itch." But the itch is to be free, not necessarily single. My aim is to show you how to *feel free* while "married."

Keep in mind, my form of address is sometimes androgynous. Sometimes it's difficult telling the wives from the husbands. That's because I'm talking to both. I'm deliberately non-sex specific: The way we *function* in marriage usually has nothing to do with whether we are male/female. It has everything to do with our being human. So, if you are comfortable saying, "How like a man!" or "Isn't that just like a woman!" then this book is bound to perturb.

This book is about hanging tough and taking pleasure in love and work. People with tough jobs and into tough love don't act any differently on the job than they do at home: Life is not a series of hermetic boxes.

"Don't give me any backchat. Just do it *my* way!"

Has your boss ever said that to you?

A certain kind of boss is likely to act in a certain kind of way. And we are likely to *react* in a certain kind of way. And remember, it doesn't matter whether you work for a man or woman (or whether you *are* a man or woman). Managers of either sex behave on the job in much the same way. And we react to authority (regardless of its gender) in much the same way. The same in marriage: The way we act and react with each other has far less to do with our sex than you might think.

So, by examining our actions both with our spouse, our boss, and our colleagues we can find out a lot about ourselves. Understanding how we react on the job helps us understand how we react at home: A working wife who can't fire her secretary at work probably is up-tight dealing with her babysitter at home; a man who hides behind his newspaper and won't talk to his wife might hide behind his work and knuckle under to his boss.

So, if your boss checks a red mark after your name if you are five minutes late to work, the chances are you work for an intimidator. Hell's bells, you might be married to one, too!

So this book is about human psychology. But I'm neither a psychologist nor a student of it. But, like you, I'm a people-watcher: Life is truly funny. Absurd. Not serious. Except when it's no longer funny. That's tragedy.*

The psychology and sociology of marriage is a subject largely reserved to academics, social scientists, psychologists, clergymen and an occasional philosopher. And women, my Gawd the women! Is it an-

---

* I'm grateful to Leslie Sanders, M.D., for this illuminating observation in his talk given to *Parents without Partners* at their Washington Chapter, later republished as "Divorce: Why Does It Happen? What Does It Mean?" in their monthly magazine.

other example of woman's historic oppression that she writes about marriage as if her life depended on it? Thus, there seems room for another point of view.

This book is about the taproot, trunk and crown of the marriage tree. I leave to more competent authority to differentiate amongst marriages: I want to touch on how every working couple's marriage is *like* every other, not how every marriage is *unlike* every other. It's a book about normal behavior, remember, not abnormal psychology. Thus, if before having sex with your wife, it's necessary for her to wear *your* galoshes, then I'm much afraid you must look elsewhere for help.

The focus of this book is on each person who reads it. No, not on you *and* your husband, not you *and* your wife. The book is neither for him nor her but you! I'm not interested in saving marriages; I'm not even interested in saving you! I am interested in you saving yourself. And that might mean getting a divorce, pronto. Simple observation reveals that if people are unhappy with each other and neither wants to change (or only one), then it's Splitsville. Same on the job: If our job turns sour, or we turn sour and we try our best to turn the situation around and it doesn't work, then far better to cut our losses and find other work.

At the same time, I'm alarmed by people in traditional, companionate and "dual-career" marriages who crumble in the face of difficulty and frustration. And the mindless jobhopping which masquerades as personal growth but reveals a feeble spirit. Anyone in midmarriage and midcareer, like myself, has been troubled by the rising tide of divorce. Of six ushers at my wedding (late fifties San Francisco rococo), five are divorced. Of my wife's six bridesmaids, four have been deep-sixed. Moreover, my thousands of interviews reveal that people just entering, midway into, and nearly at home plate in their careers find that the wreckage of their personal lives isn't helping their working lives.

So, there's a painful but obvious result of two-paycheck marriages: Divorce is more frequent. One reason is clear: Both partners make a living; they are economically independent. They don't *need* each other. A working wife especially feels free to give her old man his walking papers. And men no longer feel as "responsible" for working wives. Result: The divorce epidemic. But it's not so gloomy as it seems. People are no longer satisfied with the second-rate. Divorce—being able to exit from a miserable marriage—is a godsend. Freedom is enhanced. And the way is open for men and women to *want* each other. The difference between *needing* someone and *wanting* someone is another major theme of this book.

Money marriage is the norm rather than the exception. And anyone who is both working at a tough job and involved with someone who is working too, tells you it's tough. But many, who are just plain married, say it's tough as well. The money marriage is modern; the traditional marriage is in decline. But it's for each person to decide whether the money marriage is desirable or not. To be realistic, many wives *must* work to keep families financially afloat. My own opinion, although you didn't ask, is that there is much to be said for the traditional set-up. My problem (and yours, too) is my wife and I can't afford it! If you can, congratulations! Write a book!

My qualifications to write this book? Well, most importantly I wanted to write it. That's the most important reason for doing anything. Secondly, I interview for a living—hundreds of people every year. I've talked to thousands of people about their jobs. Lately, I've been talking to them about their marriages. And what people want is both a good job and a happy marriage. Love and work. Finally, I work and I'm married to a woman who works. We have taken pleasure both in a money and a traditional marriage, enjoyed employment and suffered unemployment, sailed on prosperous seas and into stormy weather: Marriage has been both a taffy-pull and a domestic symphony.* All of which "qualifies" me. But my most important qualification, indeed a reason to write a book, is to explain to myself a subject which has kept my interest for twenty years and always will, whether I divorce tomorrow or celebrate a golden anniversary.

What are your qualifications to read this book? Well, as if you read my mind, tough-mindedness helps. Readers unwilling to accept the condition of life ("Life is tough"), those wanting swift fixes to hard problems, and those who cope with problems by elimination or

---

* Easily the finest musical reflection of the reality of marriage is Richard Strauss's *The Domestic Symphony,* which captures, as literature can't, the high drama of family life.

evasion (circumvention is the longest distance between two points) won't like what I write. So having spirit is an important qualification.

One reason life is tough is that we all make mistakes. Mistake-making and learning from mistakes is how we grow. Thus, you aren't qualified if you can't admit mistakes and grapple with the guilt. In our civilization, all of us are up to our armpits in guilt. Another qualification of readership is being able to play with the pain of guilt. Accordingly, are you able to handle pleasure? Guilt accompanies pleasure down every lane. Thus, a lot of pleasure-hating married types cling to their disillusionment and show contempt. On the headstones of a million unhappy marriages is writ: "Here lie the remains of two people who died of contempt." That's because taking pleasure in each other's company causes guilt—more on this heavy stuff later. Finally, patient reader, intelligence, good humor, an open mind (and a mind of your own) are important qualifications. Since you obviously check out, read on.

If you're like me, you loathe self-help books. Well, we have something in common: I'm no expert at marriage and neither are you. That's another qualification of yours and mine. Experts mix up our lives by changing their minds every five years. Moreover, the American penchant for an expert opinion for every problem is simply the Utilitarian Tradition run amok. The Ben Franklin virus. On the job and in marriage and reconciling the two, there is no way we won't have problems. Experts try to solve problems. But the point is that living is a problem. That's reality. And co-operating with reality* makes more sense than trying to change it; refusing to co-operate with reality in marriage or on the job is lacking the expertise for either tough jobs or tough love. And no expert can help us.

"So, this book won't help me," you ask? No, it might help if you are willing to help yourself. Just what you learned in Sunday School; except you didn't believe it because you learned it in Sunday School! Well, if you help yourself it means thinking through what ails you on the job and in your marriage. And reading this book isn't

* Frederic Flach, M.D., in his book *A New Marriage, A New Life*, repeatedly uses the expression "cooperating with reality." It's superb and accurately reflects the reality of marriage (and life).

any help unless it helps you *think*. But, remember, thinking isn't doing any more than a concept of a poem is the poem itself. "Between the idea and the reality . . . falls the shadow" (Eliot). But if reading this book *does* help, well, yes, Doubleday/Anchor forwards packages; my favorite color is green. I love chocolate, and your checks and money orders will be cheerfully acknowledged.

Finally, Rule #1 (it's the only rule): Marriage doesn't count, people do. The spotlight is on you. "What am I getting out of this marriage?" you ask at home. And on the job you ask, "What am I getting out of my work except a paycheck?" And at home our mate asks us, "What's my pleasure in this marriage?" And on the job our boss asks, "What am I getting out of you besides your time?"

The answers to these tough questions are simple.* What we want most on the job is a sense of accomplishment. And at home what we want is the pleasure of someone's company. Feeling no sense of achievement on the job and taking no pleasure at home means you are, according to Herr Doktor Freud, unhappy; finding fulfillment in work and pleasure in love means you are happy. Unhappy people are abnormal. Happy people are normal. But normal people are a minority. It follows that the vast majority of working marrieds are crazy! Disillusioned. Impotent. Burned-out.

But it's people who make themselves unhappy, not "society." And as for the "times," "May you live in interesting times," is a well-known Chinese proverb. What's not so well known is that it's considered a curse. And we are cursed with our times as our great grandparents were cursed with theirs. But the spirit prevaileth in every age. Into every life a little rain must fall: And in some of our lives it's a goddamn downpour. But love and work are great umbrellas.

So, this book is for people tired of sleeping around, tired of being unhappy, tired of being tired. Mine is a cheerful proposition: If everyone is much unhappier than they seem, everyone can be much happier than they are. This book is for trend-buckers: It's for women who genuinely dig men, men who love women, people who

---

* Two other books worth reading if you want other answers are: *The Two Career Couple* by Francine and Douglas Hall and Caroline Bird's *The Two-Paycheck Marriage: How Women at Work Are Changing Life in America.*

are crazy about kids. It's about people in tough jobs and into tough love; finally, it's for people who find it difficult to love and be loved or who can only work in a state of resentment.

If working at a job is natural (like eating, drinking, and lovemaking) why do people make such a hash of it? If living with another person is natural (like sleeping, laughing, talking) why do people botch it? For the answers (well, *some* of the answers) let's enjoy between the covers of this book the pleasure of each other's company.

Attitude Is Everything

"Work consists of whatever a body is obliged to do, and Play consists of whatever a body is not obliged to do."

TOM SAWYER

"I love making my wife happy."

"My wife loves to make me happy."

"My job is more important than hers because I make the most money."

"His job is more important than mine because he makes the most money."

"Every morning I focus on what I 'ought' to do."

"When I bring home my paycheck I feel like I'm working for my mate."

"When I go to work each morning I say, 'I'm off to the salt mines.'"

"Working around the house (cooking, cleaning, paying the bills) makes me feel like I'm working for my mate."

"When he wants to make love, it's my duty to oblige him."

"When she wants to make love, I feel it's my duty."

"Happiness is forgetting the work ethic and following the fun ethic."

"I love making my wife happy."

Sure, you make her happy and then suddenly she's unhappy and . . . guess who is blamed? Well, it's you, my friend. And you can't bear being blamed (See *Conscience Doth Make Cowards*) for her unhappiness. So, you punish yourself and make yourself miserable. That makes two of you; another marriage made in heaven.

So, go to the blackboard and write a hundred times, "I'm not responsible for anyone's happiness."

Humor, like happiness, is something we yield to. Nobody "makes" us laugh; something inside of us causes us to laugh. Feeling free to yield to pleasure is the secret of pleasure. Protecting ourselves from pleasure earns us a reputation for having no sense of humor. The world is a funny place. If we begin to take the world—marriage and jobs—seriously, we close ourselves off to the pleasure. We cease to feel. But we don't "make" people laugh any more than we "make" them happy. Something in them causes them to laugh; causes them to be happy. We scratch the itch, but we don't cause it.

"My wife loves to make me happy."

Not strictly true.

It's truer to say you "make yourself happy with her." Otherwise it's but a short step to believing she is responsible for your misery. And since she hates to be blamed as much as you, everybody's miserable.

A great spirit—a tough ego—can be happy with someone who is miserable. An unlikely condition among the newly married but not uncommon among those couples who have "become separate."

Becoming separate is quintessential in marriage. That's because people in tough jobs and into tough love face stormy weather on the job—pressure, deadlines, bottom lines—and bring the storm clouds home with them. Frustration on the job overlaps into the home. Squalid. Facing up to bad days on the job, means facing down blaming our mates and, above all, blaming ourselves. Our working wives aren't responsible for our happiness and, try as we will, we can't make them so. Nobody can *make* us happy; we make ourselves happy with somebody.

It's impossible to genuinely please somebody and not please yourself at the same time. But people admonish you to please others and discourage you from pleasing yourself. Taking pleasure in love and work is to risk pleasing yourself every day. On the job, it's a great pleasure exercising your skills; at home it's a pleasure taking pleasure in the company you keep. Having people in for dinner is a pleasure if we invite them for the pleasure they bring us; having people in for dinner is a burden if we invite them because we "owe" them. Going out to dinner with friends is a pleasure; going out to dinner because friends "owe" us is a drag.

Sex is the best example of how focusing on your own pleasure is pleasing to others. The more focused on your own pleasure the more pleasing you are to your partner. Potency. The more, however, you focus on your partner's pleasure the less pleasing for both. Impotency.

"My job is more important than hers because I make the most money."

A common enough thought to most working men: Money is might; might makes right; he, therefore, calls the important shots.

Hmm.

So most men are wary of women who make more money than they do. "Let my wife make more money than me," he thinks, "and she'll call all the shots."

Attitude is everything. And if we think our self-worth is measured by the money we are paid, we value ourselves by the price other people put on our services. And letting other people establish our worth isn't feeling free.

It's reminiscent of Joe Stalin asking how many divisions the Pope could mobilize. It's like weighing the greatness of a nation by its land mass or measuring the value of a person by his height. So long as money is the measure of all things, we know the price of everything, and the value of nothing (Wilde). The quality of a money marriage has more to do with equity than equities. Money isn't the most important thing; it's the second most important thing (See *Money [and Time] Management*).

"His job is more important than mine because he makes the most money."

Working wives are no different from their heavy hitting husbands. "Money is power; he makes the most money, I am, therefore, powerless."

Working men of the world, awake!

It's possible that if you are younger and married, that her earnings might exceed yours. As a matter of fact, if you are middle-aging, it might happen. And for mentally robust people, it can't happen too soon!

Working couples earn two paychecks. If her paycheck is more than mine, combined with mine, we both *earn* more! The threat of my wife taking over and controlling me is *my* problem. For my wife to back off and earn less because she is *sensitive* to my feelings is bushwa.

Working couples need to straighten out on this point. Income is community property—it belongs *equally* to both parties. So if I make $10,000 per annum as a free-lance writer and my wife earns a cool $50,000 as a corporate lawyer, who's ahead? Both of us, dummy.

For me to think that my wife *controls* me (she makes more money), for me to think I'm controlled by my wife is crazy. Nobody controls anyone else.

Marriage is a fifty/fifty proposition. If my wife earns ninety-five percent of the income, I still count fifty percent. If I inherit a cool million tomorrow (don't I wish!), my wife still counts fifty percent. Thinking otherwise is a question of attitude. "I have the most money, therefore, I'm in charge." But nobody ought to be in charge. Who wants to live with someone who is in charge? Nobody wants to feel in another person's control.

"Every morning I focus on what I 'ought' to do."

Of a working day, most working couples focus on what they ought to do (and the list of oughts is endless) and rarely focus on what they want to do (indeed, there might not be a list!). Working couples, responsible people, are especially cursed. Between jobs and the home, there is no time for themselves (See *Money [and Time] Management*). But an important reason to work is to buy the time to savor it (Ellen Goodman).

Working couples who are merely married without feeling separate are filled with resentment. And a lot of people, single and married, can't work *except* in a state of resentment. Responsible people are caught up in fulfilling the needs of others and unaccomplished at fulfilling their own wants. What they want to do isn't what they ought to do. Anyone would feel resentment.

The essence of this condition is a working couple's suspicion about pleasure. The clinicians have a word for it: Anhedonia. The hatred of pleasure. And at bottom, a lot of working couples simply don't have any fun. But the whole point of being married is the pleasure we take in each other's company.

"When I bring home my paycheck I feel like I'm working for my mate."

Whenever we work for somebody else, we don't feel free. Working couples, thus, often can't take pleasure in each other's company: A husband in a traditional marriage, hating the responsibility and the economic burden of taking care of others, splits; his family is a millstone around his neck.

In money marriage, the situation is not so acute; both partners are independent and take care of themselves. Self-esteem is a product of taking care of oneself. Moreover, children without parents hovering about wiping noses and succoring needs might become more independent themselves. It depends on how successful mom and dad are in fostering self-reliance (See *Children's Hour*).

But if a working wife or husband thinks, "I'm working for my mate," it's no big secret why love and work aren't fun. Same on the job: Most working people feel they are working for their employers because they "need" to. People who stay in marriages because they are *needed*; people who work because they *need* to, don't feel free.

"Irresponsible" people feel enormous resentment: They live for others. But "response-able" people live for the self, have sex for their own pleasure, eat for their own delight, and hew wood and haul water to be warm and quench their thirst.

And breadwinners needn't feel guilty about not making enough money. There is never "enough." Nor should either partner feel guilty about spending "too much." The source of all the quarrels isn't about spending too much or earning too little. Quarrels are caused by the guilt each feels.

Stress is often a result of feeling guilty. Guilt diminishes effectiveness: Self-esteem suffers if we help others but never the self. The collapse of self-esteem itself causes more stress.

To reduce stress, become more self-aware; sense your separation from your environment; stop being responsible and be "responseable" instead.

Plenty of working wives—independent women—are complaining about their husbands' inability to cope with "the new woman." And plenty of men are complaining about "irresponsible" wives and mothers. Working wives bitch about men neglecting homemaking chores; working husbands *kvetch* about being the good wife to their wives!

It's confusing: Let a working wife try to be a "good homemaker," let a husband try playing the "good househusband" and both are likely (although not necessarily) to live and work together in a state of resentment. People who do what they *should*, hate it: They don't feel separate. "Good" people feel they have but one *other* choice: To be *bad*. Nice or nasty.

So, if attitude is everything, working couples have every reason to change their attitude about love and work. A good start is to focus every A.M. on one thing that day you want to do *least* and do it *first*. Everything we do the rest of the day will seem easy. Think about the thing you hate doing most and do that *first*: Always do first what you want to do *least*. If you must fire someone, do it first thing in the morning. Do you have a complex budget to work out? Do it first and let those letters and phone messages wait. Should you call your branch manager in Ypsilanti and chew him out? Don't put it off, do it! The wish is the father of the deed. Everything else the rest of the day will be a snap. Not putting first things first, not to selectively neglect lesser matters makes everything standing between you and an important task seem that much more difficult.

Doing what we want to do least first thing in the morning raises self-esteem, strengthens the ego, increaseth the human spirit.

"When I go to work each morning I say, 'I'm off to the salt mines.'"

Thus, you're serving a forty-year sentence at General Electric. Attitude is everything and your attitude smells to high heaven. To work at what we do and call it labor, to earn money for our family (and not for ourselves), to put everyone first but ourselves is contrary to human nature.

Everyone has a free will but most people won't admit it. To do so would be to take responsibility for their own happiness. But that means giving up blaming General Electric and our wife for our unhappiness. Ah, but taking responsibility for our happiness has its price! *Happiness* (take notes on this) *gives pleasure.* The price of happiness and pleasure is guilt. It follows, if we feel no pleasure on the job nor with our mate, we won't feel guilt either (See *Conscience Doth Make Cowards*). The perfect way to avoid paying the *price* of pleasure is to do what we "should" (go to the salt mines).

Figuring out what we want is a bitch. That's why most people do what they "should." It saves so much anxiety and thinking. And deciding what we *want* cannot be done *alone.* That's why marriage is such a help.

"Working around the house (cooking, cleaning, paying the bills) makes me feel like I'm working for my mate."

Feeling free.

We forget that when we cook dinner, rake the leaves, and negotiate with the plumber, we are working for the self. Plenty of women in traditional marriages, programmed to fulfill other people's needs (husband's darning, children's homework, PTA busywork), go berserk. The runaway wife, like runaway children, is a feature of our interesting times.

Women run away to "find themselves." "If I wasn't married to the bastard," she thinks, "I would be the premiere ballerina of the New York Ballet!" Traditional wives often resent their dependence and envy their husbands' independence. The homemaker's attitude is the counterpart of the breadwinning husband's. Each feels oppressed and hates it. They bug out: he to a bachelor pad, she to a women's commune. Both want their "freedom."

Household tasks, like workplace responsibilities, are not obligations we *must* perform unless we think so. And nothing is, but thinking makes it so. To iron our husband's shirts because we *must*; to budget family finances because we are *required*; to mop the floors because we *should* is oppressive.

So, we *want to* cook dinner for the family; we *want to* darn our husband's socks; we *want to* help our children with their homework. But we are free *not* to do these things. We are free to choose. It's our attitude about love and work which is everything. More important than *who* we love or *what* we do.

"When he wants to make love, it's my duty to oblige him."

"I need to make love," says this person.

"I want to make love," says that person.

What's the difference?

Well, it's attitude. The first person is willful; the second is willing. Our effectiveness on the job, our happiness in marriage, and our potency in bed depend on recognizing the difference.

To oblige our partners in the bedroom is the silly advice of dated marriage manuals. The whole point of lovemaking is the pleasure we take in it. And if we take pleasure in lovemaking we might give it. And that's a pleasure, too.

"When she wants to make love, I feel it's my duty."

When I say, "I need to mow the lawn," it's not the same thing as saying, "I *want* to mow the lawn."

"I *should* play tennis to stay in shape," is not the same thing as saying, "I want to play tennis and whip her ass good."

Using no-no verbs like *ought, should* and *have to* is thinking like an idiot. And working couples are crazy if they think there is any other purpose in marriage except the pleasure of each other's company. When it comes to work, being dutiful makes us lazy; when it comes to household tasks, being "responsible" makes us resentful;

when it comes to sex, being obligated makes us impotent. If we have a bad workout on the job, a bad workout on the tennis court, and a worse workout in bed, the problem, sports fans, is in our attitude.

So the message is *feeling free* to work, play tennis, and make love because we *want to*, not because we *ought to*. Going to work tomorrow because we *must* makes us hate our jobs; playing tennis because we *ought* could give tennis a bad name; making love because we *should* is simply self-immolation.

"Happiness is forgetting the work ethic and following the fun ethic."

A Puritan is someone who suspects that someone, somewhere, somehow is having a good time (Mencken). But the last Puritan died in this country *circa* 1948. Their grandchildren have turned the nonsense inside out. The fun people suspect someone, somewhere, somehow is taking real pains with his work, working up a healthy sweat, feeling a sense of accomplishment.

The work ethic is properly dead and buried; the fun ethic is dancing the valse triste. But the worth ethic is alive and well. The first died from a sense of duty; the second is dying of self-contempt; the third is living in the hearts of people who want to love and work.

The work ethic died from no enjoyment; "Doing my duty was my only happiness" reads its epitaph. The fun ethic is dying from mainlining sensations; "If it feels good, do it!" The trouble with the old work ethic was that people worked because they "should." The trouble with the fun ethic is that people work if it's "no sweat." But the fun ethic, like the work ethic, doesn't work. To work from a sense of duty defeats pleasure; to work strictly for fun wrecks our self-esteem.

Attitude is everything. But it's not an easy thing.

Baby, to Have or Have Not

Who is there whom bright and agreeable children do not attract to play and creep and prattle with them?

EPICTETUS

"Younger working couples should put Careers before a family."

"Having a child should be a rational act."

"Men are assuming an equal share of child management responsibilities in money marriages."

"Superwives have it all: Great careers, big bucks, sensational sex lives and polite, adorable children."

"Couples without children invariably have richer careers."

"Having a child ensures our immortality."

"Having a child ensures a rich old age."

"Working wives should have children when
   (a) they are young."
   (b) they are middle aged."

"Children limit personal growth."

"Having a child will save our marriage."

"It's OK to change our mind about children."

"Having a child shows faith in the future."

"Younger working couples should put Careers before a family."

Well, plenty of them do—education and work require an investment in emotion and time neither partner can make in a child. But
younger working couples make this tradeoff because they *want to*.
Other younger working couples may begin a family immediately;
one party might finance the other to a graduate degree; still another
couple might opt to work their way around the world. The point is
to figure out what you want.

To marry or not to marry?

To divorce or not to divorce?

To bear children or remain childless?

Crucial and painful decisions: It's understandable why we delay
and evade such decisions. Many people loathe themselves, put themselves down, and suffer dreadfully because of decisionphobia. But
some people are being too hard on the *self*. Not making a decision is
a decision. People's gut level feelings are saying, "Whoa, wait a minute!" And that's helpful. We need to know the "why" of a decision
before we make it. This means talking through all the elements of
baby, to have or have not. It's doing "market research" on the self.
It's establishing the price you must pay and asking yourself whether
you are *willing* to pay it.

Each of us in marriage and on the job needs to think through
what we want *without* taking into account our husband/our wife.
And if our decision requires our boss's/our wife's co-operation, well,
we consult, confer, conference—call it what you will—with them.
We do not issue Edicts nor do we feel subject to them. At work, our
boss is our colleague; at home, our wife is our partner. And a collegial atmosphere at work and at home is a free environment. So you
can't *order* your wife to have a baby; she can't command you to give
her one. What both can do is *discuss* it.

A working couple (he's a stockbroker in Minneapolis, she's a lawyer in the Governor's office) want to have a child. The risk is giving
up her income and depending on his commissions to pay their way.

Both must face the fact that they might be disappointed. Risk-management means coping with disappointment, rejection and mistake-making. The stock market might take a dive; motherhood could be a big bloody bore. But coping with mistakes, disappointment, and frustration is a definition of tough love.

"Having a child should be a rational act."

Procreation, like lust, which is its vehicle, often defies analysis. Don't ask me for a definition of the life force, but there is large agreement that it's irrational. Many working couples have babies against all the evidence of formal logic, elementary economics and common sense for reasons shrouded in mystery, wrapped in an enigma and tucked inside a puzzle.

The classical, religious understanding of parenthood, "Be fruitful and multiply," which so much offends the family planning types, encouraged the propagation of the species. Thank God most of our parents didn't believe in zero population growth! But working couples these days are foregoing children entirely or barely reproducing themselves. The advent of a live, bouncing baby is often cause for a minor riot.

So many reasons are advanced for the short fall in births (although demographers are noticing some interesting blips on their radar screens) that we forget the decision to have (or have not) a baby is a profoundly private and sometimes inexplicable act. Thinking through whether to have a baby is Topic #1 among many money marrieds and like every major transaction in life it should depend on our free will.

The greatest circumstantial cause in the baby bust is inflation. People "concerned" about the family had better start "caring" about the economy. The devastating effects of a thrice devalued dollar and the heedless debt-management required to keep most families afloat is destroying people's confidence in the future. People without confidence in the future lose their nerve.

People who lose their nerve don't want to bring children into a world bound to be worse than their own. And the upper middle class in this country is committing self-imposed class genocide: It's not reproducing itself.

*"Men are assuming an equal share of child management respon-
sibilities in money marriages."*

That's a sick joke, son.

Don't depend on men becoming mothers. Anatomy is destiny.
Women conceive, gestate and nurture children from womb through
graduate school and often long after. (And it seems to be taking
children longer and longer to leave home. That must be because it's
harder and harder for them to cope with frustration, i.e., become
independent, self-reliant, tax-paying producers [See *Children's
Hour*].)

No, children are generally *first* careers for working wives; children
are almost always *second* careers for husbands. If the money marriage is going to survive, however, this situation has gotta turn
around. Plainly, working couples each have a job. But their Career
is each other and their children (See *Ethics, Work and Worth*).

Think through this whole business of baby (to have or have not)
before filing a joint return. Otherwise it's trouble, trouble everywhere. Money marriages are often childless. If children distract us
from what we love to do, where's the pleasure in children? If he
wants a child and she doesn't, why consider marriage?

Yes, we can have love and work, there's a time and a place for everything. But we can only have what we want *one thing at a time*.
Otherwise we are setting ourselves up for the Superwife/Super-
man syndrome.

*"Superwives have it all: Great careers, big bucks, sensational sex
lives and polite, adorable children."*

Don't believe it.

Superwife is the figment of the overheated imaginations of the
New York media queens; she is as big a fiction to them as the
Cosmo girl. Working wives in money marriages who are both effec-
tive executives and effective mothers are anything but glamorous.

Feeling free means choosing between desirable objectives. Saying
"yes" to having a child means saying "no" to less desirable things.
And working wives who believe they can have *it all now*, are being
set-up for unhappiness. And a husband who believes his wife can be
all things to him (mother, mistress, friend, counselor, fix-it-gal, and

dual-career partner) is doomed to disillusionment. And disillusionment is the common state of the unhappily married.

"Couples without children invariably have richer careers."
Maybe so; maybe not.

Plenty of people feel strongly about the work they do. We might feel guilty because children don't figure in our plans. But feeling guilty is our problem. Inevitably, doing what we want causes guilt. So, conversely, if we take pleasure in our children, we could neglect our "careers." That, too, makes us feel guilty.

No matter how you cut the deck, so long as we do what we want, guilt raises its ugly head (See *Conscience Doth Make Cowards*). Self-esteem is central to human happiness. What's not so agreeable is coming to grips with the guilt associated with self-esteem—any kind of pleasure.

The courage to be happy with or without children means coping with the guilt which is pleasure's constant companion. No joke. Plenty of people have children *without pleasure* in order to avoid the guilt; plenty of people deny themselves children *without pleasure* in order to avoid the guilt. To act or not to act, to have baby or no, on the basis of avoiding guilt is the coward's way. Happy are the brave.

To have children today is to buck trends. It's an act of optimism. It's saying "yes" to the future. It's an act of faith. And the future belongs to those who have faith in it.

Younger men, determined to keep options open, overlook the sheer pleasure of fathering. Younger women, determined to become independent, repress the joy of mothering. Childless couples have no one to *love* but each other; couples without children have no one to *resent* but each other.

"Having a child ensures our immortality."
Forget this old chestnut.

It's said we live on through the lives of our children long after we die. But once dead, we can't be conscious of our children, although, heaven knows, they are aware of us (See *Momism*). Is that any reason to have a baby? King Tut isn't taking a Nile cruise to see his pyramids; we don't commute from the grave to our children's duplex apartment.

The reason to have a baby is because of the pleasure baby brings. To capitulate to grandparent desires, propagate for propagation's sake or bear a baby because "other people" are doing so (or not doing so) is hardly feeling free. And feeling free to have a baby or have not is central.

"Having children ensures a rich old age."

In olden days, in traditional cultures of extended families, children were the economic support of parents and grandparents. The young provided the social security for the old. But in our times, the boom in the nursing home industry evidences the decay of the extended family. And we are advised by learned counsel never to live with our children.

Hmm.

We quarrel about the merits and demerits for the decline in the family in America. But plainly we can't depend on our children wanting to (or even having the means) economically or socially to enrich our sunset years. And there is much evidence to suggest that if we *need* our children to sustain us in the final lap we resent them for it; and they might resent us.

"Working wives should have children when
  (a) *they are young."*
  (b) *they are middle aged."*
Women ambitious to fast-track to the top in an organization might miss the bus if they buy into motherhood in their twenties. But women who postpone children until midlife risk missing the bus in midcareer when they have the best shot at advancement. And if women delay children to midlife, they might forego children entirely.

Either way, if a working wife wants to mother in a semi-traditional manner, she is limiting her "career" development. But if children are part of her Career, then the price in "career" advancement is traded off for the pleasure of child development.

And for both working men and women, children can be a burden if they come before one or both have made their mark (earning a living doing what each wants). But if children are postponed until "careers" are underway, then parenting is by remote control. The sheer emotional exhaustion and physical displacement (the sixteen-hour-a-day marathon/the Monday morning red-eye special) obviate the pleasure of each other's company and the joy of parenting (See *Money [and Time] Management*).

To have a baby (or have not) is confusing. It depends on what each person *wants*. And if we think our "career" is circumferential (rather than linear), then children are part of our Career development (See *Ethics, Work and Worth*). If working couples want children, they factor it into the Career equation. That means defining our Career circumferentially (who I am is more than what I do). The care and feeding of kids—far from being a burden on our "careers"—are their capstone.

Particularly for working mothers, trekking off to the job each day tests the ability to separate from the child, to become a caring parent rather than a concerned one. Children are experts at exploiting parental guilt: "Mommy, why do you have to go to work today?" As for dad, he might be no help: Fathers often think children are their wives' responsibility.

Especially in the early years, fathers are protectors. This is not a corny proposition. Working wives are especially vulnerable to the demands of both a job and children; they love all the help they can get. And fathers who don't pitch in and help out risk losing the children to their mother. Mom simply finds more satisfaction in junior than in pop. And any man who wants to protect *his* self-interests wants mom to be interested in him!

So that means dad stays home from work when young Priscilla has the croup and the housekeeper is snow-bound or the day-care center is closed while working wifey catches the commuter train. For many working fathers, this is an "irresponsible" idea. Isn't it their responsibility to go out and nail those bearskins against the wall? Well, no longer: Working couples in money marriages are *both* moneymakers and homemakers. Each has his/her job. But their "Career" is the home.

"*Children limit personal growth.*"

Children don't limit us so much as shape us. It all depends on our attitude. And having baby for the pleasure the child brings is the right attitude. Having baby for any other reason is the wrong attitude.

Children are a stage in personal development. Parenting follows marriage as surely as marriage follows adolescence. But for working couples still in emotional adolescence, having a child is irresponsible. Responsible parents want children for the pleasure they bring. Taking pleasure in another person (marriage) and extending this pleasure through children is real parenting. It's a joy. We love the responsibility of children because of the pleasure they bring.

She has her career, he has his job, but the home is their "Career" (See *Ethics, Work and Worth*). That's why the housekeeper's flu is a greater crisis than your upcoming hernia operation. Why the money marriage is literal: Each partner works to earn the scratch to pay for services (like a housekeeper) you normally wouldn't want or couldn't afford if only one partner worked.

Flexibility marks the working money marriage and co-operating with reality, the housekeeper's flu, means dropping everything and finding a pinch hitter *now* to substitute for your housekeeper.

Pinch hitters are grandparents, au pair girls, friends and neighbors. And if they aren't available, it means thrashing out with your spouse who minds the home.

Self-management is the way to manage a crisis. Our attitude is everything. How we react to pressure from outside events depends a lot on what's going on inside our minds. Straightening out the confusion inside our heads precedes crisis management.

"*Having a child will save our marriage.*"

Oh, forget about the marriage!

Children no more than money save marriages. Thinking a child can save your marriage is no different from thinking not having a child can save it. The point is, do you want a baby or don't you? And does your mate agree? And if not, are you both talking about it?

Answer these tough questions:

(1) Are you both able to make a living doing what you want?

(2) Do you take pleasure in each other's company?

(3) Are you *willing* to have children?

If what we do dissatisfies us and we take little pleasure in our mate, why extend this unhappiness to children? Such children are truly unwanted. Everybody agrees that we owe it to ourselves *to want* children in the first place.

What about second marriages?

Second marriages, according to the conventional wisdom, are more successful than first. But why do forty-seven percent of them fail? And what about the children in second marriages?

A baby is a powerful way to transform his *first* family and *hers* into another family. The wicked stepmother now has her chance to be the "good" mother (See *Breaking Up* [*and Starting Over*]). Having a child in a second marriage shows you have hope for the future. But if you have second thoughts about it, hold off on baby—especially until you have the stepparenting knot untied.

"It's OK to change our mind about children."

It's OK to change your mind anytime about anything. No commitment is unbreakable even to the person we are married to; that's why there's divorce.

But changing my mind about baby doesn't mean my wife is going to change her mind. Everyone wants to have a mind of his or her own. And what we want at age twenty-six isn't necessarily what we want at thirty-six. Hanging tough in love and work means in the marrow of our bones knowing what I want doesn't mean my mate will want it, too. But taking pleasure in love and work means feeling free to express our wants.

So, if your wife wants a baby and you don't, think about a divorce. But it might be useful before you call a lawyer to check with a psychiatrist. How can you be *sure* you don't want a baby? (See *Therapy, the Uses of.*)

And if wanted children become unwanted, clearly a divorce is indicated. Children accompany the parent they want and who wants them. And if it's neither parent, it's either the extended family or the State which must take over. Tragedy. An unwanted child is crippled for life. A definition of heroism is an unwanted child who overcomes this misfortune through the strength of his spirit.

"Having a child shows faith in the future."

And faith in yourself. Taking pleasure in children and liking their company is a blessing. Joy isn't rational. Try to analyze it and you kill it. But deep down inside, we know we are eternal (Wilde). And we know it in the company of our children as we know it with no one else.

Becoming Separate

> He who binds to himself a joy
> Doth the winged life destroy
> But he who kisses the joy as it flies
> Lives in Eternitys sun rise

WILLIAM BLAKE

" 'Becoming separate' is a question of separate vacations."

"Marriage is greater than the sum of its parts."

"Being married is a question of my wife becoming what I expect her to be."

"Becoming separate is being dependable."

"Being married is a question of my husband becoming what I expect him to be."

"I hate being nagged for every nitpicking thing."

"I hate nagging my wife to do things I can do myself."

"I often feel free with complete strangers and inseparate with my family."

"If both of us have a crazy day on the job, our marriage goes crazy!"

"Our marriage is more like a business partnership than a marriage."

"Becoming separate is becoming the person I want to be."

"Every successful marriage is a 're-marriage'" (Frederic Flach).

" 'Becoming separate' is a question of separate vacations."

It depends. Everything that's important, *depends!*

If I say, "I want to get rid of my wife," it translates "I don't feel separate at home." I don't feel separate at home and I think separate vacations is the way to separate in my head. Much better I say, "I want to go to Greece and check out the Parthenon," and my wife says, "I want to go to Aspen for the summer music festival." Both declarations are authentic expressions of the free will. But if our plans for the holidays are simple rationalizations to physically eliminate our mates, no dice. Attitude is everything.

Separate vacations, like separate tables and separate bedrooms, is no way to become involved. Some people who yearn for separate vacations don't feel separate at home. And probably never felt separate from mom (See *Momism*). True separation is a state of mind, not a geographical matter.

"Marriage is greater than the sum of its parts."

Score: My Marriage: 72
        Me: 6

Ignore the marriage! That way each partner *is as important* as his mate.

Why?

Well, each partner wants to feel free, separate and involved. But if both partners feel like a team, it's bad teamwork not playing the marriage game. But marriage is no game. It's not a team sport. It's simply two people taking pleasure in each other's company. And nobody can take pleasure in other people if they don't feel separate.

"Being married is a question of my wife becoming what I expect her to be."

A certain sign a marriage is on its second lap is when the partners to it create a mutual Rehab Society. People want their partners to change into the person each wants the other to be. This is surely the funniest and (when it's no longer funny) the tragic aspect of "being married."

"Men are April when they woo, December when they wed: maids are May when they are maids, but the sky changes when they are wives" (Shakespeare). After we set up house together, well, the sky changes. I'm still perfect, of course; it's my wife who needs shaping up.

A working wife can't become what her husband wants her to be unless *she wants to;* a husband can't become what his wife wants him to become unless *he wants to.* The essence of being separate is to focus on what he wants and let her focus on what she wants. This is responsible. If we shift the focus and insist our partners become what we want them to be, this is irresponsible.

"Well, I'm nearly perfect," he yells, "but you need shaping up!"

"That's just the way I am," she screams, "but you need to change!"

Trying to instruct, reform and enlighten our mates is the main business of the merely married. It's compulsive behavior—we seemingly can't help ourselves. And there's no pleasure in it. To undertake the reformation of our spouse is irresponsible. He insists she become responsive to him in order to avoid his own sense of responsibility to himself.

"Becoming separate is being dependable."

If you're a working wife and you can't
   change a washer
   start a lawn mower
   file an income tax return
   check the oil in the car
   deal with the plumber
   change a fuse
and a hundred other things you depend on your husband to do, then it's time you learned. Acquiring a proficiency in trivial tasks is a great boon to self-esteem. And teaches, as nothing else does, that there is nothing in marriage which is trivial.

If you're a husband of a working wife and you can't
   boil an egg (and peel it!)

stock a refrigerator
thread a needle
cope with the cleaning woman
arrange a dinner party
write a thank-you letter

and a hundred other things you depend on your wife to do, then it's time you learned. And your self-esteem grows, too.

Both partners in a money marriage want to be able to take care of themselves. If each can take care of the self, both are bound to feel separate with the other. She no longer needs him; he no longer needs her. Rather, she now *wants* him; he *wants* her.

So, the point is to *catch* yourself nagging. Know thyself. And being self-aware means examining *why* you launch a nag attack on thy spouse: You don't feel separate. "That's her job," he says. "That's his responsibility," she says. Nobody feels free.

Giving up feeling dependent means becoming separate. Husbands cannot be fathers to their wives; wives can't be their husbands' mothers. Emptying the garbage, feeding the three-year-old, weeding the rock garden *yourself* is a way to impress the self (take care of yourself). If you still feel resentful (and you will, you will!), it's because you still don't feel separate. Free. Doing what you expect "other people" to do and never letting them forget it is being a nag.

"Being married is a question of my husband becoming what I expect him to be."

You want your husband at various times to be:

Gary Cooper (when you hear a burglar downstairs).

Rhett Butler (on a summer night and after your second gimlet).

Sigmund Freud (when your therapist is on vacation).

the Marx Brothers (when you want some laughs).

John Paul Getty (when you fancy a three-month oriental vacation).

What wife hasn't thought as much while married? Surely, she thought the same thing about mom and dad and maybe brother and sister. She didn't feel separate from them (See *Momism*) and she doesn't feel separate from her husband, either, so, she tries to shape up her husband, but it doesn't work. And she knows she's a nag and hates herself for it!

The antidote to nagging your husband into being what you want him to be is becoming the person you want to be. That means being self-aware (See *Know Thyself*). A self-manager. Becoming responsible for your own happiness—so easy to say, so hard to do—is feeling separate from the person you live with. It's what younger people call space. But the space you want is inside your mind. The space is your sense of separation without which you can't feel free to be involved with your partner.

So, the lesson is that she can't change him and he can't change her. We are not responsible for each other. We are, however, responsible to the self. And the way to promote change in the person we live with is to change ourselves. Moreover, we might change into a person our mate no longer *needs!* Don't expect people necessarily to *like* the new you! But the new you forces your mate to adjust to your new moves. And this person can't adjust unless he learns some new moves, too!

A lot of men caught up in responsibilities forget one purpose of both work and love is to have fun. The idea might never violate their minds. And they might, therefore, be jealous of wives who know how to have a good time. They might envy them being "irresponsible." Feckless. Dizzy. Is it why they married such women in the first place? Crazy women attract sober men. Sober men arouse crazy women.

Well, she's probably crazy like her mom; he's probably an old sobersides because of *his* mom. She feels he will make her more responsible and he thinks she will make him happy.

Attraction between opposites causes an electrical short. Suddenly this marriage doesn't throw off sparks. The sympathy between opposites becomes antipathy. A drag.

The drag we feel is our own anchor chain scraping bottom. But each thinks the other is the drag. He must give up thinking it's his duty to take care of her; she must give up thinking she needs someone to take care of her. The focus is on the self, never each other. Otherwise he simply feels a greater responsibility and she a greater dependence. But if each zeros-in on the self, the thrill of self-discovery ("Golly, I can so have fun!" and "Gee, whiz, I can so make a living!") frees both parties to take pleasure in each other's company.

"I hate being nagged for every nitpicking thing."

If we look deeply inside ourselves, we didn't much like being nagged by mom. She was always after us to do something. And married types are always after each other to do something. It's easy to understand why we don't feel free. Henpecked as kids we peck like hens while married.

So, if you catch yourself talking to your husband just like your mom talked to you or if you nag your wife to do something your mother always did for you, that's a start. Most people resented nagging when they were young and resent it now that they are older.

But, if . . .

> he's as blind as a bat and insists on driving (and she doesn't raise a row)
>
> she makes the worst cup of coffee in the Commonwealth of Massachusetts (and he's afraid to tell her so)
>
> he's as tight as a tick (and she hesitates to call something by its real name)
>
> she's a practicing hypochrondriac (but he backs off telling her what he thinks)

you have a problem being critical, and being criticized.

The unwritten pact between many working couples is, "Don't fault me and I won't fault you." Nonaggression pacts aren't peace—they signify cold wars. Besides, peace between marrieds is usually indifference. People no longer care: "Married" people.

Married people who smoke the peace pipe bore each other to death. But it's nice having a man about the house she can resent; it's nice coming home to a woman he can complain about! Enjoying each other's company means being tough enough to criticize and bear criticism.

Criticism isn't necessarily nagging: It often helps us become separate. We are made aware of what we are blind to in our unreal character. Another reason why marriage helps you to feel free. Single people have no one to point out the egg on their necktie.

So, my responsibility, when I catch my wife using my straight-edge razor to shave her legs, is to raise a row. It's a first step forward, a boost toward her becoming self-critical: She catches herself using my razor. Once she is *aware* of herself she can do something about herself. My wife's responsibility to herself is to raise a little *quiet* hell when she catches me using her toothbrush. That way she helps me become *aware* of myself.

"I hate nagging my wife to do things I can do myself."

In money marriage, the economic independence of the partners doesn't protect either from the perils of dependent conduct. Indeed, the close coordination between both partners often makes each feel more dependent than ever on the other. The chances of a nag-attack are augmented; the opportunities for becoming a nag yourself are increased.

And don't believe nagging is a female complaint. Husbands nag wives and children are often accomplished masters. Nagging and being nagged is often the main form of conversation in marriage. But nobody admits to liking it; everybody affects to hate it. Yet what we really hate is our dependence on another person and/or his/her dependence on us.

Blaming unhappiness on what is outside of us (rather than inside) is like blaming the foul weather for our gloomy mood; sure a cloudy, rainy day reinforces our own poor mood or dampens our happy disposition: It affects us, but it doesn't cause gloom. The same with the person we live with.

"I often feel free with complete strangers and inseparate with my family."

Brief encounters; one-night stands; entrancing Epiphanies.

We are surprised by joy. Potency (on the edge of our consciousness) is suddenly the center of our being. Brief encounters prove men and women are naturally potent; impotence is an acquired and carefully indoctrinated state of mind. Government, Business, the Trade Unions, Churches, and Schools (above all, Schools!) train people to be docile, dull and dependent. Many married people are a monument to the triumph of impotency. But impotent people are unable to feel pleasure and sure as hell can't give it.

Often before we marry, what attracts us to another person is whether we are attractive. "She needs me," he says to himself. But after we marry, being needed is a burden. Before she marries, she says, "I need someone to take care of me; I'm attracted to him!" After she marries, she begins to hate being dependent on Mr. Big Man. It's suffocating.

But with strangers, we feel separate; with family and friends we feel inseparate. Indeed, the pact within families is *don't challenge me*. Don't reveal my weaknesses. Don't humiliate me. Don't let me see my impotence.

"If both of us have a crazy day on the job, our marriage goes crazy!"

Oh, fie on the marriage!

It's you who are crazy; the marriage is fine! Of course, if he blows a case in court and she botches the inventory at work, neither is going to take pleasure in the other. Each person's self-esteem has taken a lickin'! Tough love means in moments of defeat hanging tough with each other. If neither party blows up at the other, it's a miracle. If both parties blow up *at* the other, it's a marriage. Tough love means we have someone to resent when our jobs turn sour and that our companion is tough enough to take it. But if both partners to a working couple's marriage can't stand the heat in the kitchen, then neither is qualified for tough love. The marriage of strong wills means playing with the pain. If we stub our toe, we say "ouch!" If we suffer from a bad blow at work, we say "ouch!" And our partners hear us howl.

"Our marriage is more like a business partnership than a marriage."

It requires an accountant, a travel agent, a day-care worker, a psychotherapist, a gardener, assorted cooks and bottle washers and a first-rate plumber. Well, marriages *are* business partnerships (ask any divorce lawyer or CPA). But the point of this outside expertise is to buy the time to take pleasure with ourselves and each other. Forgetting the ends of marriage and focusing entirely on the means is a definition of fanaticism (George Santayana). We are invested in the Marriage and no longer vested in ourselves.

Burned-out.

Small wonder we burn out! "I'm not getting anything out of this marriage," this guy complains. "I'm not charged-up on the job anymore," that gal moans. And it's usually our attitude; we don't feel separate.

People who feel separate and free on the job become *involved*. Married people who feel separate and free become *involved*. Thus, we are able to say both "yes" and "no." A burnt-out case has no choice; he can't answer. Saying "yes" means being *committed*; saying "no" means being *selfish*.

In my marriage, both my wife and I work *part-time*. That adds up to one *full-time* career. The price we pay is reduced income; the pleasure we consume is more time with ourselves and each other. Start saying "no" to "success." If our jobs consume us, life together won't work. "There will be no marriage today because of a lack of interest," the announcement reads in the paper.

"Becoming separate is becoming the person I want to be."
 Tough.
And it's impossible doing this alone. It's possible but still difficult while married. And the point of being married is to increase your freedom, not diminish it. But nobody can be free while married who doesn't feel separate. Feeling separate is feeling free. Tough love— married love—won't thrive unless both parties feel separate. And unseparated partners don't feel free to become involved.

Check yourself out: See if you're feeling more separate from the person you live with. Saying "yea" to every one of the following statements means (a) you're either an incorrigible liar or (b) uncommonly happy:
 "Becoming separate in my marriage is feeling
   Pleasure *and* pain (apathy is feeling inseparate)."
   Free to divorce (no commitment is unbreakable)."
   Guilt (becoming separate causes pleasure *and* guilt)."
   Free to do what your spouse normally does for you (becoming a
     dependable person)."
   Free to disobey (thus, you are free to obey)."
   Free to focus on self-interests (otherwise you can't protect your
     interests)."

Free to love (the inability to love is a definition of hell)."

Free to show anger (the inability to show anger means you aren't free to love)."

Lovable (self-contempt is intolerable)."

Responsible to yourself (feeling responsible for other people isn't feeling free)."

Free to say 'yes' or 'no' (always saying yes/no means you don't feel separate from other people)."

Free to give up feeling in control and being controlled (nobody is in control)."

Free to change yourself (and not change your mate)."

Able to support yourself (people love taking care of the self)."

Free to be co-operative (unseparated people can't co-operate)."

Free to take pleasure in your mate (nobody is free alone)."

"Every successful marriage is a 're-marriage'" (Frederic Flach).

Most marriages are between emotional cripples. The rocks in his head fill the holes in hers. And each party often changes into what the other one doesn't *need:* The reasons we marry are no longer the reasons we stay married.

There are three results: (a) Both partners sink into apathy; (b) both fly to Haiti for a quickie divorce; (c) both become separate while married—remarried. Becoming separate is becoming the person you want to be. But lots of folks go to the altar and retire. Home safe. But no one is safe in marriage.

"Being married" is being lonely together. Becoming separate—remarriage—is being alone together.

Being My Own Boss

"Why, Hal, 'tis my vocation, Hal; 'tis no sin for a man to labour in his vocation."

SHAKESPEARE, *King Henry IV* (Part One)

"Being my own boss means depending on my wife's salary."

"Both of us becoming self-employed is too risky."

"Two big salaries means we work part-time for Uncle Sam."

"Being my own boss means using other people's money on behalf of my enterprise."

"Being my own boss means taking a sharp reduction in income."

"Being my own boss means being able to price my product or service."

"Being my own boss means learning from my mistakes."

"Being my own boss means being self-disciplined."

"Being my own boss means being able to take risks."

"Being my own boss means living with and learning from disappointments."

"Being my own boss means working alone."

"Being able to cope with success is a part of being my own boss."

"Being my own boss means depending on my wife's salary."

Being your own boss is the dream of most working Americans. The money marriage makes it possible. Living on one paycheck serves as a *base* to become a peanut-futures speculator, a fast-food franchiser, or a self-employed consultant. Conversely, if we become our own boss, our earnings become a *base* for our wage-earning partner to do the same.

Well, before plunging into the capital markets, writing a stock prospectus or buying a wholesaler's license, it's smart thinking through whether you have what it takes to be the boss. We know eighty percent of new entrepreneurs fail because of insufficient capital and/or poor management. What's not so well known is the kind of personal characteristics most successful entrepreneurs possess.

The most important characteristic is the ability to manage oneself. Self-management. Plenty of working people in big organizations thrive on being managers or on being managed. But being our own boss is another story.

In money marriages, plenty of partners can't bring themselves to *depend* on their mate's salary. Many men "lose control" of their lives; many wives prefer salaried jobs to self-employment because they want to help other people. The key to being our own boss is our attitude: If we can't be *dependent* on others (banks, clients, staff, husbands/wives) or we can work for other people and not the self, we aren't cut out for being our own boss.

In business, as in life, we are dependent upon others and are depended upon *by* others all the time. But *being dependent* can cause resentment; being *depended upon* can be a burden. Truly responsible people are those who are dependent and dependable without feeling a loss of freedom. People often resist working co-operatively, fearing a "loss of control"; being dependent on others often makes people think they are being "taken care of." Either attitude is a disqualification for self-employment.

"Both of us becoming self-employed is too risky."

It's better to become self-employed *one-by-one.* As soon as one partner has earnings su. ient to make the mortgage payments and buy the victuals, it's time for the other to do his/her thing. This keeps the anxiety quotient at a manageable level.

Anxiety—the fear of failure/the fear of success—is a major hurdle for the self-employed. Anxiety is paralyzing. It clouds clear thinking and cripples executive action. We are unqualified for self-employment if we can't manage anxiety.

Less than eight percent of the working public today is self-employed and the figure is falling. That includes small farmers, businessmen and women, and self-employed contractors. But money marriages are the perfect institutions to promote self-employment.

If working marrieds want to be their own boss, each needs to look at the world of work and ask what the "world" wants done. Fulfilling needs, doing what other people will pay you money to do, is the secret of finding good jobs. And it's the secret of making your own job—being your own boss.

The risk is failure. That is, being *wrong* about what the world wants. But in thinking through what they want to do and meshing it with what the world wants doing, potential entrepreneurs are training themselves to think about themselves and work in a far more realistic manner than most job-seekers who are caught up in fulfilling employer needs but not their own wants.

"Two big salaries means we work part-time for Uncle Sam."

Whether you drive an eighteen-wheel Mack truck (and your spouse works as a school dietician) or you're a vice-president for corporate finance (and your spouse is a department store buyer), the time you clock for Uncle Sugar is staggering. That's why one (and eventually both of you) ought to consider being your own boss.

The price you pay for the pleasure of being your own boss is often a drastic reduction in income. One of the curious things about going into business for yourself is the difficulty in making money! That's the bad news; the good news is that Uncle Sam lets you take five years! Also, every dime you make which is a business expense is nontaxable. Any accountant, lawyer or self-employed person can give you a clear picture on how Uncle Sam helps us become self-employed. No other country in the world offers as many self-employment opportunities as America. In money marriages, self-employment is often *the* answer to myriad problems of careerism, time-management, housekeeping, and, yes, even child-care (plenty of self-employed people manage cottage industries at home and watch the kids at the same time).

The pleasure of being your own boss goes without saying. The price of pleasure—reduced income, dependency, risk—are talked about altogether *too* much. But what nobody talks about at all, buckle your seat belts, is the *guilt* of becoming successfully self-employed. That's right. Pleasure for many is inevitably accompanied by feelings of conscience. "I should be putting in time at ITT, not lollygagging about doing my own thing," we say. Thus, doth conscience make cowards of us all.

"Being my own boss means using other people's money on behalf of my enterprise."

Plenty of otherwise capable people can't spend money on themselves. A debt to others (or a debt to themselves!) is a no-no. But using other people's money (and our own) is a qualification for self-employment.

Again, the dependency ghost spooks us out. The responsibility to others (creditors) defeats us. But the problem, as in marriage, is in our minds. The paralyzing sense of responsibility is itself the enemy, not the fact that we need a $50,000 line of credit. And being a responsible person, like being a responsible parent, a responsible husband/wife, heaven help us, is the source of the problem. Until we give up being "responsible to others" we won't be responsible to ourselves.

And being our own boss means being responsible to the self. That's the major qualification—self-management—in being able to use "other people's" money. An entrepreneur is somebody who uses other people's money on his own behalf. Effective entrepreneurs know how to make money using other people's money.

"Being my own boss means taking a sharp reduction in income."

Entrepreneurs plow back earnings into the business. Real income —our salary—is often drastically reduced. If spendable earnings are a measure of our self-esteem, our feelings about ourselves could plummet. But the real compensation in becoming our own boss is psychic: Being self-reliant is worth more than a paid vacation on somebody else's payroll.

Moreover, our reduction in spendable earnings, if we become a going concern, is temporary. Sure, making money is the toughest aspect of being self-employed: It takes time. But in time our spendable earnings could double or triple.

"Being my own boss means being able to price my product or service."

Tricky.

The vast majority of people who try self-employment and fail— *under-price*. They don't pay themselves back for the cost of being in business nor for the risks they take. Nor do they cost-out the time it takes to make an idea work and factor it into the price. *Time, risk,* and *being in business* are the hidden capital expenditures of ideas entrepreneurs put into action.

Still another problem is the inability of a lot of people to be *profit oriented*. The plain truth is that our educational system is graduating people into the economy with no understanding of or sympathy for the point of profits in making a free society *work*. To take a profit on our labor is considered a heinous sin; to make a profit is to steal. "You first" people have no business becoming self-employed: They are unqualified.

"Being my own boss means learning from my mistakes."

Becoming the boss means making our own decisions. Making decisions means making mistakes. People who can't make decisions don't make mistakes but can't become self-employed. Being able to drop the gate on a great idea (which isn't working), firing our best friend (who isn't paying his way), and cutting our losses is essential. The essence of being our own boss is not making money, as such, but in ceasing to do what is *losing* us money. Entrepreneurs are bound to make some right decisions (about one in three times). The trick is to *stop* doing what is preventing us making money.

Mistake-making.

Being able to make mistakes in marriage, on-the-job, and in your own business is essential. Being your own boss means there is no one to pass the buck *to,* no one to cover our ass *from,* no "system" to blame. Taking responsibility for your own failures (and successes) is being able to respond to the self, not to others.

There is an abundant literature written by women, for women, and of women the theme of which is the need for risk-taking. Everywhere a woman turns there is some authority pronouncing on the subject. A disguised premise is that *men* know how to take risks (and that women must *acquire* the same *skill*).

Well, for openers, taking risks is not a skill, it's a state of mind. Second, men spend a good deal of time *reducing* risks. Thirdly, the greatest risk is never taking risks. Fourthly, the reason people evade risks—quite properly—is that, in Lenin's phrase, objective conditions aren't propitious. Finally, the inability to take risks is usually a product of a wasted will and a lack of courage. Existentially, our greatest risk is being born; it's inevitable we die.

Anxiety is the problem. Too much of it and we can't make decisions, much less take risks; too little of it and we sink into a state of apathy, loathing the security of a risk-free life. Striking a proper balance between liberty and security (a risky and a risk-free existence) is crucial.

"Being my own boss means being self-disciplined."

Everybody hates discipline. Becoming our own boss means becoming our own worst critic, censor and taskmaster. We compete against ourselves: Our record. Self-discipline comes from within. Being disciplined comes from without.

This matter of self-discipline is tough on people trained to be impotent. That is, trained to respond to other people: Unless they are in somebody else's control—on somebody's payroll—they feel *out of control.* Undisciplined.

The undisciplined mind is not innate: It's scrupulously fostered by parenting and schooling. The message is, "Serve others." Therefore, to "Serve Thyself"—become self-employed—is a message which arouses enormous anxiety.

Self-discipline is rooted in desire: Doing what we want. Such an idea is not alien to human nature; it *is* human nature! So the trick in being self-employed is focusing on desire, self-interest, pleasure and self-fulfillment: In desires begin responsibilities.

Finally, a lot of people, your friends included, might try to put your ideas down. But nobody can put you down; you do that to yourself. The point is that friends and neighbors might be jealous of you acting on your free will. These people don't feel separate from you. For them to succeed, you must fail. If you should succeed, you won't make them look good (to themselves). Avoid these folks at all cost. And if you are married to a person who puts your ideas down, stand up and give your partner a piece of your mind.

"Being my own boss means being able to take risks."

Most self-employed types are considered risk-takers. But most successful entrepreneurs are risk-reducers. They practice their high-wire act with a net. This means doing market research on yourself and matching yourself against the market.* If nobody wants what you can do or you can't do what somebody else wants, you aren't in business.

The best way to reduce risks is talking to people who have made the mistakes you are bound to make, i.e., other self-employed people doing approximately what you want to do. Also, as a by-product of obtaining good advice, we discover from others what they did "right." Remember, to be successfully self-employed only one out of three decisions need be on target. Find out from others how they hit the target.

Another way to reduce risks is to *multiply by two* your start-up costs. Insufficient capitalization is one of the two major reasons we fail. "Capital" is the money we "waste" making mistakes. And since we all make far more mistakes than we think (Murphy's Law), we need twice as much money as we think to afford these mistakes.

Finally, ask yourself if you have what it takes to be a self-manager. Don't put yourself down if you don't have it. But by the time you hit your thirties and forties, the idea of self-employment is more realistic than in your twenties. The older we get the better we

---

* See *Go Hire Yourself an Employer* for a far more complete version of how to identify and market skills.

get, and the more attractive a self-managed life becomes. And, remember, a risk-free life is a dull existence.

"Being my own boss means living with and learning from disappointments."

Becoming your own boss means coping with disappointment. The fantasy of self-sufficiency (no self-employed person is self-sufficient), the impatience for success (it takes years to build a business following), the expectation of riches (remember, you plow back earnings), causes disappointment. But that's reality, too. And co-operating with reality is the essence of self-employment.

In a money marriage, disappointment with yourself infects your partner: You become a pain in the ass. Disappointment in business makes you a disappointment at home.

Gird thy loins. Feeling free is becoming separate: Separate from mom, colleagues, business associates, husbands and wives. Otherwise burnout is the result. And your partner finds no pleasure in your company, because you find no pleasure in yourself.

Effective self-managers guard against guilt. To be disappointed in ourselves often is a case of feeling "irresponsible." If we aren't bringing home the bucks, we feel "irresponsible." We feel guilty about our mates paying our way while we start up a string of greenhouses, a smart haberdashery, or a scheme to sell hook rugs. Moreover, the sheer pleasure of being self-employed causes guilt if our spouse is still belting the commonweal on salary. Talking these problems out with thy spouse—real talk—is the way to solve problems. Hand-holding is part of marriage and self-employment.

Your husband is turned down for a job in favor of a whiz kid imported from the West Coast.

Your wife graduates *cum laude* from a school of pharmacy and she self-destructs because she expected *magna cum laude*.

Your son is cut from the basketball squad a week before the season begins.

Your new restaurant business is unable to qualify for a liquor license for two years.

All examples of life's little sticky wickets. The door is slammed in our faces precisely at the moment we expected entry. Disap-

(a) *"When my wife left me, I learned to cope!"*

The formerly married don't need anyone to cope. Most single people cope very well, thank you very much. Learning how to take care of yourself *again*, like the teenager who discovers the pleasure of earning his own way in the world, puts a new bounce in your step.

Ex-wives learn how to change the oil in the family car, paint the bedroom, file their own tax return; ex-husbands learn how to bake angel food cake, scrub out toilet bowls, and throw a cocktail party.

Coping raises self-esteem. If the formerly married remarry, the trick is to continue to take care of yourself. Being able to take care of yourself might have saved you in your first marriage. To think you couldn't cope might be why you collapsed! Also, plenty of married people arrange it so their partners can't cope; otherwise they don't feel needed.

But coping alone in the long run (and in the long run, "we are all dead"—Keynes) is no pleasure. Coping with life isn't living it. But taking care of ourselves is a precondition to living it. And becoming responsible for ourselves—becoming separate—is essential in "remarriage."

(b) *"When I left my husband, I felt he couldn't cope."*

That might be why it took you so long to leave! Your sense of responsibility to husband hamstrung responsibility to yourself. Remember, feeling responsible for others causes unhappiness. And if someone feels responsible for you, your husband, for example, his company is bound to be no pleasure. Runaway husbands and runaway wives are often running away, not so much from each other, as from Responsibility.

(a) *"When I dumped my wife, I felt guilty."*

The old demon.

But guilt is no more natural than impotence. Guilt is imposed on us by the culture. Guilty folk are easily controlled by other people. Indeed, wives provoke guilt in husbands (all the more easy to control them, my dear) and husbands promote guilt in wives (all the more easy to manage, my boy). Thus conscience doth make cowards of us all. But no one can make us feel guilty; we make ourselves guilty.

(b) *"When I ran out on my husband, I felt to blame."*

Working wives, far more than husbands, feel more to blame when marriages collapse. And if they initiate the break, the blame is far worse. Self-defeating.

Working husbands, far more than wives, feel more responsible when it comes to making money. If they don't make "enough," they hold it against themselves. Self-destructive. Even irresponsible men, men who can't hold a job, are simply the same character structure turned inside out.

But the Reign of Conscience is unacceptable: Many wives stay with men they take no pleasure with; many husbands work at jobs they take no pride in: Both do it from a sense of duty. Duty to whom? Thus, it's our sense of responsibility to others which destroys our chance to be happy.

And if we bring into our second marriages this malignant sense of responsibility, our remarriages will be similar to our first.

(a) *"I felt terrific the day my divorce was final."*

As many people feel joy on the day of their divorce as on the day of their marriage. Many won't admit it, of course: People are *supposed* to wallow in shame, failure and guilt. But giving up a bad marriage like giving up a boring job is often a cause for joy not sorrow.

As the day we married, the day we divorce we feel free. Being in love is feeling perfect freedom. There is no freedom in the world like love. No longer loving—no longer feeling free—is miserable. Divorce is elating: We are free to love again!

Exiting from a miserable marriage, like leaving a bad job, won't cause joy but sorrow if you don't feel separate: Separate from your former partner. If you continue to press the sour grapes of wrath, it shows you don't feel separate. Free.

To feel separate is far more mental than physical. Physical proximity doesn't mean we are together any more than physical displacement means we are alone. Attitude is everything: If we continue raking up memories of a bad job or a bad marriage, it means we don't feel free to find a good job/make a happy remarriage.

(b) *"I cried the day my divorce was final."*

Good grief!

The trouble with being formerly married is that the past is never past (Faulkner). To *remain* in a state of resentment and hostility is hardly the way to open up to the possibility of starting over.

Mourning is often a necessary part of being divorced. We feel enormously sorry for ourselves. There is no one to *resent!* The resentment is turned on ourselves and acute depression is the result. Most depressed people going through a divorce should hire a therapist tout de suite.

Now, of course, hostility helps us separate from our mates. If there is such a thing as an amicable divorce, it can only be because of a banal marriage. So people going through a divorce are naturally going to be angry with each other. That's a necessary part of breaking up. But continuing to be angry means we are spiritually still wedded. Inseparate. Unfree. With no one about to hate but ourselves, it's painfully clear to the formerly married that a life alone is unacceptable. That's a big step to starting over.

(a) *"Breaking up means being free to start over."*

Now you are free to start over.

But plenty of people are shattered by divorce. They either feel dumped, rejected, and put on the scrap heap, on the one hand, or overwhelmed with guilt on the other. The formerly married vow, "Never again!"

Remarriage is out of the question. Until, of course, our needs, those damnable constants like sex, companionship, and love, force us —usually in the dead of night—to realize that nobody is free alone.

A lot of the formerly married appear invulnerable. To defend ourself against our need for other people, we deny our need for them. Unattractive. We don't *attract* other men/other women because we deny our need.

Unattractive, invulnerable, hostile, the formerly married can't start over because they haven't broken up. They don't feel *separate* from previous spouses. And obviously before we can start over, we must give up (feel separate from) previous mates. Tough (See *Be-*

coming Separate). Otherwise we can't become attractive, vulnerable and loving to our next mates.

(b) *"Starting over is better than giving up."*

Starting over is better than giving up. Playing it cool, denying your need for another, being irresponsible to your own feelings with all its attendant consequences: listlessness, drift, private fantasies and public rebellions, cultivating-your-own-garden—that never works. No glamour career nor celebrity nor exotic life styles compensate if the single life is an emotional desert.

(a) *"The formerly married often remarry duplicates of first spouses."*

Indubitably.

Hidden forces, dependent needs, compel us to search out and find someone just like our ex. That's why computer dating services are such a farce—they can't program people's hidden needs. So, if you're among the formerly married, hire out a therapist and find out why you can't, for example, resist willful women; find out why you can't, for example, resist helpless men. Take a hard look at yourself. And you can't do that alone. Thus, our need, as Ann Landers says, for "professional" assistance.

(b) *"The formerly married often remarry opposites of first spouses."*

We jump from the frying pan into the fire, quit our job in the whorehouse and take up residence in the vicarage, turn our backs on Tammerlane ("The Terrible") and embrace Oscar ("The Fool"). It's easy to see why. "If he's not like my husband, this must be love!" But whether we marry photo copies of our ex or opposites, it's surely not feeling free. Go see a psychiatrist—now. Do not pass Go. Do not collect $200 (See *Therapy, the Uses of*).

(a) *"I love my second husband but I can't stand his children."*

You are the wicked stepmother.

The children of your new husband (when they come to visit and live with you) naturally resent the new gal in his life. "You're not my mommy," they scream. And you're not; so don't play the fairy stepmother. Don't capitulate to the emotional blackmail of your husband's children. Friendship can slowly grow between stepparents and children, but you can't be their mother or father.

Pain is inevitable in stepparenting. But pain is inevitable in life. We do not pass from birth to death without inflicting and receiving pain. To think so is to embrace apathy; we pump novocaine into our bloodstream and call ourselves pain-free, when what we are is walking zombies.

So, whether you are stepparenting or considering doing so, beware. Showing caution doesn't mean never to remarry ("The kids will be hurt"); wisdom doesn't mean remarrying ("The kids need a mother/father"). Being hesitant does mean that the children issue could be central to your happiness. The divided loyalties ("I love my new wife but my kids hate her."); the natural hostility between rivals ("Daddy loves his new wife more than he does us."); and the feelings of rejection ("My husband cares more about those bratty kids than he does me.") are bound to trigger many an explosion. Worse, there may be no explosions: Everyone—including the children—puts on their Sunday School clothes and lives unhappily ever after.

(b) *"My children loathe living with my second husband."*

Why shouldn't they? Hamlet threw a fit about it: Something rotten in the state of Denmark. And what stinks to high heaven is mom bedding down with someone not dad! Children can't feel separate from mom, feel jealous of her new love, and raise hell. Thus, stepparenting is a helluva row to hoe for children, parents and stepparents alike.

To think our children won't feel the pain of our remarriage is believing our children are grown up. And even grown-ups often have unadmitted problems with stepparents. But to back off remarriage because of the pain our children feel is as unreal as our children themselves backing off marriage because of the pain it causes us. Dads don't like giving up daughters, mothers don't happily give away sons.

The answer is we don't *own* our parents nor our children. We are separate. Separating is going to cause pain. Indeed, if it doesn't cause pain, we aren't separating. Hostility between stepchildren and stepparents is natural. But once the separation is complete, when stepchildren and stepparents alike become separate, they have a chance to be happy with each other.

(a) *"Children suffer the most in a divorce."*

Sure, it's documented, children from broken homes go through hell; but it's undocumented and just as true that children within unhappy marriages go through another kind of hell.

Children, above everything else, want a happy mommy and daddy. Thus, it's truly irresponsible to stay unhappily married for the sake of the children. If mom and pop do file for divorce, however, children often feel responsible.

His daughter says, "Oh, if I had only been a good girl, Daddy would still be with me." Well, children aren't strong enough to feel separate from parents. Indeed, children can't function except in terms of other people. That's why peer pressure is so ironclad among kids.

But it's parents who can help children free up from this sense of responsibility. And feeling responsible for your children's happiness isn't helping them from feeling responsible for your divorce. It's a parasitic arrangement; children and parents alike feed off each other's dependency and sense of responsibility.

So, if you're married and considering divorce don't paper over your differences for the children's sake. Fish or cut bait: Either divorce or pitch in and try to take some pleasure with your spouse. Married types unready to change but unable to divorce don't do any favors for their kids. They don't do any favors for themselves! Sure, kids suffer in divorce. But your unhappiness is a terrible example for your children.

To divorce our wife (and feel guilty for the sake of our children), to stay married and miserable (to avoid the guilt for the sake of our children) are both cop-outs.

Hang tough.

Don't take your children into account if you are contemplating a divorce. Focus on yourself. Separate. Feeling responsible for their happiness is certain to ruin your own. And whether you stay in the marriage, divorce and remarry, or divorce and remain single, don't carry this corrosive sense of responsibility with you.

Feeling free to divorce our mates is quintessential to feeling free to live with them (See *Marriage Half-Truths [and Hard Truths]*). But the focus can't be on other people: Our wife, our husband, our children. Focusing on yourself will cause you to feel guilty; you feel irresponsible. But it's not your children which cause the guilt; they might arouse it but you cause it.

So, divorce, like marriage, must be a free-formed decision. A free-formed decision takes into account your feelings, not those of other people.

(b) *"I feel awful when I visit my children by my first husband."*

Do yourself a good turn and start hating this unreal sense of responsibility (See *Conscience Doth Make Cowards*). To visit your children in a state of guilt is awful for you and no fun for kids.

Don't expect any help from your kids: Children play into your sense of responsibility. That's because they don't feel separate from you. They're dependent. But unless you can shake guilt, you won't be able to take pleasure in your children. The guilt causes plenty of divorced parents to ignore children from a previous marriage entirely.

Irresponsible.

Finally, if you are considering divorce, the toughest decision of all is deciding which parent the child(ren) will live with. *Answer: Ask the child.* If the child prefers mommy that doesn't mean he's been a bad daddy; if it's daddy, it doesn't mean she's a bad mommy. Kids have a need for mom and dad at different stages in life.

And if you're a child from a broken home (or are married to someone who is), the implications are worth considering. Whether it was your mom (who left dad) or dad (who left mom), chances are better than even that in your own marriage the *threat* of being unwanted is never far from your mind. In fact, it's buried deep in the psyche working overtime.

Abandonment is a child's greatest fear: They carry this fear with them. Living through the trauma as a child, they are conditioned to the threat in marriage. So, hire a therapist if your parents' divorce spooks you in your own marriage.

Burnout

"If all the year were playing holidays,
To sport would be as tedious as to work."

SHAKESPEARE, *King Henry IV* (Part One)

"*I often burn out on the weekends and can't figure out what I want to do.*"

"*Some days on the job I can't face another client, patient, customer, student, employee, et al.*"

"*I look forward to business trips away from my wife.*"

"*Every day at work and at home seems much like the day before.*"

"*I often find reasons to work evenings and weekends.*"

"*All my friendships are habitual and routine.*"

"*I don't feel challenged on the job.*"

"*I care more about my job than my husband.*"

"*On vacations, I feel I ought to see my relatives.*"

"*During my vacation, I'm frequently bored and not with it.*"

"*My boss is a workaholic and I am, too!*"

"I often burn out on the weekends and can't figure out what I want to do."

To switch from focusing on others (on workdays) and on oneself (on weekends) is tough. People *need* you during your work time but nobody needs you during your free time. So you set it up so that you are *needed* all the time. And burn out.

Freedom leaves a lot of working couples helpless. But helpless people feel enormous rage. That's why so many blow-ups occur on weekends. Ask any cop; the domestic homicide rate soars on weekends and holidays.

How often have you said to yourself, "I want a job where I'm needed?" And the love-starved say, "I want someone to need me." Well, our dreams come true and we enter into a life of service. And marry someone, no doubt, who needs us. Then we have no free time. Focusing ten hours a day on other people's needs and another eight on our family's—working wives are the worst victims*—is setting yourself up for a case of burnout. Being pleasing, accommodating, and nice to everyone but yourself eliminates the self. Nice going. No wonder you pop greenies.

Burnout is especially obvious in the "helping professions": Social workers, clergymen, nurses, teachers, and counselors. But everyone suffers mildly from the disease to please. So stop fighting everyone's battles but your own, become separate. No, separation isn't separate vacations, separate hobbies, and separate residences. The space you want is in your head.

"Some days on the job I can't face another client, patient, customer, student, employee, et al."

If I spend every day fighting other people's battles, who is fighting mine? Protecting other people's interests and never your own is alien to human nature. The whole idea is imposed on us by schoolmarms, clergymen, humanists and other refractories. Mother lovers, every one of them (See *Momism*).

Being able to say "no" to potential clients, sick patients, impatient

* See Jessie Bernard's excellent book *The Future of Marriage,* in which she documents how marriage actually "makes" people ill.

customers, eager students, and dependent employees means to separate from them. But if we can't say "no" to them, we say "no" to ourselves, and burn out. Guess who isn't effective on the job anymore? And guess who senses we don't care? Well, it's clients, patients, customers, students and employees!

The antidote to burnout is saying no to other people's needs (that means you can say "yes," too) and the result is:

a renewed interest in your work (you now feel separate from it).

greater self-esteem (you no longer eliminate the self).

more fire in your belly (you no longer throw cold water on your desires. And in desires, remember, begin responsibilities).

"I look forward to business trips away from my wife."

A lot of reasons.

First, you learn to function alone, take care of yourself. You don't *need* her. Result: You feel free. Second, away from your "in" box and absent from your wife's demands, nobody *needs* you. Third, feeling separate is forced on you by circumstances; you have no choice but to act independently. Finally, while traveling, you don't feel responsible.

But coming back home and going back to work is tough. Suddenly you become dependent on your wife (and she on you); your "in" box is overflowing; and you can't act interdependently with your wife. You no longer feel free. Separate.

Result?

A big fight. That way you can still feel uninvolved. Unintimidated. The last angry man. And you think, "This marriage is a burned-out rocket." But there is nothing wrong with the marriage. There is something screwy about your attitude. And until your attitude changes, you are bound to feel burned out.

The question you need to answer is, "Why can't I feel free both away from home and on the job?" Well, why can't you? And you can if you become separate from both. Separation is self-awareness. And becoming a self-manager is the result. That means giving up feeling responsible (See *Conscience Doth Make Cowards*).

"Every day at work and at home seems much like the day before."
Time becomes a blur.

That's why punctuating your life with frequent mini-vacations, dining out, and taking a three-day pass from fulfilling other people's needs makes sense. Time away from home time renews perspective and recreates our sense of separation. Grab time for yourself. Learn how to "savor" it (See *Money [and Time] Management*). Remember the unimportance of being earnest.

"I often find reasons to work evenings and weekends."
Often we work best when we are least expected to. That's because we feel free with ourselves. Working when we are not "supposed" to eliminates the sense of responsibility. And, thus, we work more effectively.

And frequently we feel free to take pleasure in our marriage during those times we are least expected to. Monday evening, for example. Plenty of working couples escape from each other and into themselves on weekends and come back together on week nights. We act contrary to our responsibilities: We aren't *expected* to work weekends; we aren't *expected* to take pleasure in each other on worknights! Crazy.

"All my friendships are habitual and routine."
Is it because who you see socially, you see on the job, too? Boring. No separation of work and home: Your life becomes a floating staff conference.

At your place of work, greet your colleagues off the job once a year: During the company's annual picnic. Steal into the night on the eve of every workday and pursue your own pleasure. No wonder it's such a pleasure to work with such free-spirited colleagues: You might burn out, but not with each other or because of each other.

"I don't feel challenged on the job."
No longer tested, pushed to your limits, extended, you become bored with yourself and sense you're less effective. The answer is to delegate routine responsibilities and undertake new challenges. The challenge of every job is making it more challenging. Find a new

task. That's how to make our work life more interesting. But it means being able to "let go" of some other responsibility.

Challenges are what we create for ourselves—a new hobby, career, vacation or project. Self-created challenges tax and test us, push us beyond our limits, the result is self-fulfillment.

Think about it!

Reflect on the peak emotional experiences of your life, and I'll bet my bippy those were your "learning" experiences! One of the greatest challenges, one which we freely accept or evade, is the challenge of tough love. No trip you will take, no job, no public office you win, no celebrity you enjoy equals the satisfaction of taking pleasure in another person.

"I care more about my job than my husband."

(1) She finds herself enjoying her job more and him less. He finds working on Saturday afternoons not the drag he thought it would be. Why are these two people so evasive?

(2) She looks forward to lunching out at work more than the evening with her husband. He joins an exclusive health club and "works out" with the boys two and three times a week. Why don't they like each other's company?

(3) She nags and corrects him about his clear deficiencies as a conversationalist. He wonders if she has what it takes to be a mother. Why do they hate each other?

(4) She feels dependent on his income, coerced by his dominance, unfree with their friends, and overcome by the "marriage." He feels her dependence is a millstone, her lack of confidence gauche, her job an escape, and his "marriage" a burden. Why don't these people get a divorce?

At work, they feel power; at home, they feel powerless. On the job, they feel in control; at home, they feel controlled. At their desks, they feel in charge of their environment; in their living room, they feel their surroundings surround them.

But attitude is everything.

To work evenings and weekends in order to avoid unhappy home situations isn't cooperating with reality. And if they perceive they are in someone else's control at home, the trouble is not in their stars but in themselves. Changing their attitudes and learning some new moves is the way to fight burnout.

"On vacations, I feel I ought to see my relatives."

Well, if it's what you *want*, fine; if it's what you "ought," watch out.

Working couples—responsible people—are often emotionally black-mailed by parents, in-laws, and kissing cousins *on their time.* Keep in mind that grandmothers come to your house rather than you going to theirs. Your older and retired kith and kin have more *time.* Insist they pay you a visit.

Putting relatives *second* guilt-trips a lot of working couples. But it's a pleasure breaking free of relatives and doing your own thing. That's the price (guilt) of pleasure.

The same goes for your kids who see too much of you anyway. (Well, actually, maybe not enough, in which case reverse what you are about to read.) Separate vacations for kids is a great holiday for their parents, and builds self-reliance in them as no other experience can. The secret is becoming separate from your children: The anti-dote to parental burnout.

A last word on burning out in love and work. As you make progress separating the self from the job, your mate, friends and relatives, you'll feel freer, suffer guilt, and, hold on to your seat, feel rage. That's right.

Feeling free, becoming separate, taking responsibility for the self, causes you to hate the old, unreal, used up "you." "Why don't I have fun all the time," you say when your vacation is over? Transla-tion: "Why don't I feel free all the time?" Well, why don't you? That means you burn like a flame most of the time and burn out none of the time. The point is to try to impress yourself. And if you feel so good about the self you can't stand it, don't worry: Personal change, even in the smallest matters, often causes pleasure, guilt and rage (in that order). The rage is the rage to feel free *all of the time.* Thus, the rage is the way you know you can *so* change: Become sep-arate. Feel free.

"During my vacation, I'm frequently bored and not with it."

A vacation is recreation.

And if you are bored and not with it, it's easy to blame your unhappiness on the vacation itself. But it's usually your fault. Plenty of people have a problem putting the self first. Unless people are doing something "useful," "constructive," or are engaged in a "learning experience," they feel bored. That's particularly true of those who spend their daily lives fulfilling other people's needs—working couples. Lives spent in scheduling hassles, crisis management and catch-as-catch-can home management feel at a loss on vacation. Burned out.

Being free to do what you want seems like a burden. Nobody needs your help, nobody depends on you. Working mothers especially buckle. And some working men are no better. They call their office daily, take "working vacations" and like nothing better than spending time poolside within reach of a telephone.

Hmm.

Some people can't wait to get back to work. Playtime is "wasting time." Wasting time tickles the Conscience. So it's back to work with a heigh and a ho. The point is to leave your Conscience at home along with your watch. Happiness is the unimportance of being earnest, and a playful attitude toward both work and play means taking a vacation from time, obligation and Conscience.

Still other people can't go on vacation at all; they stay at home and shape up the house. So long as it's fun, swell. Some people have no problem making what they "ought" to do what they "want" to do. But most people, hung up on screening the verandah and shaping up the clothes closets, would rather be scuba diving at Point Reyes. They don't "burn always with this hard gem-like flame" (Walter Pater); there is nothing to burn!

"My boss is a workaholic and I am, too!"

No working couple will go full-term without being touched three or four times by workaholism. Whether we or our mates go over the brink, remember it's a contagious disease. You carry the dreaded bacillus home and contaminate thy spouse. The antidotes are many; hobbies, good sex, mini-vacations, climbing down-the-ladder-of-responsibility, self-awareness, therapy, jogging, executive sabbaticals. But above all, another job or another working way of life might be necessary. Moreover, a little-discussed aspect of the problem is that most workaholics don't *want to* kick the habit—not because work is wonderful, but because their homelife is hell. Workaholics often become managers; working for them is a twenty-four hour a day assignment. If you value your life, say "no" to the boss and find other means of employment. A person dominated by a boss who loves working nights and weekends is no different from the husband whose wife demands twenty-four hours of his attention. When your love and work life begin to list to port, you have no choice but to choose the self.

Finally, don't bring office work home with you. You won't work effectively or feel free to have fun. Home is the fun place, not the work place.

Caring Is Not to Worry

Inasmuch as I needed to love and be loved, I thought I was in love. In other words, I acted the fool. I often caught myself in a question which as a man of experience I had previously avoided. I would hear myself asking, "Do you love me?"

ALBERT CAMUS

"I hear myself asking, 'Do you love me?' "

"Caring is not to worry."

"Working couples are responsible people."

"My mother was a 'concerned' parent."

"Being 'concerned' makes me feel needed."

"Happiness is serving other people."

"The 'concerned' are unloving."

"A caring person is a loving person."

"I'm concerned about my husband because I don't know what pleases me."

"Working couples compete with each other."

"My husband is a very caring person."

"I hear myself asking, 'Do you love me?' "

"How much does a yacht like this cost?" someone once asked J. P. Morgan. "Well," he replied, "if you have to ask the price you can't afford it!"

And if your partner asks whether he is loved, well . . . the answer is *no*. Being asked, even nagged, sets up both for a bad case of shinsplints. It violates our freedom. Husbands and wives *should* love one another? But the evidence indicates many don't! And that's because they *"ought to."* With all the votes counted, Cupid loses in a landslide.

ITEM: I can bring myself to the table groaning with a weight of delicacies. (That doesn't mean I *will* eat.)

ITEM: I sit down at my desk and attack my "in" box. (That doesn't mean I *will* work.)

ITEM: I open and look at my anatomy text. (That doesn't mean I *will* study.)

And I can say to the world, "I love my wife." (And not love her.) Nobody can *will* love if it's a "duty." In tough love, we don't ask our partners if we are loved; it's the silent language we "sense." Don't ask if he loves you! Tell him, "I love you." Focus on what *you* feel. That's being responsible to the self. Give up being concerned about what other people feel. Separate! Be a caring person.

So that brings us to our old friend, dependency. In no other transaction in life are we as dependent on our partner as in sex. And no one is more dependent on us than the person in bed with us. Women need men; men need women. And needing anything, being dependent on someone to provide it, makes us feel unfree. Needy. Concerned. Resentful. Helpless.

"Caring is not to worry."

A caring mother isn't concerned.

A caring boss isn't a worrywart.

A caring wife isn't a nervous Nellie.

A caring husband isn't intimidated (or unintimidated).

CARING	WORRYING
"I care about what I do."	"I worry about what I do."
"I care about how well I'm doing."	"I worry about how well others think I'm doing."
"I care about my boss knowing what I think."	"I worry about what the boss is thinking."
"I care about what's right."	"I worry about who's right."
"I care about winning my staff's loyalty."	"I worry about commanding the loyalty of my staff."
"I care about my staff making decisions."	"I worry my staff will make mistakes."
"I care about being successful."	"I worry whether I'm successful."

Attitude is everything. Caring is not to worry. A truly caring person feels separate from what he cares about: His wife, his children, his job, his boss. Caring isn't concern. A concerned person feels inseparate from what she worries about: Her husband, her children, her job and her boss.

Becoming separate.

Give up being needed on the one hand and feeling needy on the other. Becoming separate means you begin to value other people (instead of being needed). It's, among other things, a definition of friendship (See *Friends in Need* or *Friends Indeed*).

"Working couples are responsible people."

Pound-for-pound and square-inch-for-square-inch, people in money marriages are the most responsible class in the country—producers, taxpayers, parents. Working couples are the glue which holds the nation together. They repair the social fabric ripped by destructive people. And like concerned and responsible people everywhere, they fret about the cost of pork loin.

Working couples take pride in being concerned citizens, responsible parents and producers of products and services other people need. Working couples "work" at their marriage.

But working couples who work at marriage don't take pleasure in it. Responsible people are often miserable, oppressed, burned-out—the harried married. The whole point of love and work is the pleasure of each other's company and the pleasure we take in exercising our skills on the job.

Taking responsibility for other people's feelings and being irresponsible to our own is being concerned: Concerned folk often don't know what they are feeling.

"My mother was a 'concerned' parent."

Nobody, as we shall see (See *Momism*), is entirely free of mom. Those least separate from her are usually those who buck most at the thought of mom being alive and well and rolling around in their brain pan. But becoming separate—being a caring rather than a concerned person—is often a result of our success in separating from the big "M."

As children, ours was an apparently indissoluble bond with mom. But growing up is dissolving that bond: Growing up is becoming the person we want to be even if this is the same person our mom wants us to be!

But on a continuum from right (complete identification with mom) to left (complete independence of her) everyone is either right or left of the median. To the extent we are "concerned" spouses, parents, and workers, we are right of the median. Thus, becoming separate from our spouse is tough. To the extent we are caring husbands and wives, parents and employees, we are left of the median. Therefore, becoming separate from our mate is easier but still tough.

Husbands and wives become surrogate mothers. A husband depends on his wife (as he did with his mother) and his wife fights to feel free with him (as she did with her mother), and vice versa. This eternal back and forth, now involved and engaged, now separate and independent is the heart of marriage. It's why hanging tough in love is so tough. He wants to be involved with his wife, she wants to be separate—today. Tomorrow, she feels dependent on him and he feels independent of her. It's not much different from living with mom.

Happily married people are nonconformists. "We happy few," they say, echoing Shakespeare. But how many of the happy few are happy all of the time or even most of the time? Well, we don't know. So, if someone asks you if you are happily married, an honest reply is, "I was dreadfully happy Monday, unhappy Tuesday, relatively happy Wednesday, Thursday was a downer, Friday a glory and the weekend mostly fair."

We are enjoined by Scripture to love our neighbor. But if I have a toothache, it's unlikely I will love my neighbor or anyone else. My toothache is *real*. I feel miserable.

Message?

It means accepting the inalienable right of everyone to feel miserable from time to time. That doesn't mean my wife needs to be miserable, too!

And is there anyone who would disagree that life can be miserable from time to time? Living with our own misery and not taking responsibility for another person's misery (much as they try to make us) is what is meant by feeling separate. The same with happiness: Why can't I be happy while my wife is working on a migraine?

And the astonishing consequence of feeling aware of our own feelings ("Ouch, my bicuspid is killing me!") and feeling separated from the feelings of other people is that our caring capacity is expanded. Compassion is extending ourselves to others *without fearing the loss of the self*.

Clearly being a loving person isn't easy; being open to love isn't either. And our inability to love (and be loved) is a not so modern definition of hell. "All I want is love," is the slogan of the harried marrieds. Love is what everyone wants and few people get. People who want to love (and be loved) envy those who do; people who are able to love—tough lovers—are fortunate indeed: Something special about their mommies no doubt.

Loving people have a gift, a talent, a fortune—the Rockefeller brothers are poor by comparison. Why most people are unfortunate and few are able to love (and be loved) is a riddle. Surely, the loving person owes a lot to his or her parents. But most of us had "good enough" parents who could have (if they would have) loved each other more. The trouble with married love is simple; neither partner loves the other "enough." Mom and dad didn't love each other "enough." They tried to control each other. We try to *control* other people by making them take responsibility; people try to control *us* by making us take responsibility.

And like their mothers, husbands and wives try to control each other. Mothers controlled their children by extending and withdrawing their love. If we tried to break free of mom—become separate—she withdrew her love. If we needed her love (became dependent) she extended it—just like marriage!

But, of course, nobody can control *me*, nobody can control *you*. And being married and doing something which benefits our spouses doesn't mean we are in their control; working for our bosses doesn't mean we are in their control.

Caring isn't being concerned, caring isn't being in control. Caring is to value someone quite apart from his/her needs (and ours). Nobody who wants to control others can be a caring person.

"Being 'concerned' makes me feel needed."

A concerned mother hates seeing her children grow up, become independent, and leave home; mom is no longer needed. A husband hates his wife going off to work and taking care of herself; he no longer feels responsible. Our boss hates us to show initiative; his supervision is no longer necessary.

Being needed is feeling in control. People come to depend on us. We feel responsible, needed, useful—miserable. A traditional homemaker is especially afflicted. Children, spouses, in-laws, and the folks next door come to *lean* on her and become a burden. She wants to shuck them off, become separate, feel free. But what she wants to shuck is her sense of concern, the responsibility she feels toward others, her need to be needed. To rid herself of her unreal self, she wants to find her real self. But her unreal sense of responsibility to others was imposed on her by mom. It isn't real. Mom, too, was a "concerned" parent. Thus, becoming a caring person isn't being like our "concerned" parents.

Don't blame mom; that's a cop-out. She had a mom, too. The point is our whole civilization until fairly recently was predicated on the idea of helping others. "The vocation of every man and woman is to serve other people" (Tolstoy). But civilized people are discontented (Freud). Thinking our vocation is service to other people robs us of our free will. We become prisoners to other people's needs. Unhappy.

Look at the result: The golden rule has been turned inside out:

"Love thyself and screw thy neighbor." That doesn't work either, nobody is self-sufficient. Selfish people are prisoners of their own needs. Unhappy.

"Happiness is serving other people."

Many employers go glassy-eyed listening to the young job-seeker's typical refrain, "All I really want to do is help people." It's not a laughing matter. Young people today often feel useless, unneeded. A teenager's self-esteem soars once he lands his first job and feels independent. That's the point in growing up, feeling free. Being needed is a big step for kids, it sure beats being dependent. Being needed is the opposite of being dependent and in need.

But grown-ups put childish things away. Being needed is no longer a reason to love or work. A life in service is a rotten philosophy even for a servant!

A first-rate servant serves his master or mistress and takes pleasure in it. It's the same with every job. We take pleasure in using our skills. And, yes, in the process, we "help other people." But working solely to help other people makes us discontented. We don't feel free. Separate. We take our work *seriously* and a serious attitude is deadly to pleasure.

Concerned parents, worrywarting managers, and harried marrieds aren't as effective as caring parents, effective executives, and loving partners. Concerned parents take no pleasure in their children; worrywarting managers are concerned about bottom lines because they can't care about other lines; harried marrieds are hagridden by responsibilities to other people.

Becoming a caring person is growing up; remaining a concerned person is staying a child. Whether you are a "you first" person or a "me first" person, neither way works. Both the "unselfish" and the "selfish" must give up (a) being responsible to others, and (b) being irresponsible to others, in order to be responsible to the self.

"The 'concerned' are unloving."

Being concerned is disabling. Anxiety paralyzes free feeling. Concerned people consumed in filling other people's needs forget their own, and are filled with suppressed resentment. Children are especially quick to sense this in their parents.

Truly caring people are loving. They feel separate from what they love. Thus, they feel free to become engaged. But "concerned" people don't feel separate. Therefore, they don't feel free to become involved with their work (work is love made visible); involved with their children (parenting is extending the power of pleasure to our children) and involved with their partners (taking responsibility for pleasure in their company).

A caring person is attractive. We are attracted to strength, a free will, a great spirit. We want to lean on such a person. But a truly caring person makes people stand on their own two feet. Caring people care about others becoming strong. Concerned people fear other people will become strong.

"A caring person is a loving person."

As we have seen.

But it's more complicated. A loving person can't care about someone who doesn't care about himself. A child in a rage, a wife in a snit, a husband in a pout are unlovable.

Frustrating.

A miserable wife, a moody husband, a temperamental child, all can put us off our feed. They *make* us unhappy. But it's truer to say we make ourselves unhappy with them. Strong egos and great spirits can be happy in the company of the miserable. But it's tough. A strong sense of separation is required. And who of us is strong enough?

This is the test of tough love.

Hanging tough and playing with the pain of being miserable and unlovable, on the one hand, and becoming separate and feeling free in the company of someone who is miserable and unloving, on the other—that's reality. But it's also true that tomorrow our wife is a joy to live with, our husband whistles while he works, our children light up our life and we ring that old bell at work.

A concerned person always worries about tomorrow. His glass is always half empty. A caring person knows tomorrow is not today. His glass is always half full. Guess whose cup runneth over!

Tough love is the profoundest emotion felt while married. It's a matter for poetry, not prose, a Bach cantata, not a rock opera, reality rather than romance. Tough love celebrates the "is" of life, the shared sufferings and joy of two lives commingled and separate.

"I'm concerned about my husband because I don't know what pleases me."

OK, if you love giving pleasure. But if you are concerned about other people's needs and ignore your own, you become dopey with resentment. And who needs any more resentful wives?

So, if you are always pleasing your husband (and never yourself) it follows you do the same with children, in-laws, employers and sorority sisters. No wonder you want a long vacation away from it all!

Well, it's easy to be cynical about this problem but much more difficult to do anything about it. Know thyself. That might mean hiring a therapist. Maybe you have no training, upbringing or conditioning in focusing on the self or maybe you think it's selfish. But self-awareness isn't selfishness; the most thoughtful people in the world are the most self-aware.

Keep in mind, too, that to be professionally concerned *all of the time* causes depression. Airline stewardesses, inn keepers, public relations types all suffer inordinately high levels of depression. Why? They are paid to please! They are constantly controlling their feelings. Pretty soon they cease to feel at all. And they are always tired.

Moreover, it's displeasing or it promotes displeasure to be continually in the company of someone who is concerned to meet our every need. And Miss Congeniality is notoriously a bitch in private. Mr. Nice Guy might beat his wife.

So, if you feel free giving pleasure, pleasing other people, making people feel at home—Godspeed. But if you increasingly resent other people, feel a lack of self-esteem, and feel fatigue, turn on to yourself for a change, and start caring about the self.

"Working couples compete with each other."

It isn't a marriage, it's a junior achievement competition. Especially if both partners practice the same craft, work for the same organization, attended the same graduate schools, or work together in their own business (See *Being My Own Boss*).

For married folk in noncompetitive crafts and with disparate organizations, competition isn't so obvious. Each partner is separated from the other and is as likely to take pride in his or her partner's accomplishments as to feel envy.

But it's difficult for her to enjoy his success when she so desperately wanted success herself. Hang tough: "Goddamnit, that's the job I've always wanted!" is frankly confessing her envy and becoming free of it.

Many a working wife backs off success on the job (a *little* success is OK) from feelings of responsibility for her husband's feelings with attendant irresponsibility to her own. Worldly success causes many working wives to think their husbands won't love them anymore—indeed no man will ever love them! Crazy. Any working wife who values herself is going to kiss off any man who believes her success is his failure.

Competition, jealousy and occasional envy are a consequence of feeling inseparate. And trying to promote competition in your mate is being a five-star bitch/bastard. The solution is to break free from measuring his progress against hers by becoming separate. If that doesn't work, see a psychiatrist and find out why your mother made you a competitive and concerned and not a caring and loving person.

"My husband is a very caring person."

Such people say, "I'm married to a very supportive person." And to be a supportive person these days is considered a compliment to our sensitivity. Many people think supportive people are caring people.

But one way to "support" people is to challenge them. An effective manager always gives *more* work to his staff than they can do. And the work is done and done uncommonly well. An ineffective manager never gives enough work to his staff and is woefully overstaffed. And the work never gets done and is done uncommonly bad!

A truly caring person challenges his staff, his wife and his children. A caring person is not so interested in being supportive as he is in helping people support themselves. On the job, a caring person is neither nasty nor nice and twice as effective. At home, a caring person is never dominant or submissive and is therefore twice as intimate.

Children's Hour

Parents are the bones on which children sharpen their teeth.

PETER USTINOV

"Parents should love their children."

"I worry about my kids."

"I loathe working at home with the children underfoot."

"Children of working parents are more self-reliant."

"Working couples are able to give their children all the 'advantages.'"

"Building self-esteem in children is important."

"Working parents must keep up a common front with their children."

"Children should learn the difference between 'right' and 'wrong.'"

"If my children ask why they can't do something, I say, 'Because I said so.'"

"Loving my wife/husband is more important than loving my kids."

"Parents should love their children."
    Nobody, least of all the experts, is entirely sure how to raise chil-

dren. But all of us are experts to the extent we were once children. So look inside yourself for guidance. Looking outside to the "experts" (me included) suggests that experience isn't the best teacher.

"Expert" opinion fifty years ago, for example, asserted that "Every mother loves her child." Q.E.D., you are a mother, therefore, you love your child. Good logic but a lousy premise: No mother living or dead loved her child all of the time and some loved their children none of the time.

Expert opinion fifty years later says every parent should be effective. But the mystery is why "effective" parents with "advantaged" kids have happy and unhappy children in the same proportion as "good enough" parents with "disadvantaged" kids. The heart of the mystery is love. Some parents simply love their children more effectively than others.

But if you feel you *should* love your child, you won't. Attitude is everything. If you feel free to love your child, you will. But that means feeling free to dislike your child, too. And isn't that a guilt trip! Part of feeling free to love is "letting go." Give up being the "concerned" parent and become a caring parent. And, as we have seen, that means feeling separate from your children in the first place.

"I worry about my kids."

Well, let's focus on the difference between caring about our children and merely worrying about them. Caring, remember, is *not* to worry.

CARING	WORRYING
"I care about my children having a good time."	"I worry my children will climb a tree and break a leg."
"I care about my children becoming independent."	"I worry my children won't need me."
"I care about being happy with my children."	"I worry about whether I make my children happy."

"I care about my children fight-   "I worry my children can't fight
ing their own battles."   their own battles."

"I care about my own feelings."   "I'm responsible for my chil-
                                                 dren's feelings."

"I make my children face the   "I worry about my children
consequences of their actions."   knowing right from wrong."

"I care about my children taking   "I worry about my children be-
responsibility for themselves."   ing responsible to others."

"I care about taking time off the "I worry I'm not taking enough
job to be with my kids."   time off to be with the kids."

"I loathe working at home with the children underfoot."

In plenty of money marriages, each partner often makes arrangements with employers (See *Organizations [and the Working Cou-
ple]*) to work at home from time to time, part-time, or even most of
the time. Lawyers prepare their briefs, editors bluepencil copy, sales-
men schedule appointments and make trip reports—at home.

Working at home with the children underfoot scares people. It
seems "unprofessional." There is no separation of shop and home.
But to be effective working at home is to separate not in space but in
your mind. Strong-willed people know how to deal with distractions.
And people who know how to focus and concentrate are strong
enough to separate from work to diaper baby. Every productive person should work a fifty-minute hour. Children who distract us ten
minutes of the hour help us focus the other fifty.

The weak-willed can't eliminate other people (especially their
children) from their minds. Other people are a burden. If our children are an interference, dimes to doughnuts we perceive people at
work an interference.

Europeans work at home more than Americans; doctors, architects,
lawyers and consulting engineers often have their offices in their
homes. Working at home saves energy, commute time and "down-
time." Executive productivity has sloped off badly since 1968: A lot
of the slack is due to the *kaffeeklatsch*, grab-ass, entropic sociali-
zation which takes place in so many white-collar working environ-

ments. Too many people are coming home from work these days not so much tired as nervous. Four hours of *real* work at home beats eight hours being a talk-show host.

"Children of working parents are more self-reliant."

Nobody knows; maybe so, maybe not. Working couples' children are necessarily no more self-reliant than children of traditional marriages are necessarily more loved. But it's in the working couple's interest if their children become more self-reliant. And children are more likely to be self-reliant if their parents are self-reliant. Children learn by imitation.

Self-reliance is where dad is so important. Apart from pitching in and helping mom, dad's job is helping his children break free of her. If dad isn't there (or doesn't *care*) or is afraid of his wife (his mother?), then he's no help to his kids. Fathers stand up to mothers and do the downfield blocking to help children rely on themselves. That means helping them be less dependent on mom. And that's a big help to mom.

Mothers emotionally dependent on children, children emotionally dependent on mothers, won't "let go" of each other. Children without a strong father are left to break free of mommy *alone*. And that's impossible for a child, and the reason building self-esteem and self-reliance in children is so tough. All the more reason for a strong father.

"Working couples are able to give their children all the 'advantages.'"

But what are "advantages"?

Self-reliance, self-esteem, self-management: Those are the values working couples want to communicate to kids. That's truly loving your children. But one reason many children are taking longer and longer to "grow up," why kids leave home later and later (or leave and come back!), why so many children are having trouble focusing on what they want is because so many of them have been protected from frustration and difficulty. Reality. As children, they always had a sufficiency of things, services, entertainments. Children become accustomed to being taken care of, and people who are taken care of can't take care of themselves. When they grow up they look to others to take care of them.

Adolescence is wretched because teenagers feel *useless*. On family farms, the acute pangs of unworthiness are not so obvious—young people work at helping the family survive. As children become older, helping them become *useful* is helping them become separate. To help your children become self-reliant:

Make children contribute all their earnings into the family treasury; dole out allowances from the common pot.

Set up household chores on a rotating basis in which children and adults alike participate on the basis of work commensurate with abilities and desire.

Train young people to cook, garden, do tax forms, keep checking accounts—manage a household.

Show your children how you make a living! Take them to the office. Let them read through your "in" box, go on a business trip, attend a meeting. No joke: Many middle-class kids haven't a clue as to what their working parents *do*. Children don't see, therefore, the connection between their "advantages" and the money you make. And when they grow up they are long in learning the connection between work and survival. They look to others to take care of them: Schools, Uncle Sam, "Movements," Corporations.

Finally, spend time with your children. In many two-paycheck marriages, we provide *things* but forget to provide ourselves—that might be true, too, with our mates. Time is more precious than money in money marriages. Finding the time to be with our children is a question of saying "no" to our jobs. And, yes, that might mean less income. But if our family is our Career, that's the price we pay for the pleasure of our children's company.

"Building self-esteem in children is important."

Strictly speaking, parents can't build up anyone's self-esteem except their own. But loving parents can sure as shootin' encourage it in their kids.

To help build self-esteem in your children is not to forget your own. Setting limits with conviction is the way parents help children cope with reality. Parents who consistently communicate what they want help children communicate what they want. Sure, setting limits, saying "yes" and saying "no" and being a strong-willed parent is tough. Tough on parents who are separating from their children; tough on kids who aren't strong enough to feel separate with parents. But a strong mother and father also please children. They have something to push against, someone to disobey!

Disobedience is important. Nobody who doesn't disobey is going to break free, become separate. That doesn't make kids free, but it's a start. And children who cope with frustration, difficulty, and pain come to understand the terms and conditions of life ("Life is tough") far quicker than children protected from frustration, difficulty and pain.

Sure, a willful parent overwhelms his child and diminishes his child's sense of self. But a spineless parent underwhelms his child and defeats his spirit. The "good enough" parent is neither willful nor without will; the good enough parent has a will! That means feeling separate from children. In reality, we are separate: Children don't own their mommy and daddy, parents don't own their kids.

Plan, therefore, for a lot of ego-tripping in your happy family. Shouting, tears, laughter, point, counter-point. Strong wills find the means to express themselves and mark the happy home.

"Working parents must keep up a common front with their children."

That's not becoming separate.

To be sensitive to our children playing one parent off against the other causes us to think of ourselves as a unit and not as separate souls. To feel we are in our children's control unless we are united is to believe we are out of control if we are not. But nobody in a family is in charge, especially its weakest members—children.

Children break free, become separate, and start taking responsibility for their own happiness if they have two models to copy. But a dependent mommy and a dependent daddy, good team members both, makes it difficult for children to separate. We know children grow and change and start taking responsibility for themselves when they take something of daddy, something of mommy to make someone of themselves. But if mom and dad function dependently with each other their children are likely to remain dependent, too.

Kids have divided and ruled for years. That's not because there is no *common* front; it's because there is *no* front. Working couples are going to quarrel about their children like everything else. If the quarrel involves the children why not involve them? Ask your kids what *they* think. That's making them take responsibility. But keeping up a common front is being irresponsible to your own feelings (because you take into account your partner's feelings) and everyone's a loser.

"Children should learn the difference between 'right' and 'wrong.'"

Children are extremely self-conscious, which is the opposite of self-aware: Children define everything in terms of other people. Adults have problems in this department, too. But from the time a child first says "no," he is breaking free of "other people."

Parents help children when they make them less self-conscious and more self-aware. This means making children understand that responsibility is not toward other people but toward themselves. It means helping children think for themselves, think through the consequences of their actions (not the right or wrong, the bad or good of an activity), so they can recognize the importance of having a mind of one's own.

Parents who manage children by trying to control behavior through appeals to Conscience, who make a totem of the word Responsibility, reinforce children's ties to other people. Children's behavior thus is copied from other children. Happiness is considered to be outside in the world at large and not inside each person. "Society" is blamed for everything that goes wrong.

My son charges through the front door and bangs the screen. I say, "Bad boy!" But he isn't being bad; he's high spirited! The point is not to bang the door when his hardworking daddy is taking his nap. Let my son pay the consequences, but don't let him think high spirits are bad!

There is no more important work for working couples than deprogramming children from the right/wrong, bad/good, black/white mentality. A good start is deprogramming yourselves from explaining the universe in terms of bad and good. Otherwise we and our children are the victims of our civilization's morality fables. The Conscience is fed good red meat when we are kids and drinks our blood when we are older. "Clean up your plate," his mother orders, "there are starving Armenians in the world." But that's no reason for a boy to clean up his plate! A far better reason is that mom won't serve the chocolate pudding and hard sauce if he doesn't clean up his plate.

Honor, truth, beauty, valor, integrity, excellence are all marvelous values. But educators and moralists, mother-lovers every one, indoctrinate us with what's right—Excellence, for example—say it's *good* for us and we turn ourselves off. In a word, inculcating moral behavior in our children turns them off and turns them on to so-called immoral behavior.

Attitude is everything. If you lay down your life for your country, it's noble; if you lay down your life for your talent, it's honorable; if you lay down your life for your children, it's divine. But it's all nonsense if you feel you have been "sacrificed."

A man dies for his country; in its defense he realizes the self; a woman expresses her talent; without which she is not faithful to the self; parents protect their children; otherwise they would destroy themselves. "Self-sacrifice" in marriage and work is not necessarily the elimination of self but its realization. The difference between self-sacrifice and love is the difference between people ruled by responsibilities (on the one hand) and the ability to respond to the self (on the other). So, if you turn down a promotion at work, follow your husband to his next assignment, stay put for the children's sake, you do so for the self's sake. Self-sacrifice is life denying; love is self-fulfilling.

So, the eternal verities—honor, truth, beauty—are not for the sake of other people but the sake of the self: Self-esteem.

"If my children ask why they can't do something, I say, 'Because I said so.'"

Working couples with tough egos who know what they want won't let their children push them around. But plenty of couples with weak egos are plainly bullied by their own children. Such parents are constantly being blackmailed. Children sense their parents are namby pambies: They constantly "test" their parents and find them wanting.

Pollyanna parents don't feel free; they don't feel separate from each other and certainly not from their children. They are "concerned" parents but have trouble truly caring about their children. Crawfishing parents suffer from poor self-esteem and communicate this highly infectious disease to children.

Their children have enormous difficulty thinking through what they want. Their own *willingness*, a true desire to *do* something, has been frustrated by parents who gave them everything. Children who don't know what they want are over-protected—they want to break out. But how can they break free if they live in a fur-lined rut? Well, they can't and they won't if parents are too weak to say "yes" and "no."

Concerned parents are doubting Thomases; they look outward to "experts" for help when they should look inward. And if we look inward, take responsibility for our own feelings, recognize that both parents and children are separate, we won't hesitate to say "Do so because I said so!"

"Loving my wife/husband is more important than loving my kids."

What's central in a family is love between mom and pop. A love affair between parents is what children want most, it's their best security. Mom is so crazy about dad, she's not hassling the kids. And dad is so crazy about mom, he's not afraid or uninterested in helping his kids to break free of her. A loving feeling between mom and pop helps their children separate, feel free, take responsibility.

No man is a philosopher with a toothache. And no one in a money marriage is a philosopher when the TV set blows a fuse, our second child comes down with the flu, our boss wants us to fly to Detroit tomorrow, our husband bollixes the income tax return, our wife's checking account is overdrawn, and friends are expected for dinner. Moral? People are often miserable in marriage. But it often has nothing to do with who we are married to or whether we are married at all! Single people have troubles, too!

Yes, she has her career and he has his job and *both* manage the home. But if both partners are so caught up in the job, her career flourishes, he doubles his income, where is the pleasure, what is the profit, if our children run wild (or grow wan) and the center of our life—the family—falls to pieces? The human comedy becomes a tragedy. Life is no longer funny. Life is no fun.

Whether the money marriage endures depends on our children. "Children begin by loving their parents; after a time they judge them; rarely, if ever, do they forgive them" (Wilde). And it's our children—taking a hard look at working parents—who will judge whether the two-paycheck marriage shall endure. The evidence so far suggests it will. Plenty of younger people, now in early man- and womanhood, never remember mom not going to work. And some kids nowadays find it passing strange their mothers don't work.

But children of parents who don't love each other are denied what they want most. Thus, parents overinvest in their children: Mom loves sonny more than pop and depends on her son's support. No wonder the kid doesn't feel separate, and why he feels responsible for his mother's happiness!

So, we come full circle: Taking responsibility for our own happiness. If each partner in a working couple's marriage has what it takes—a strong ego and a great spirit—their children, the little copy cats, might simulate them and be happy in love and work too. And if they don't, so what. Everyone must take responsibility for his or her own happiness whether their parents helped them or not. And meanwhile, back at the ranch, parents have their own lives to live alone together.

Conscience Doth
Make Cowards

When you prevent me from doing anything I want to do, that is persecution; but when I prevent you from doing anything you want to do, that is law, order, and morals.

GEORGE BERNARD SHAW

"Happiness is having a clear Conscience."

"Let Conscience be your guide."

"In every family the weakest rules."

"I can't say 'yes' and I can't say 'no.'"

"Sometimes saying 'no' to others is saying 'no' to myself."

"Saying 'yes' to myself often means saying 'no' to others."

"My wife dreads being wrong and hates to face mistakes."

"Whenever my wife says 'no' to what I want, it's frustrating."

"I'm secretly pleased when I displease my wife."

"If I do what I want, I feel bad!"

"I hate myself when I make a mistake."

"If hubby makes a mistake, I make sure he knows it."

"If I'm at fault, I blame my wife."

"I can't seem to fire anyone at work."

"Happiness is having a clear Conscience."

The Conscience has a good press. We believe it stands between us and skid row, between doing "good" and being "bad." Our Conscience, we think, saves us from ourselves. Appeals to our Conscience are made in a thousand messages to us every day. And, as if they didn't have enough on their minds, we appeal to the Consciences of other people a thousand times a day. "Take care of me," is one message. "Make me happy" is another.

People feel best about themselves (and each other) if Conscience takes a holiday. The trouble is our Conscience is always on duty. Think about everything you "should" be doing this very moment and if your Conscience is your guide you won't finish reading this page.

If our child says, "Bad mommy!," well, chances are mom feels bad. But that's mom's problem. Nobody makes us feel guilty, we make ourselves feel guilty. And in marriage there is no pleasure in each other's company.

Feeling pleasure, as you close readers know, promotes guilt—a major reason there are few happy marriages. But being unhappy and miserable is our crazy way to avoid feeling guilty. Unhappy are the innocent; happy are the brave. The courage to love is to take pleasure in our work and our marriage. But it means wrestling with Demon Conscience.

"Let Conscience be your guide."

"All effective executives work on Saturdays. I'm effective, therefore, I shall belt the commonweal this weekend."

"All good wives iron their husbands' shirts. I am a good wife, therefore, I will iron the sonofabitch's shirts."

"All nice little boys take piano lessons. I'm a nice boy, therefore, I will practice piano."

"Nice guys don't challenge their wives. I'm a nice guy, therefore, I won't criticize my wife."

These are the wacky syllogisms of the Conscience. The game plan of the Conscience is to help you defeat yourself. Letting your Conscience be your guide—doing what you should—is no way to toughen your ego: It breaks your spirit. No wonder you don't do what you want; small wonder you don't know what you want!

If you catch yourself practicing this kind of mind control, it's high time to recognize your Conscience as a loathsome terrorist. It's a policeman, teacher, Sunday School teacher, and parent. The Conscience censures your thoughts, polices your manners and morals, judges your every thought and action and finds you guilty. The Hangman cometh.

Feeling "responsible" is how you shall know Conscience. Conscience is the bull-whip of the human race. The next stage in the evolution of civilized men and women is the elimination of Conscience in our daily lives: Eliminate your Conscience and raise your Consciousness.

"In every family the weakest rules."

The weak appeal to the Conscience of the strong. Children, therefore, are Dutch masters at promoting a sense of responsibility in parents. Husbands, down with a bout of the flu, are no slouches at making their wives into resentful nursemaids and working wives are postdoctoral fellows in guilt-tripping.

"Look what a mess I am," he says to his wife. "Help!" Weak people want other people's pity the better to control them. So if you catch yourself appealing to another person's Conscience, it's despicable: you come to despise yourself. Self-contempt.

But self-contempt, like guilt, is intolerable. So we turn our contempt on our mate and, presto! there goes the pleasure of marriage. In money marriages, both partners have ample opportunity on the job and with each other to feel sorry about themselves. Therefore, working couples must be particularly alert. Self-awareness is our best defense against being sucked into our partner's contempt.

The way to help the weak is to help them grow strong. Challenge them! Potency, the ability to respond to a challenge, is inside of everyone; impotency, the inability to respond, is outside of us.

Contempt is not incurable, but tolerable and reducible if given time, some bed rest, and plenty of attention. Shaking the habits of mind of our parents (and grandparents) is Herculean work; comparatively, cleaning out the Augean stables was a cinch (See *Momism*).

Hanging tough and taking pleasure in love and work, putting the self first, loving the honor of God (i.e., Freedom), raising the Consciousness, becoming a caring person, loving children, friends and your mate for the pleasure they bring and becoming separated from them in order to become involved with them has been the message.

So when you woke up this morning you read of an earthquake that killed 20,000 people in Peru. When you try to start your car you discover your battery is dead. Question: Which is most important *to you?* Well, if you answer "the earthquake," you qualify for a dubious sainthood. If you admit it's your dead battery, you are cooperating with reality and bringing the Conscience to bay.

So instead of consulting your Conscience—as you have been trained to do—far better to take into account reality. And co-operating with reality reveals that if you rob a bank you might go to jail, if you commit adultery you might face divorce, and if you kidnap somebody you might live in infamy. Focus on the *consequences* of your actions and let the Conscience be damned.

"I can't say 'yes' and I can't say 'no.'"

Ours has been called an age of conflict, an age of analysis and an age of anxiety. And it's all these things: My moniker for our interesting times is the age of the wasted will. "What do I want?" is the correct question.

The reason the answer is so tough is the bloody-minded Conscience. "Is what I want right or wrong?" we ask. But it's the wrong question. The right question is, "Am I free to become what I want?" It's why people have trouble both in saying "yes" and saying "no." There is no free answer to the question so long as the Conscience does all the talking.

To say "yes" to the PTA, the Republican Party, and your husband might mean you can't say "yes" to the self. You don't feel separate. Unseparated people are sitting ducks to be zapped by guilt if they even *think* about saying "no." Bringing the Conscience to bay and polishing it off is a lifetime job. Everyone hears the beast howling in the night.

People who say "yes" often feel locked-in, trapped. To be committed to anything causes them to back off involvement with other people. Therefore, they hang loose (they never hang tough) and keep options open (never make commitments). These folks hate to make "mistakes." Saying "yes" to others means saying "no" to the self. Unseparated.

There are no risk-free marriages. The chance of divorce these days is actually about *even*: the chances of unhappy marriage without divorce are greater than even! Given the odds, a lot of people avoid marriage entirely. That, too, is a risk. Like the person who can't leave a marriage because it's *wrong*, another person can't go into marriage because it might be a mistake!

The unseparated feel in other people's power. Oppressed. Victims. But saying "no" to the self when saying "yes" to others is screwy. So if Jake knows what he *wants*, he could frustrate Jill; if Jill knows what she wants, she could stymie Jake. And that's OK; married types aren't living together to accommodate each other's expectations (Frederick S. Perls).

But can any of us be *sure* we *want* what we say we want? Is what we want simply a way to please our partner? Is what we want simply to displease our partner? To either please other people without pleasing ourselves or to displease other people solely to please ourselves is decadent.

So sometimes, most times maybe, saying "yes" to others, is saying "yes" to the self:

"He wants sex (Will I sleep with him?)."

"She wants companionship (Will I dine with her?)."

"My boss wants the work done (Shall I put it out?)."

So to fill my nattering *needs*, as they say in the therapy biz, I need someone to co-operate, to say "yes" to my desires. So it's a question, here's our song again, of attitude. To "need" anything is to feel dependent; to want something is to feel independent. In the first case, we feel inseparate, unfree; in the second instance, we feel separated and free. Easy it isn't, but too tough it's not, unless thinking makes it so.

To be "told" to do something drives some people up the wall and out of their minds. They don't feel separate. They feel in another person's *control*.

So, we do what we *want* (and think we are free), don't do what she wants so we are not in her control, please ourselves by displeasing her, ignore what she wants and take what we want. Impotent. We have a problem and can't obey simple commands (our boss is *paid* to give orders, our wife has every right to make demands, husbands have a free will).

Thus, our husband or wife assumes the role of rule-maker. That's not their fault, we foist it on them. And if we obey the rules ("We fulfill our responsibilities") we do so resentfully; if we disobey the rules ("We feel irresponsible").

We know mothers try to *control* their children by withdrawing their love; we know wives and husbands try to *control* their mates by doing the same thing. It's clear we learned this at our mother's knee. The solution is to give up our state of mind which *requires* us to love or to be loved. Nobody can function in a marriage who is *required* to be loved or be loving.

We say of *that* married couple, "She wears the pants." Or we say of *this* married couple, "She won't make a move without her husband." We establish who is *dominant*, who is *submissive*. And plenty of marriages function on this basis; each thinks, neither partner can *help* being submissive/dominant.

Saying "yes" to others and their saying "yes" to us is co-operation. Two great spirits (strong egos) in synch. Together we make love, money and music. But people who can't say "yes" don't make love, money or music. It takes two to make love, decision-making is the essence of making money, and music is the harmony of two chords. So, if thou hast trouble co-operating with thy spouse, you probably feel in that person's control: You co-operate while he operates.

Be tough enough to accept demands made on you. To resist or accommodate other people's demands is not the problem; it's feeling free to demand (and be demanded of) on the job and at home.

"Sometimes saying 'no' to others is saying 'no' to myself."
So, we *don't* co-operate when we say to ourselves:
"Who needs sex (my husband's a lousy lover)."

"Who needs companionship (my wife's a lousy talker)."

"Who needs this job (my boss gets all the credit)."

Self-defeating, self-destructive and self-immolating. And it's our self-esteem which takes a nose dive: We've placed the *responsibility* for our lousy sex life on our husband, our loneliness on our wife, and the quality of our job on our boss. And—puzzle within a paradox department—we are often charged with being selfish. Our husband says, "What a selfish bitch"; our wife says, "What a self-centered creep"; our boss says, "What an operator."

"Saying 'yes' to myself often means saying 'no' to others."

I want my wife to balance her checkbook; she wants to study for her law boards.

My wife wants me to transplant the strawberries; I want to start a compost heap.

I want my wife to pick up the dry cleaning; she wants to balance her checkbook.

My wife wants me to start a compost heap; I want to watch the fourth game of the World Series.

Hanging tough.

Back to basics: Qualifying for tough love—married love—means feeling separate from the person we married. If we have trouble saying "no" to our husband or our wife, it's just as true we had trouble saying "no" to mom. We didn't feel separate from her; we don't feel separate from our partners.

"My wife dreads being wrong and hates to face mistakes."

People who need to be "in control" hate being wrong and loathe making mistakes. They think they are losing control. They are not effective managers and they have terrible marriages.

To be in control is to be a slave to Conscience. Thus, many managers are constantly appealing to rules, to operation manuals, and to higher authority. If they try to control you, they themselves are controlled by the "rules." And, we know as if life were a game, it's against the rules to make mistakes.

Same at home.

But making mistakes, being "wrong," making a left turn when

you should have turned right, is as much a part of life as the air we breathe and we can't breathe in marriage or on a job, if we are forbidden to make mistakes.

That's the problem in government. Civil servants who make mistakes suffer; civil servants who don't make decisions don't make mistakes, so they don't suffer. But everyone in government service complains of being stifled, breathless.

People in jobs and marriages who suffer are far better off than people who don't. The first feel pain. Pain is important, it means we are alive, we feel. The second feel neither pain nor pleasure. They are nonfeeling—dead.

"Whenever my wife says 'no' to what I want, it's frustrating."

Hey, gang, just because I know what kind of job I want doesn't mean I'm going to get it! Just because I know where I'm going doesn't mean I'm going to get there!

Life is tough.

Of course, if I can't get what I want, I'm going to be frustrated. Sometimes mad as a hatter, maybe mad as a wet hen, occasionally madder than mad. Passionate. And a passionate response to frustration means we are alive and well and know where we are going. A dispassionate response to frustration might do permanent mental damage.

So the message for working couples is to put out and don't shut up. Put your feelings up front and show disappointment. Don't clam up and play the martyred bride, the long-suffering bridegroom. Who wants to be married to Mr. or Ms. Grundy?

Living with another person—hanging tough—is a hassle. If you can't hack through hassles, you aren't qualified for tough jobs/tough love.

"I'm secretly pleased when I displease my wife."

Inseparation syndrome.

To deliberately displease your wife is to fear being in her control; to please her is to capitulate to her control. Crazy.

That's the result of people taking responsibility for each other's happiness. "My life can't be entirely meaningless if I can make my wife miserable today," says the five-star bastard. And his wife might play into the hands of his problem by becoming miserable.

It's possible but hardly probable that two people could live side by side, the one miserable today, the other miserable tomorrow. If so, it means each partner has a strong ego. But in most marriages we blame our unhappiness on each other. We think we have the power to make people happy or unhappy.

Feeling free and separate means trying neither to please nor to displease our mates but trying to please the self instead. But if a state of war exists between two people, neither feels free to please (or be pleased).

"Gee, I could be happy with my wife," is impossible for a man to say who doesn't feel separate from her. Feeling separate from her means refusing to take responsibility for her feelings, and allowing himself to become vulnerable to his own.

More men than women are frightened of feelings. And more women than not, eager for men to express feelings, are disappointed when men let it all hang out. Is it really their husbands' feelings which interest wives so much as male reassurance?

The intimate know how to love and be loved: There is a fixed bridge over their moat into the castle. They are unprotected, they can be hurt. They play with pain. Pain is important. Avoiding pain is avoiding feeling. But who is hurt most in love, he who closes himself off to it or she who is open to it? Well, both are hurt. But far, far better to be hurt by others than to hurt ourselves.

The unintimate are emotional cripples: They hobble themselves by protecting themselves from their own feelings. The intimate are strong enough to lower their guard.

So, a man needs to go the extra mile and show his feelings ("Talk to me," says his conversation-starved wife). And a wife needs to hang tough (what the old man has to say might curl her hair).

But the pleasure of giving pain is sadism. Too much "truth-telling"—letting it all hang out, saying what we really feel—promotes pain. Taking pleasure in giving pain is not feeling separate. As we shall see, we can't be tender unless we are tough, we can't love unless we hate, we can't qualify for tough jobs unless we have strong egos; we can't take pleasure in our lives unless we can cope with the pain of guilt. A tough aspect of money marriages is this constant in-and-out, inseparate/separate, uninvolved and very much involved interlocking of two people. If both partners have a high intimacy index, the pain of separation is often intolerable. And if both partners have a low touchy-feely quotient, the painful inability to become involved is unacceptable. In the first and smaller group, each must find the courage to break away from the other; in the second much larger group each must find the courage to love the other.

The serpentine nature of the money marriage requires two great spirits. The strong are tender. The weak-willed don't have the strength: They are too weak to separate, not strong enough to become involved. Each partner feels inseparate, neither partner feels free.

"If I do what I want, I feel bad!"

Irresponsible.

To do what others want is responsible; to do what you want is irresponsible. The former is realistic; the latter isn't being realistic. Conscience doth make cowards of us all. Thinking so makes it so.

ITEM: A working wife and mother takes time "off" to attend her evening class in computer sciences; she is plagued by her Conscience: Hubby must prepare the evening meal.

ITEM: A working husband accepts a great job which will keep him on the road more than ever; he is conscience-stricken about not seeing enough of his children as is.

ITEM: His boss wants him to work over the weekend to complete a report (his boss was to have finished it a week before). It's the weekend he's booked for a tennis clinic in the Poconos.

Note: If you do what you *want,* you frustrate what other people *want,* if you do what you *should,* you are thwarted by what other people *want.* In the former case, you feel guilty; in the latter, miserable. In no case do you feel free. Separate.

People of Conscience are never free. Separate. They can't make free decisions. But a strong spirit prevaileth. If you work this weekend (and don't go to the Poconos), you damn well *want* that report done; if you go to the Poconos, you damn well *want* to work on your backhand. If you reject a cool promotion which means more travel, you damn well *want* more time with your kids; if you accept your promotion, you damn well *want* to succeed. If you take time off for a computer programming course, you damn well *want* another tool to master your job; if you stay home and feed your family, you damn well *want* the pleasure of their company.

The focus is the self, the free will. Knowing what you want and saying so might or might not please others. But letting your Conscience be your guide is certain always to displease: To love and work is out of the question; to be able to love and work means confronting what other people want. That requires courage: The courage to love thyself.

"I hate myself when I make a mistake."

"You told me if Debbie got her bike, I could have a dog!" your youngest son wails. "Oops! I made a mistake," you think. "Now I'll have to do what my son wants." Thus, you feel in his control. Unfree. Inseparate. Unhappy. But it's not your son who "controls" you; it's your bloody-minded Conscience. The Conscience doesn't forgive. So, the point in life is to be perfect. Don't make mistakes.

Perfectionists are an unhappy breed; they are always in a shortfall position. Mistakes are mortal sins without benefit of absolution. The way to avoid the blame of mistake-making is never to make decisions. Thus, perfectionists are often ineffective on the job (they can't take risks for fear of making mistakes); unable to make or spend money (they might lose it); miserable at home (they hate their imperfect selves).

Educators and parents have a lot to answer for: They transmit the message to children that it's *wrong* to make mistakes. Children are often protected from the chance to make mistakes. And can't live with their Conscience when they do. Conscience is imposed on us from the outside.

Impotency, like the Conscience, is outside of us; Potency, the human spirit, is inside of us.

But in many money marriages, Conscience often ruleth. The spirit never prevaileth. So many things can go "wrong," working couples are whipsawed by guilt. There is no profit in trying to be perfect: If she burns the roast, he brings home a colleague unannounced, their oldest flunks trigonometry, *someone* is to blame. So what? To be at blame is not to be bad, unless thinking so makes it so.

Fortunately, people hate being unhappy, too. Since most of the human race's unhappiness is caused by feeling at blame, the enemy of happiness is the Conscience. "Please, somebody, say I'm right!" is a cry of help to set us free. Marriage counselors are beset by clients who insist their marriage partners are at fault, to blame, guilty of cruel and barbarous conduct. But nobody can help us get off the hook except ourselves. Nobody is to blame for your unhappiness except your Conscience.

"If hubby makes a mistake, I make sure he knows it."

"Watch out," she screams, "you're driving up a one-way street!" He hates it when she yells at him this way, but what he really hates is making a mistake. Because he made a mistake—drove the wrong way—he is to blame. Guilty. And for every crime there is a punishment.

"For God's sake," he yells, "you don't have to scream like a banshee!" Cleverly, Mr. Never-Made-A-Mistake has shifted the blame. His wife must take the blame because she raised her voice. She is guilty and will be made to suffer.

In marriage, if each partner isn't allowed to make mistakes (and if we don't allow ourselves to admit mistakes), it's due to our Conscience. We hate it so much we can't stand it. Nobody can stand hating himself. But it's not ourselves we hate; it's our Conscience.

But if Conscience is our Character, Character is Fate (Heraclitus). But Conscience is not our character; it's imposed on us by parents, schools, churches, and governments, not to mention the Junior League. In marriages where Conscience rules, it's prosecutor, judge and jury. Someone is either right or wrong, someone is at *fault*. This person is to be arraigned at the bar of justice, made to accept blame, and punished!

"No-fault" divorce is a popular concept. It's because nobody wants to admit being to blame. But there is no such thing as a no-fault marriage. Plenty of grounds for divorce—being at fault—are apparent within a few days of being married (Robert Anderson)!

"If I'm at fault, I blame my wife."

That's your Conscience talking to you. Feeling blame is intolerable, there are no guilty men in prison. And there is no one at fault in marriage, it's our partners who are to blame. So, that's right, make your partner bear the rap, feed her Conscience. But you don't *make* her guilty, her Conscience makes her guilty.

Everyone who examines his thoughts discovers how he hates his Conscience. "I'm not at fault," we say at home. "I'll cover my ass," we say at work. It's other people who are at fault.

But shifting the blame doesn't work. The Conscience is a hot potato, nobody wants to handle it. So, we are blamed and thus blame our spouse for some *other* act of commission or omission. Try thinking about what your last fight was really about! Well, what it was about was your malignant consciences.

The core of the functioning marriage is the elimination of the blame of mistake-making. As long as partners can't face up to mistakes (they are faced down by their Conscience), neither has anywhere to go with the other except into a state of antipathy and apathy; sympathy is out of the question.

It's the same on the job: You won't qualify for tough jobs unless you are able to make tough decisions. Many decisions are mistakes. Admitting these decisions were mistakes is a qualification for filling a responsible job. And at risk of being pseudo-profound, being able to admit many things in our civilization are mistaken is the best thing about civilization. The worst thing in our civilization is its Conscience.

"I can't seem to fire anyone at work."

You feel responsible.

Managers complain that having to fire someone is the worst part of their job. But managers who can't fire people, eliminate the self instead. That's right! They fire themselves! That way they won't feel guilty. Their Conscience is kept at bay, the beast is on his leash.

If you can't fire your secretary at work (for not meeting deadlines), it follows you can't punish your son at home (for driving his moped through your rose garden). In both cases you feel responsible!

But why are *you* responsible for your secretary meeting deadlines? Why are *you* responsible for your son trashing the rose garden?

Make people take responsibility for themselves. That means they must take the consequences of their actions (and their inaction). Making people pay the consequences is what managers and parents *do!*

Plenty of working people who can't bring themselves to fire people complain of migraines, insomnia, back pain. They literally give the self a pain in the ass. And they call the people they would fire a pain in the ass! To eliminate the pain, they need to fire their secretary. Eliminating the self—not firing their secretary—causes the pain.

To get rid of the biggest pain in your life, get rid of your Conscience. It's making you a minion manager, an ineffective parent and a lousy lover. The free will is engaged in a great war with Conscience. To be great, paraphrasing Shakespeare, is to start a quarrel with the world. And to be happy is to start a quarrel with your Conscience.

Ethics, Work and Worth

Our problems in life begin when we know what we want.

JULIAN HUXLEY

"Money marriage isn't linear."

"Money marriage is circumferential."

"Career counseling is an extension of marriage counseling."

"I follow my husband wherever his job takes him."

"I follow my wife whenever she is reassigned."

"Any husband who stays at home is no kind of man!"

"My husband practices corporate law in Los Angeles and I'm an air traffic trainee in Denver."

"Absence makes the heart grow fonder."

"I work regular business hours and my wife's on the night shift."

"My husband and I constantly play 'my turn now, your turn next time.'"

"Who I am is what I do, not where I do it."

"What's most important is the children's happiness."

"The toughest part of money marriage is sometimes putting the job first."

"Money marriage isn't linear."

Two-person careers are rare, traditional marriage is in decline; money marriages are on the increase. The form of marriage is changing, but the content of marriage is the same. The way we work has changed. The form is different, but the content is the same. The linear career (college, grad school, corporate training program, entrance level professional, middle level manager, assistant manager, General Manager, Assistant Vice-President, Vice-President, Group Vice-President, Executive Vice-President, President, Chairman of the Board, Chairman of the Bored) is the traditional route in work. But it's no longer normal nor modern.

Neither marriage nor careers are simple straight lines. Moreover, there is no longer a consensus on what it is to be "successful." But there *is* a developing consensus on what it is to be happy: Most people agree the quality of life is more important than the quantity. But nobody is saying quantity, i.e., money, isn't important. Money is the second most important thing.

Happiness is the new success ethic.

Let's look at a young couple more "normal" than you might think. Note the non-linear aspects of both their love and work life; the zig-zag, pert-path, serpentine character of their mutual involvement and separation.

Himself first: A college drop-out, he drops in to the Colorado Rockies and supports himself as a bartender while he masquerades as a ski bum. Of course, he checks out an attractive cocktail waitress and in time they are "living together." Come the Summer season, he starts completing applications to return to Cornell. In Ithaca, he works part-time as a bartender and goes full-time to school. The lady in his life (following up on a good thing) joins him in his last semester and together they celebrate his graduation and hitchhike around the world supporting themselves teaching English. After a year they settle in Taiwan, he studies Chinese and gains admission to a stateside graduate school. Eventually he earns his Ph.D. and does a stint at the JFK school in Cambridge. His first "job" is with a foundation in Indonesia. Oh, I forgot to mention that he finally ties the knot with his live-in companion somewhere in the middle of his

Ph.D. orals. Together they go to Djakarta and when his two-year gig is over both move to Hawaii where he writes a book.

What about Herself? Well, when she meets her live-in companion, she's graduated from college and is on her year "off." After reaching Ithaca, she supports herself working as a research assistant and she finds herself learning silk-screening techniques in Taiwan which she uses to establish a stateside business while Himself finishes his Ph.D. His job in Indonesia is a perfect base to expand her operation. Oh, I forgot, she pops a baby in the South Seas and in Hawaii she's giving some thought—having sold her business—to going to graduate school.

Note the point when each *co-operated* with the other, where the points on her compass coincide with the points on his; where each did what each wanted mostly in tandem, sometimes out of synch with each other:

(a)   To live or not live together?
(b)   Live together in Ithaca?
(c)   To work while he studies?
(d)   Hitchhike around the world?
(e)   Stopover in Taiwan?
(f)   To take up silkscreening? To learn Chinese?
(g)   Back to Ithaca? She works? He studies?
(h)   Two years in Indonesia? Business venture?
(i)   Baby?
(j)   Sell business?
(k)   Hawaii?

There is nothing traditional about this marriage; there is nothing "glamorous" either. There is constant confrontation, conflict, resolution. Two strong spirits dancing to the music of time; harmony and dissonance.

"Money marriage is circumferential."

Imagine yourself to be a circle; imagine your mate to be a circle. Now overlap each circle. If there is a perfect overlap, yours is a two-person career; if there is far more overlap than not, yours is a traditional marriage; if there is less overlap than not, yours is a circumferential marriage.

At the point where each of you intersects with the other (for those of you into solid geometry) a *third* torpedo-shaped figure develops. To the extent each partner separates from the other each feels free to expand the circumference of the third circle. To the extent neither partner can separate, the circumference of their common circle contracts or one circle absorbs the other.

In money marriages which *work*, the points on his circular compass which touch hers mean involvement. Marriage becomes a co-operative venture; each partner knows how to operate (and co-operate). Money marriage is a confederation of equals, not a federation of unequals. Confederates are both allies and adversaries, an alliance which either can break at any time. The federated are neither allies nor adversaries, they are in an indissolvable union.

The romantic definition of marriage is the complete absorption of each partner in the other; an apathetic definition of marriage is two parallel lines which never meet. The traditional view of marriage is an overlap between the two circles where the wife's circle is increasingly swallowed up by her husband's or vice versa. The definition of a circumferential marriage is the creation of a *third* circle of involvement. But the trick is for both partners to feel separate.

Neither partner can be involved with the other so long as each feels inseparate. Each can freely choose to be engaged with the other if they feel separate. Result? Repeated confrontations. But "problems" can't be solved without confrontations.

Two-paycheck marriage is by definition circumferential since both partners have the means (two incomes) to give weight to nonorganizational and noncareer considerations (his crazy hang-gliding hobby, her string of money-losing greenhouses). Each partner's life values are meshed against work values.

The payoff is greater freedom for both partners, but the price of this tradeoff of the work ethic for the worth ethic is guilt. Pleasing the self usually provokes the Conscience.

Forty years ago young men worked at General Electric with the goal of being its president by 1980; forty years ago their wives married them to have a family. Today younger men in money marriages are concluding home and hearth considerations are *as* important as their careers; their wives believe their own careers are *as* important as the home. Linear careers and traditional marriages are being swallowed up by circumferential careers and money marriages. And the work ethic is giving way to the worth ethic.

"Career counseling is an extension of marriage counseling."

Each partner in a money marriage has his/her career. But their "Career" is each other. Tough.

Tough on employers who are finding out they don't come first.

Tough on working wives who work every day but still worry about the home.

Tough on men who worry about what it is to be a man.

Everyone feels responsible; everyone feels irresponsible (See *Conscience Doth Make Cowards*). Thus, the responsibility of job and marriage drive working couples into divorce. They run away from families and quit jobs. But they are running away from their sense of responsibility.

Attitude is everything. If it's the man's "job" to be the chief breadwinner and the woman's "job" to be the chief breadbaker, both are bound to feel responsible/irresponsible. Nobody co-operates with reality. And reality is that he has his job, she has her job and both manage the home.

Part of reality is what we think of it. Thinking we are responsible is self-defeating. True responsibility is being responsive to our own feelings. If two working people love each other, each partner's career could be secondary to their Career.

If marriage is an equity proposition, sharing money, house, and child management, then surely this carries over into our jobs as well. But, like everything else, there will never be a perfect division of labor at home ("that's her responsibility . . . that's his responsibility") any more than there is likely to be perfectly equal earnings on two different jobs. Thinking we are the chief breadwinner; thinking we are the chief homemaker—believing one party *more responsible* than the other—is not equity among equals.

It's his job to feel his job is important; it's her job to feel her job is important. That's being self-aware, becoming separate. This helps both parties focus and programs frequent confrontations, all of which promote a sense of separation and independence. And it re-establishes, time and time again, that her career and his job are equally important!

But if either party perceives the other partner's job to be more important, that's Big Trouble. Not unlike believing my wife's health is more important than *mine;* her goals more important than my objectives.

If I think so, *thinking makes it so.* That's when I begin to complain about being oppressed. But the responsibility for my "oppression" is mine. My wife can't take responsibility for my feelings.

An oppressed person oppresses himself; his job is to resist feeling oppressed. This means focusing on the self. You can't do that until you eliminate from your mind "my wife"/"my husband." And you can't if you are constantly taking into account other people: Employers, spouses, children, in-laws. Eliminate them from your thoughts. Once you have focused on the self, then (and only then) are you able to take other people into your thoughts. You become a "caring" person.

The outcome is that "other people" sense you are "responsible." It's because you know what you feel and don't hesitate to reveal it; if you don't know what you feel and can't reveal it, other people sense you are "irresponsible." You are a concerned but uncaring person.

"I follow my husband wherever his job takes him."

Wife, obey thy husband; Husband, love thy wife. The Army wife, the corporate spouse, the academic helpmate, the politician's spouse, all are enjoined to practice obedience. In return, the Army officer, the corporate treasurer, the professor of musicology, and the Congressman from the 3rd District are commanded to love.

It doesn't work. You can't obey unless you are willing to; you can't love unless you want to. So if you're married to someone frequently transferred, it's a life either willingly or unwillingly lived.

In olden days, to be sure, women followed their husbands as surely as their husbands followed the flag, the Cross, the corporate seal. Some women felt free to do, some felt unfree. It's the same today.

Working couples either feel free with each other or no. It's our attitude, not the structure of marriage, which is decisive. The more things change the more they stay the same.

The plain truth is that plenty of women become as excited as their husbands about transfers, promotions and reassignments. Army wives love to travel; corporate spouses thrill at a chance to live in New York City; academic wives willingly look forward to living in Palo Alto; politicians' wives love going on the campaign trail.

But if working wives hate it, why do it? File for divorce. That's putting the self first. No man should give up a job he loves unless he loves his wife more than his job. If not, it can't be helped (Frederick S. Perls).

"I follow my wife whenever she is reassigned."

Men accompany women on location far less frequently than wives follow husbands, but their ranks are growing. For plenty of celebrated women, their husbands are often their business managers. Still other men use their wives' salaries to start up businesses, become self-employed, realize travel opportunities.

The major obstacle for a man is overcoming his sense of responsibility. But if his sense of malignant responsibility is muted, if what he does is what he wants, if a life following a working wife gives him pleasure, a husband who adjusts to her career path can have a rich life. And, like traditional wives, househusbands happy at home are a pleasure to be around.

The major problem for working wives with househusbands is their giving up feeling "responsible" for the home. This means househusbands need to give up thinking their working wives *are* responsible. And, of course, the way these two live isn't the way their parents kept house. That's the nub: Thinking unconsciously that our working wife/househusband arrangement isn't natural, in conformity with generally accepted family principles. But feeling free is often a question of disobeying "principles," customs, mom and dad. Happy househusbands are the real revolutionaries. But unhappy househusbands, often have, like traditional wives, enormous self-esteem problems.

"Any husband who stays at home is no kind of man!"

That might be true.

Like the traditional housewife, a househusband must cope with the self-esteem issue. Plenty of traditional homemakers literally make themselves sick; the homemaker's disease. It's no use saying this problem is in our heads, psychosomatic disabilities are as disabling as physical ones.

So, househusbands, too, must address the same issue: Can your ego cope with being economically dependent on your wife? Can you live with the self? If not, don't put yourself down, plenty of traditional wives can't either; it's a major reason wives are returning to the workplace. The trick is to focus on a project which you can do at home, while you househusband, which raises self-esteem and might bring in some money besides. That way you won't feel useless. Dependent.

The toughest question asked of traditional wives in mid-passage, Oil of Olay types, is, "By the way, what do you *do*?" Plenty of traditional homemakers have an anxiety attack; househusbands go into a depression, too. But, of course, letting "other people" program what we want (a job, for example) is as unworthy of househusbands as it is of traditional homemakers. A snappy reply to that question, "What do you really do?" is to ask in return, "Well, my pleasure in life is my family and myself. By the way, is what *you* do any more important than *that?*"

I much admire traditional homemakers who really dig being mothers and wives and stand above all the bustle in the world of work; I'm speechless with admiration in the company of men who can do the same. Taking pleasure in the self, working and playing at home doing what you want, whether for money or no, is no easy thing. Only heroic egos need apply.

"My husband practices corporate law in Los Angeles and I'm an air traffic trainee in Denver."

Very unsatisfactory.

He has his career, she has her job—who is minding the home? Answer: There is *no* home to mind. How did these two occupational incompatibles come together in the first place? Well, each no doubt accommodated the other before marriage and thought about reconciling work with love *after* marriage: "After all, tomorrow is another day"—Scarlett O'Hara (Margaret Mitchell).

Bothwell's advice to Mary, Queen of Scots, is apropos, "Bed them, madame, don't wed them!" And couples in a premarital holding pattern either should have an affair and forget marriage or resolve the work/love issue and marry. No two ways about it, commuter marriage is a *temporary* inconvenience for younger marrieds and an occasional necessity for older folk. But only the non-intimate can hack a permanent sleep-alone arrangement.

Reconciling love/work issues means putting the worth ethic ahead of the work ethic. Marriage is a Career. But if his job and her job are more important than their lives together, if both want the pleasure of marriage but won't pay its price, neither is co-operating with reality. The reality is that most people would rather sleep together than sleep alone.

For younger working couples, the commuter marriage is an arrangement which temporarily "works" so long as the pleasure of the work exceeds the pain of separation. So, yes, Jane in Denver who digs aviation and Jack, in Los Angeles, who has just begun to practice law, are establishing careers each wants. But when the pain of separation becomes greater than the pleasure of each doing his own thing, someone is going to give. And traditionally, it's the working wife.

Sleep-alone partners are often artists, athletes, scholars and business careerists. As we have seen, the marriage often dissolves or one partner, usually the wife, "gives in." Sometimes it's the husband; he follows her to her good job in Albuquerque. So commuter arrangements work as long as younger people are sorting out options, establishing careers, finishing educations. And midcareerists, often because of war, short-term away-from-home assignments and on-the-job crises, are compelled to choose between the pleasure of each other's company and workplace responsibilities.

In either case, hang tough: Commuter marriage is a sometime

thing. If a full-time thing, something's bound to give and it's usually the mysterious thing two people have for each other.

"Absence makes the heart grow fonder."
"Usually for someone else" (Franklin P. Adams).

That's the rub about commuter marriages, nobody likes to sleep alone. Manufacturers' reps, pharmaceutical detail types, and road-show entertainers—the host of men and women who live one place and work many places—are in greater need than stay-at-home marrieds. And their spouses who stay at home while they hit the road have needs, too.

Sexual need is constant. That's never going to change. But plenty of marriages survive even though one partner and/or the other spends most of his or her time in airports; they survive because neither partner wills an end to the marriage. They trust themselves and each other not to play around; they are no longer merely married but are re-married.

But for the merely married, a sleep-alone arrangement must be a short-term thing. That's because two people, still growing up, need each other's ego to sharpen their own. That can't be done if he works in Tulsa and she punches a timeclock in Chicago. So, think twice (three times!) about sleep-alone arrangements. Not thinking about it could be a signal neither partner is involved with the other. Neither "controls" the other but neither is intimate either. A commuter arrangement makes sense only because neither is together in any sense. What makes more sense is a divorce.

"I work regular business hours and my wife's on the night shift."
And you meet Sunday morning and read the comics together.

Tough. Sometimes necessary. But like a commuter's marriage eventually intolerable.

Conflicting hours of work involve a lot of intra-family memo writing and home seems more like a message center than a port in a storm. The serpentine nature of marriage isn't possible. Parallel partners aren't involved with each other. Separation becomes customary and routine. Each partner functions alone and resents functioning together. A lot of fighting takes place. Either they fight to maintain their separation or fight to free themselves of their short-term involvement. In the long run, there is no pleasure in it.

The answer lies in putting the self first. And, if what you want is the pleasure of each other's company, you need to rearrange your working hours. This means one or both partners finding compatible jobs. So, she uses her current job as a base to launch a self-directed campaign to find similar work at different hours. Savvy working couples know that skills are transferable. The trick is to establish what your skills are, what jobs require those skills, research employers who hire for these skills at hours of work compatible with your partner. But most working couples feel trapped. They don't think they can find another job with a different employer. They accommodate current employers and lack the imagination to think about next employers* (See *Organizations [and the Working Couple]*).

"My husband and I constantly play 'my turn now, your turn next time.' "

Thinking about working couples and working marriages, the dilemma of his job (versus her career), his promotion (her reassignment) seems central. Everyone knows someone who has made twelve relocations in twenty-four years of marriage. Everyone tells tales of broken marriages which seemingly foundered on the inability of two people to "compromise."

The choices are simple enough: (a) Turn down any transfer opportunity; (b) accept every transfer; (c) trade off with your spouse, "My turn, your turn"; (d) establish a commuter marriage; or finally (e) establish an innovative and alternative objective. But if one or both partners don't feel separate, none of these solutions "works."

The heart of the money marriage is coping with "tradeoffs." In plain English, no, we can't have it *all* at once; yes, we can have it *all,* one thing (maybe two things) at a time.

I can't invest $30,000 in a graduate education *and* at the same time take two years off in Ibiza and write a novel.

My wife can't have another child *and* at the same time run in the Boston marathon.

* See *Go Hire Yourself an Employer* for a book-length treatment of this important subject.

Our best married friends can't start a chain of wine and cheese shops *and* at the same time expect to take a year off and see the Soviet Union.

That's reality.

Feeling free in love and work means co-operating with reality which is changing all the time (a promotion for him, a graduate degree for her, a second child for both). Consequently, working couples are often moving from one holding pattern to another, now allies (then adversaries), now temporarily living apart to pursue separate careers, now working at building a business together (and not working on salary at all), now backing off and returning to traditional jobs once the kids are ready for college.

As we have seen, the greatest gift a person can bring to a two-paycheck marriage is a strong ego, a great spirit. Who you marry should have a similar purchase on their life. Alas, how many people who marry are so responsible to the self? People's needs—sex, companionship, their need for "support"—are stronger than their egos. And they marry people who are fairly weak-willed, too.

Marriage, as we shall see, is a stage in life. It helps strengthen your ego, you test someone else's ego, you "grow up" together. As such, two people merely married who are becoming "remarried" are weaving in and out of each other, now separated and focused on the self, now involved and interdependent with their mate. Working couples are qualifying for tough jobs at work and tough love at home. That's why money marriage is the best thing going in hanging tough and taking pleasure in both.

"Who I am is what I do, not where I do it."

Foreign currency traders happily practice their craft in Hong Kong or Hollywood.

Saxophone players gladly make music in Carnegie Hall or Covent Garden.

Baseball players rejoice in shagging fly balls in Three River Stadium or the grubbiest playing field in the Texas Panhandle.

For younger working couples to put work before family is part of the same myth that working couples—once established—focus more on family than the job. Becoming "King of the Hill" on the job means staying on top of the hill. And that requires as much energy in mid-career as in the starting gate.

The person they marry needs to understand that the pleasure (and the price) of their company is a life of two for the road.

"What's most important is the children's happiness."

So you turn down a peach of an assignment in the Big Apple (you don't want your children into the dope scene); you give up a shot at a foreign assignment (until your children finish high school); you delay jumping jobs (until your children graduate from high school); you live on one income (until the children are ready for school); you go back to work (to earn the money for their college education).

Your happiness depends on how free you feel. Isn't it worth considering whether your children are equal to coping with dope and alcohol? How can you be sure your children won't benefit from a European education? And is it really responsible to delay finding a job you want until the children win their college sheepskins? And wouldn't *two* incomes buy first-rate child care for your children? And does it make sense going back to work to pay for your children's college education when it's not even clear your children want a higher education?

Tough questions.

And hanging tough in marriage means asking the self these questions. And, above all, it means *asking your children.* Helping kids be responsible is making them take responsibility for their own happiness. Putting your children's safety before your happiness is no way to raise children, and ignoring your children's safety to fulfill your interests is selfish. But thinking you always know what's best for your children and for children to think that mom and dad always know what's best isn't realistic. Nobody feels separate.

"The toughest part of money marriage is sometimes putting the job first."

So, in putting your job before marriage (or marriage before the job) you're bound to feel "irresponsible" to one (or the other). No wonder working couples suffer from a higher divorce rate than traditional couples! Working at a tough job and hanging tough with your partner inflames your Conscience. You are crucified by your sense of Responsibility. And your sense of Responsibility toward Work and Marriage destroys happiness in both.

In the world of work, men feel more "responsible" than women; in the world of marriage, women feel more "responsible" than men. This is the reason women often turn on to jobs more than their husbands; it's the reason husbands often turn themselves off on the job. But women, if a marriage fails, feel far more "responsible" than their husbands. "Husbands replace wives far easier than wives replace husbands" (Ellen Goodman).

Cruel choices which working couples constantly face are made more painful than necessary by each partner's sense of Responsibility. No matter whether you quit your job (and find another), divorce your partner (and find another), the capacity to feel Responsible and your incapacity to be "response-able" shadows you your whole life.

"He has his job, she has her career, who is minding the home?" is what people ask about the money marriage. Two-paycheck marrieds don't live like their parents. Mom stayed home and baked the bread and pop went off each day to make it. That's the traditional marriage and working couples live in its shadow.

One result is the destruction of an illusion: The dream of perfect domestic tranquillity.* Working wives particularly bear the burden— leaving undone those things at home which "ought" to be done. And men are discomfited by the increasing financial, social and sexual independence of their wives. "What is it to be a man?" is the question many men in money marriages are asking themselves today.

Nostalgia is the enemy of money marriage. But the sentimental forget the sometimes stultifying effects of the close-knit extended family, the life-in-death of a death-do-us-part philosophy, and the self-imposed oppression of home-bound wives/work-bound husbands. Everything from inflation to runaway kids is blamed on money marriage. It's charged with undermining family sanctity, customary

* For a more complete report on what Caroline Bird calls the "great revolution of our times," see her book *The Two-Paycheck Marriage,* on how women at work are changing life in America.

sexual definition, and, praise God, our "Judeo-Christian" heritage, all of which, by the way, were worth undermining. And underlying the accusation is the unspoken assumption that the old ways are the best and traditional marriages are good, true and beautiful.

Thinking that the phenomenal increase in working wives is what's wrong with our way of life isn't realistic. The changing character of technology, the economy and our culture changes the shape of marriage but not its content. So a word about criticism of the two-paycheck marriage. For openers:

> It's illogical. We can blame any undesirable social development from declining SAT scores to the increase of male impotence on two-income families.

> Value-rich reasoning ("A woman's place is in the home; a man's place is in the shop") is a hopeless task. It argues for a code of conduct true for some people and untrue for others. It's as silly as saying traditional marriages are necessarily oppressive. Some people thrive in customary marriages.

> Blaming the nature of the two-paycheck marriage for the high divorce rate is no more (and no less) valid than blaming divorce on the high rate of inflation. It makes as much sense (and is as much nonsense) to blame divorce among traditional marrieds on *one* paycheck!

> True, the sheer strain of working at tough jobs and living together is difficult. But life is tough. Conflicting priorities between love and work—the mark of the money marriage—are painful. But "becoming separate" while married helps us cope with the pain and co-operate with reality while merely "being married" doesn't. "Becoming separate"—tough love—helps us bear the slings and arrows of outrageous fortune.

Fighting Fair

Reckon the days in which you have not been angry. I used to be angry every day; now every other day; Then every third and fourth day; and if you miss so long as thirty days, offer a sacrifice to thanksgiving to God.

EPICTETUS

"I often disagree with my wife in public."

"Marital conflict is a result of incompatible personalities."

"Fighting destroyed my marriage."

"Showing negative feelings is a bad strategy in marriage."

"Being hateful while married is awful."

"Fighting fair in marriage is playing by the rules."

"At bottom men and women hate each other."

"I fight fair when I say what I feel; an unfair fight is when he tells me what I'm feeling!"

"My husband is always telling me what I'm feeling."

"Fighting fair often precedes solutions."

"A working wife shouldn't cry on the job."

"Women should be able to cry on the job."

"Working men don't like working women who make waves."

"I often disagree with my wife in public."

Working couples who agreeably disagree with each other in front of strangers are admirable. Those who always disagree with each other in public are contemptible. To feel free to disagree with your mate means feeling free to agree. More admirable yet is someone's ability to admit an error in public in front of his partner.

Knowing thyself is knowing what you are feeling and saying so. But never disagreeing with your partner in public means you are your partner's protector and nobody should protect other people from reality. Part of reality is your feelings about it. Each partner helps the other cope with reality when each tells the other what they are feeling. Protecting other people from your feelings is the way to promote unhealthy dependence.

There are occasions in public when you do *so* protect your partner. But you don't protect them from what you are feeling: You protect yourself from other people. That's self-defense. Often an attack on your spouse in public is an attack on you. On other occasions, it's appropriate your mate defend him/herself. In either event, you can't feel free if you don't feel separate. That's due to your inability to focus on your feelings and being caught up in what other people are feeling. Helpless. Dominated. Impotent.

That might be because you can't show your feelings at home.

"Marital conflict is a result of incompatible personalities."

Fighting won't make you compatible. But fighting in marriage is inevitable if there is compatibility which is a consequence of passion. Feeling free to fight is a condition of passion. Incompatibility is often a consequence of surface harmony and superficial co-operation which squelches passion.

Showing anger is feeling free to do so. The heart of marriage, remember, is the constant coming together and breaking apart of two people. Becoming separate, becoming engaged. The sign of a non-working marriage is neither partner feeling free to come together or pull apart—neither separate nor involved.

Working couples in working marriages feel passion (lust, anger, affection), the whole gamut of emotions running from A to Z. But in dispassionate marriages that don't work, emotions run the gamut from A to B, to paraphrase Dorothy Parker.

It's often more difficult to show passion in money marriages. Partners come to invest more passion in their work than each other. Thus, the money marriage is blamed for the high divorce rate. But marriages, traditional or two-paycheck, fold because passion dissolves. Eros is frustrated and finds an outlet in "careers," affairs, children, and the Monday Night Game of the Week.

"Fighting destroyed my marriage."

But a boring truce destroys marriages as well.

In either event, Eros is sent to the showers. Fighting all the time prevents you from being involved; fighting none of the time prevents you from feeling separate.

Hell is your inability to love. But your inability to love is often your inadequacy in showing anger. Love *and* anger are the alpha and the omega, the Yin and the Yang, the systole and the dystole—the heartbeat of marriage. Like love and marriage, they go together like a horse and carriage.

How many times have we heard, usually from the newly wed (or the nearly dead) that, "Jim and I never quarrel." Smug unreality. Is it possible for two people who passionately care about themselves and each other *never* to engage in a face-to-face fight? It's a crime against nature. It might even be un-American.

The proposition that love and hate are central to working marriages is discomfiting. It flies against the definition of what marriage "should be." To admit that I sometimes hate my wife, for my wife to admit she sometimes hates me is hardly encouraged by the Church, the State, and the School.

"Showing negative feelings is a bad strategy in marriage."

Co-operating with reality takes a lot of courage. Part of reality is our feelings about it. To deny your own feelings and especially the anger you are bound to feel plays into the hands of sentimentalists, all of whom have a stake in promoting the fiction that love conquers all. Well, the Pollyannas are half right. But tough love and the whole truth is that love without anger (and anger without love) won't conquer anything, except the self.

Showing "negative feelings," many people think, is *bad*. Now a bad person is hardly going to like himself. Bad people are guilty and thus punish themselves and become miserable. Miserable people are no pleasure.

A no-win situation? No, indeed.

A lot of married folks get a divorce. That's one way to solve a problem; simply eliminate it. But how can anyone find happiness *alone*. "Creative Divorce is like creative bankruptcy" (Ellen Goodman).

Another way to solve the problem is to evade it, go around it. To circumvent problems is to deny they exist. Therefore, squelch "negative feelings" and eliminate positive feelings, too. Plenty of working couples who hate anger try staying "busy." That is, become so involved with jobs, children and the garden club they avoid feelings—positive and negative.

This solution is never satisfactory. Great victories, Winston Churchill once said, are never won through great retreats. And retreating from your feelings is self-defeating.

There is a third solution.

But a warning: The third solution causes guilt on contact. So, to avoid the guilt, avoid the solution.

Feeling free to hate our mate (without feeling bad) means feeling free to love him, too. The act of hating is the opposite side of the same coin, heads I hate, tails I love.

Anger is natural; anger with whom you live helps you to separate. Feeling independent of someone allows you to feel loving. Thus, showing anger is a tool you use to "become separate" while married.

In another context, you sometimes hate your work (in order to break free of it).

You hate your children (in order to break free of their demands).

You hate your attitude in order to change it.

It's impossible to become passionate about your work, children, and attitude *if you don't feel separate from them*. Anger helps you free the self. How can you break free from your work, your mate or a bad habit (overeating, smoking, drinking) if you don't feel separate from them.

"Being hateful while married is awful."

Everyone would rather be loving than hateful. But the stark truth is, you can become neither if you don't feel both love and anger. The necessary ingredient is courage.

Courage comes from inside ourselves. We can't confront others until we confront the self. So, stop calling anger "negative!"

But there is a difference between "hating" and feeling "hateful." Hating *well* means expressing your anger in the first place; being "hateful" means suppressing these feelings. If there is in your marriage a "hateful" quality, it's because nobody feels separate. You say it's a "communication" problem, but it's more complicated. You can't communicate "negative" feelings you think. It's not *nice, good, mature.*

To discourage hateful feelings and encourage loving feelings means hating resentment. A mark of a hateful marriage is the resentment both parties feel toward each other. Nobody feels free. But revealing your anger banishes resentment and your hatefulness.

Express your anger: The very act of expression is the solution. That's why in working marriages a lot of fighting takes place. Why, when you grow angry with your partner it's a liberating (and loving) act. Somebody who cares enough to grow very angry with me must love me very much. It's why good sex is often the consequence of a good fight.

Learn to *fight fair.* Fighting unfair is turning the self off and then blaming your lack of feeling on the person you live with. But we can't turn each other off; we turn ourselves on (and off).

"Fighting fair in marriage is playing by the rules."

Making marriage work is hard work if you take seriously the mythology which surrounds the subject. Marriage half-truths are the junk food of romanticists and gothic marriage counselors. The vocabulary of the marriage myth-makers is replete with words like "trust" . . . "commitment" . . . "maturity" . . . . "meaningful relationship." Invariably, the myths of marriage all boil down to a bunch of rule makers writing still another set of rules by which you *must* live if you are to "actualize your potential," find joy in your "relationship," and make a "mature marriage."

It doesn't work.

No one completely fulfills his potential, joy is evanescent and "mature marriage" a bore. This whole business of rules is at the heart of the problem. Nobody wants to live a life, married or otherwise, subscribing to rules other people write. Rule-makers are born mother-lovers; they never broke free of mom. What's "right" and what's "wrong" isn't important; it's what's "free." Feeling free doesn't mean playing by the rules, it often means ignoring them. And if you play by the rules, it's not because the rules are right but because feeling free is right.

If you join the rule-makers (and start making a few of your own), this encourages your mate to do the same. Soon, your marriage develops its own Operations Manual; in case of dispute, refer to the rule book. Beginning with the Ten Commandments and ending with last week's advice column, there is a body of Law surrounding the subject as thick as the Sunday *Times*.

Fighting clears the air: It's the best anti-pollution abatement device available. Each partner reveals what he or she wants (a vacation home, a trip to the Far East, a business of his or her own, a chance to be with the kids). This frees your partner to reveal what he or she wants (a shot at another job, a remodeled kitchen, a chance to work at home, a fancy private school education for the kids). Working couples can't solve problems, can't have a *worthwhile* marriage, unless they fight about what each wants: The worth ethic.

"At bottom men and women hate each other."

Well, it's because men *need* women; women *need* men. Needing anything often breeds resentment, anger and rage (in that order). Being dependent on someone (and being depended upon) means we aren't free, right? Wrong. Dead wrong.

The wrongheaded think self-sufficiency is independence; the free thinking know self-love isn't love. For reasons not entirely clear to me, men are more prepared to admit their need for women, than women will admit their need for men. Is it another example of female oppression? A horny woman who admits it's nice to have a man around the house is the kind of gal every guy wants to play house with.

Nevertheless, it's *half* true that men and women hate each other. But it's altogether true to say that men and women both love and hate each other. No man feels complete without possessing (and being possessed by) a woman; no woman feels complete without possessing (and being possessed by) a man. So, what we hate is not men or women, as such, but our lack of completion. Our impotence.

"Women are good for only one thing," says the misogynist. "Men are good for nothing," says the manhater. Thus, we deny our need, rebel against our dependence, violate human nature: The responsibility of being free.

For potent working couples, it's necessary to cultivate both your Demons and your Angels (Rollo May). To love (and not to anger); to anger (and not to love) won't work. Feeling *free* to both love *and* hate the person you live with is tough love.

Thinking you must be positive all the time is being "responsible." Everybody feels lust, anger, and envy—so-called negative emotions. But emotions are neither positive nor negative; turn off the cold water tap and you turn off the hot. Turn off the anger and you turn off the love.

"I fight fair when I say what I feel; an unfair fight is when he tells me what I'm feeling!"

You don't know for sure what your boss, your husband or your child *feels!* Everyone is separate. Be *responsible* to your own feelings. Shift the *focus* from other people onto the self. Becoming self-aware is more difficult than becoming aware of somebody else; listening to your own feelings is more difficult than being sensitive to another person's feelings.

Self-awareness is looking out for the self. And you function best with people who never disguise or deny what they are feeling. You function least well with people who care about what you feel but can't tell you what they feel. These are "irresponsible" people.

But look again. Break responsibility down to three words: *Able-to-Respond.* Able to respond to whom? A lover, a companion, a husband? Well, sorry about that, *no*. Real responsibility is the *ability to respond to your own feelings*. That sounds easy, right? Wrong, again. It's tough work. Nobody taught you. Rather, you're trained to be *sensitive to other people's feelings*. But how can you be considerate of my feelings when I don't know what I'm *feeling!* Or I don't say what I'm feeling.

And how do you touch base with your feelings? By separating yourself from other people's feelings.

Is this why the old-fashioned idea of love eternal is, thank heavens, dying? Are people tired of living for someone else's feelings, losing their personality within another's, *being in love*? It's certainly a prescription for falling in love but who wants to be a prisoner of it? Shackled. Unfree. Inseparable. Dependent.

But how to fall in love without *yielding* to another person? Well, you can't and no man or woman of right mind wants to . . . But what you *can* do, once the pleasure of someone's company begins to fade, is to recover your freedom. Separate. And that means becoming self-aware. The impression of the man or woman in your life correspondingly improves. Becoming self-aware in marriage doesn't mean an end to the marriage, it means a remarriage.

So noninvolvement is not freedom, a poor sense of separation is not a marriage, feeling free isn't a solitary task, and being in love is not personal surrender. Happy people say "yes" *and* "no"; they cooperate—never capitulate. They love each other. But it's never romantic love; it's tough love.

"My husband is always telling me what I'm feeling."

He can't get it up; so he focuses on why she doesn't turn on! "My wife has no feeling for me," the unfeeling husband confesses. "My husband really turns me off," confesses the unfeeling wife. Impotent. But impotency blights every aspect of life.

To know and reveal what you are feeling is potent; to stifle your feelings or not reveal them, impotent. In bed, you accommodate each other's pleasure and your own desire goes puff. In conversation, you focus on what the other person is saying and not what you feel about what is being said: A bad listener. At work, you please the boss and displease the self and become ineffectual.

Impotency is outside of us. We are told to please other people, to be concerned about others, to be responsible. Everywhere someone preaches the gospel of *goodness*. That's why we dream about being *bad!* But feelings are neither good nor bad; they are simply real. And part of co-operating with reality is to reveal what we feel.

"Fighting fair often precedes solutions."

Two people can't fight fair if neither partner knows what he or she is feeling. An unfair fight is focusing on *the other's* feelings.

The key to fighting fair is feeling separate from the person you are having the fight with. Quarrels help us *separate* from loved ones. Remember your adolescent rebellions? They helped you break free of family. Same in marriage: Fighting helps you break away. That's why before a trip you quarrel (it makes *leaving* so much easier); and why, returning, you fight (you might resist "coming together").

It sounds simple, but it's not. Moral: You quarrel to feel separate and free, you make up to feel pleasure.

Whether on the job or at home, confrontations precede problem-solving. Fighting fair means revealing what you are feeling and being tough and tender enough to withstand what the other person is saying (and feeling). Both resentment and rage are impotent and inappropriate expressions of human feeling. They are a sign of a wasted will and an unseparated personality. Resentment marks the intimidated person, rage brands the unintimidated. But anger—on the job and at home—is intimate. Effective executives on the job and intimate marrieds at home are vulnerable to their own feelings and open to the feelings of others. Potent men and women sense that unexpressed anger finds a way to wound the self. Both rage and resentment eliminate the self.

"A working wife shouldn't cry on the job."

That's not fighting fair. But it's better than showing no emotion at all.

A few years ago (we were then living through the heroic stages of Women's Liberation) a woman advanced the notion (in the name of Men's Liberation) that men should cry on the job. "Until men learn to have a good cry," she said, "they are bound to remain emotional paraplegics."

The idea of men crying on the job won't go away. Quite apart from the humor, there is a nub of wisdom in the proposition. The challenge is separating the malarkey from the germ of the idea. Thus reduced, the proposition is that people lack passion on (or off) the job. In this form, the idea seems true enough.

What's debatable is whether tears are an *acceptable* expression of passion? And to include men, they of the strong and woeful countenance, flies in the face of human nature. Little boys despise other little boys who cry. Gary Cooper, Hopalong Cassidy, and Joe DiMaggio ("Joe, Joe DiMaggio, we want you on our side!") didn't cry in their beer. Besides, if boys give in to tears, some other boy might be watching.

"Women should be able to cry on the job."

But a woman who cries on the job isn't playing fair with men. Her tears remind men of their problems with mommy, sister, girlfriend, and wife. Men go to work each day to escape the vale of tears at home. To confront a teary female at work, too, goes against the idea of separating the shop from the home.

Still, a woman might argue, tears are a legitimate expression of human feeling. Men must cope with women and the best way is by having a good cry themselves. But if men and women both give in to copious weeping on the job, it's easy to imagine a mass reversion to the fetal position and thumb-sucking.

Besides, are tears on the job *legitimate* and *appropriate?* The answer is no, no, a thousand times no! Tears are for moments of tragic import like when the Red Sox blew the 1978 playoff game to the Yanks.

What is an appropriate and legitimate expression? Well, it's *anger,* that's what it is. Anger is good for us. It clears the sinuses, ventilates the bronchi, and raises the protein count. Anger is far healthier than jogging, which causes shinsplints.

Besides, men have an easier time with anger. It's useful as a part of their leadership style. Now, rage, that's something else again.

Rage in a man is the equivalent of tears in a woman; it's childish
. . . and impotent.

Yet people back off from this idea: Becoming truly angry on the
job is OK for men, but for women, well, it's hardly ladylike, is it? A
working woman in full wrath is considered unprofessional.

This is the core of the apple, the heart of the artichoke, and the
pit of the cherry. People are scared to death of women running
amok. Men particularly panic at the thought; an angry woman could
reduce a man to tears!

Why are men afraid of *The Angry Woman?* Well, let's sock it to
mom again. A truly angry woman reminds us all, on or off the job,
of mom. Hurricanes, until the National Weather Service got with
the revolution, were assigned distaff names, like "Hurricane Hilda."
And it's the hellish Hildas, making waves in the executive suite,
which scare the hell out of men. And women, too, are frightened of
the idea of coming on like a hurricane.

Now, it's men on the job who are most to blame. Men compel
women to accept *one* emotional outlet on the job. Tears. Women
hate themselves when they cry; men dread it. But men won't consider the alternative. And that is to promote a woman's right to be
angry.

"Working men don't like working women who make waves."

What's at stake is our collective mental health. If men and women
alike consider womanly anger unladylike, we are trapped. This
means that women (who are raising their consciousness like crazy,
anyway) need to go the final mile and cope with their anger. And
men, gird thy loins, must give up protecting women's feelings.

Men unconsciously promote tears (and discourage anger) in
women. Turning this situation around means men must give up
being *sympathetic* to women. Sympathy toward women is misplaced
and malignant.

A woman's tears play on a man's protective instincts. This protection racket feeds a woman's propensity to emotionally hold up and
blackmail men through tears. Women come to *lean* on men for emotional support. Indeed, the highest compliment a woman pays a man
these days is to describe him as "supportive." Leaners, clingers, and

dependent-passive types soon become a burden, but men are at fault for letting women lean, cling, and depend on them. And it encourages women to cry.

Being sympathetic is consistent with the way men were raised. But if a man completely accepts an *angry* woman, he is truly being loving. Women have it no way as easy as men in expressing true anger. It's why Katharine Hepburn is so much admired; she has a quality of anger about her which is truly fine.

Moreover, what men fear most, a raging Valkyrie rampaging through the Accounting Department, is fictitious. Rage, a temper tantrum, a volcanic eruption are destructive. Anger is constructive. Anger stands between smoldering resentment on the one hand and a towering rage on the other. If people feel free to be angry on the job, they are happy and effective.

Why?

Well, human happiness is a product of feeling free. If we don't feel free to show anger, it's understandable why we don't feel free! But tears and temper tantrums are out of bounds. Both are a result of bottling up anger. They are the specialized and childish expressions of emotions favored by people who bear resentment. And resentful people on the job don't feel free.

To promote a woman's freedom to become angry means men must show more anger themselves. Especially with the women around them. And women must feel free to express anger especially with the men around them. The crux of the matter lies in the apprehension both men and women feel toward expressing passion. A passionless attitude toward our work and the people we work with is a definition of a bad job. A passionate response to our work and the people we work with is a definition of a good job.

Friends in Need or Friends Indeed

Favors cease to be favors when there are conditions attached to them.

THORNTON WILDER

"Friends of mine have been jealous of my success."

"All my friends are going to be strangers."

"Friends in need are friends indeed."

"All our married friends are splitting."

"I have a lot of acquaintances and few friends."

"I maintain opposite-sex friendships now that I'm married."

"All my friendships are with people of the same sex."

"I'm still friendly with premarital associates."

"I treat married friends as couples, not as individuals."

"My friendships from a previous marriage have disappeared."

"I depend on my friends when I'm in trouble."

"I feel friendlier with other married couples than I do with my mate."

"Friends of mine have been jealous of my success."

Another baby, a choice job, a sudden inheritance—even a new mate—causes friends in need to envy you and yours. Everyone has the strength to withstand your misfortunes but your prosperity is intolerable!

All your "friends" are going to be strangers. Who needs or values a "friend" who fails if you succeed? Separation syndrome: Your "friends" don't feel free with you; they are tracked by values, totems and shibboleths established by other people.

If you play into this inseparation propensity, you might back off from good fortune. Success. Power. Money. Worse, you might scramble after the same totems as your "friends" in hopes it will make them envious! It's clear why you are inseparable!

Envy is in the eye of the beholder. Other people's envy causes you to feel guilty. "Oh, if I *hadn't* won that contract (Jim would still be my boyfriend)" . . . "been awarded that prize (my best school chum would still write me)" . . . "raised such a talented child (Jack and Jill wouldn't have such hard feelings)." Any "friend" who begrudges you wealth (success, beauty, children) is no friend. All your friends are going to be strangers.

"All my friends are going to be strangers."

Try defining what a good friend is and it's as difficult as trying to figure out what a good parent is. Moreover, the nature of friendship varies so from one country to another, one culture to another, it's impossible to establish a universal definition: In Russia, friendships are intense; people are not so much friends as true soul brothers. In America, friendships are so catch-as-catch-can, tentative and abrupt, most of us can count on five fingers friendships which have survived school, the military, eight jobs, three careers and twelve relocations.

In America many of your friends are likely to be strangers. You change; they change—life moves on. At Christmas we catch up. But because of distance, time, and the nature of work and serial marriages, friendships often end. Divorce contributes to the high turnover rate. Moreover, after marriage, couples tend to be friendly with *couples,* not individuals.

At bottom, the mobility of two-paycheck couples has left many with a sense of emptiness at the center of their lives. Fortunately, in the last ten years, there is abundant evidence to suggest many people are saying "no" to a life which moves on and up and away. And "yes" to a life where we don't shuck friends like corn husks.

At the same time there is something to be said for a society so rich in options, places to work, things to do and people to know that collegial associations come second to love and work. Ours is a free country and feeling free often means trading old associations in for new ones.

A lot depends on what you want. A new job on the West Coast? An overseas assignment? A dramatic career change? A big change causes us to pull up roots and plow new turf. And new turf revitalizes us. But everything has its price: The price includes giving up friends who helped us put down roots on other turf.

Americans are always beginning new chapters. And new beginnings cause pleasure and pain.

"Friends in need are friends indeed."
  Quite the opposite.
  Sure, everyone *thinks* he wants to be needed. But in reality we want to be *wanted*. A big difference. It's the reason most people only have a few true friends in a lifetime. Everyone, for heaven's sake, is in *need*. Friendship isn't necessarily a mutual aid society. Common miseries—shared grievance, adversity, and pain—are powerful catalysts. Old Army buddies, schoolmates, and ex-colleagues all shared experiences together. That doesn't make them good friends.
  True, such people *might* become friends indeed: True friendship, no longer fulfilling each other's needs so much as enjoying the pleasure of our friend's company.
  That's the key to friendship. Pleasure. Friends indeed feel free with you; you feel free with them. Nobody is filling out a report card; my good fortune is not his misfortune. You *want* the pleasure of each other's company but don't *need* it.

"All our married friends are splitting."
  Nobody married today can escape the fact that in a few years fifty percent of those married will divorce. The evidence is everywhere:

Every weekend city zoos are packed with displaced fathers, the real estate market for the formerly married is booming and social clubs and packaged vacations aimed at the newly single and single parents are thriving industries.

The zooming divorce rate is lessening the social pressure to stay married. The ubiquity of divorce ("Everybody is doing it") suggests that plenty of people are following the crowd. Circumstances have changed and it's fashionable to split. To be middle-aged, married twenty years and middle class is to be some kind of a freak in trendy circles. Old married hands are made to seem somehow dowdy: There is a suspicion they are delaying some fundamental step in personal development; without the "creative" trauma of divorce, old married hands are somehow retarded.

But patently to divorce because "it's the thing everyone is doing" is as silly as marrying "because all my friends are" (See *Options, Keeping Open*).

"I have a lot of acquaintances and few friends."

"One friend in a lifetime is much; two are many; three are hardly possible" (Henry Adams). For working couples, the message is simple. Wherever you go, whatever you do, whatever your circumstances, you make new acquaintances. Don't make decisions about jobs, reassignments, and new opportunities on the basis of giving up old connections. The pleasure of change is the chance to meet new people. That doesn't mean we forget older ties. And in all events acquaintances who ripen into friends indeed are rare.

Acquaintances are people met en route who might ripen into true friends: Friends indeed. But our greatest need in an absurd society which trains us to be impotent is to establish a continuity, a thread of meaning, a plot with a narrative line. That's where true friends, friends indeed, supply our greatest need. Our true friends remember who we *were* and rejoice in who we become.

"I maintain opposite-sex friendships now that I'm married."

Old beaus and flames were friends in need; these people might be in touch but they can't touch. Acquaintance, yes; working partners, of course; social friends, indeed. But forget the touchy-feely stuff: If you can't, there is something wrong at home.

It's perfectly natural, of course, if denied needs at home, to look outside to others. The impotent want to be potent (See *Sexual Politics*). But the price you might pay is the end of your marriage either in a divorce court or in a state of apathy. So, while you might step out on your wife/be unfaithful to your husband, recognize the consequences. And take action: Time to find out why you get it up with your old flame but go limp with your wife; time to find out why you turn on to your husband's best friend while you turn yourself off to your husband.

"All my friendships are with people of the same sex."

It's probably truer that most of your associations are of the same sex. While everybody needs opposite-sex involvement many prefer the safety of same-sex involvement. It's men and women *together* who keep each other sane. Same-sex involvement is boring. Other men reinforce *macho* conduct in men; other women play into each other's *macha* propensities. But men and women together transcend each sex's limitations.

"I'm still friendly with premarital associates."

When you marry, you often give up your many acquaintances and invest your emotion in one true friend. This is tough on premarital shipmates and colleagues (who feel abandoned and unwanted) and who often disapprove of Mr. or Ms. Right on the provable grounds of having been *replaced*. Many married people, encountering "friends" from the single life, wonder why they no longer click.

Simple.

Dependent associations have been replaced by a dependent marriage; the new person in your life fulfills your needs. Perfectly natural.

Carrying premarital acquaintances into marriage can be childish. It's an indication you are unable to separate from a few associations and move on to marriage with one person. Now, of course, you don't want to slam the door in the face of your bachelor pals and your movement sisters, but don't be surprised if your involvement is different.

As for your partner's premarital pals, don't feel badly if you don't easily warm-up to them. After all, you are the chief person fulfilling your partner's needs. So you don't necessarily become friends of your partner's friends any more than your partner can become a friend of your friends. But that doesn't mean you won't. Friendship, like marriage, is in nobody's control.

The mutual satisfaction of needs should be satisfied inside your marriage. But quite apart from mutual needs fulfillment is the idea of value. Good friends simply have a value greater than dependent associations. Friends indeed are our ties with the past, our memory, bases we touch en route. We are no longer in need of them and they are no longer in need of us. That's true friendship.

"I treat married friends as couples, not as individuals."

When entertaining other marrieds, *always* separate couples; married folks don't come to your soirée to talk to one another.

When traveling by automobile with another married couple, *separate.* Let this wife's husband sit with that man's wife; let that man's wife sit with this wife's husband. Don't segregate the sexes, either: Man/Woman; Woman/Man.

Always introduce wives as Joan ——, Barbara ——, Carol ——; skip the Mrs. routine; it couples people who want to feel free and equal in social situations.

Stop thinking married friends are *units.* If a divorce happens, treat each party separately and don't take sides. Don't talk about the "Johnsons." (Talk about Jack Johnson and Carol Johnson.)

"My friendships from a previous marriage have disappeared."

After divorce, the formerly married begin new friendships. That's often as much from necessity as design. The cruelest moment for many once-married people is the termination, not only of the marriage, but of the friendships that accompanied it.

Why?

Well, for openers, a lot of married folks don't want to catch what you have: Divorce. Moreover, many married folks who think of you

Housekeeping

Viele Hände macht die Arbeit leicht.
(Many hands make light work)

Old German Proverb

"Husbands who can't get it up around the house, can't get it up in bed either."

"Most of our fights are about some trivial housework responsibility."

"Working wives should domesticate the male animal."

"My big problem is doing more things around the house than he does."

"Every working couple needs a wife."

"If one of us must stay at home and negotiate with the telephone repairman, it's always the wife."

"My wife does the housework; I do the yardwork."

"Housekeeping gives me a sense of accomplishment."

"My partner and I fight about what to keep and throw away."

"Whenever he does something around the house, I say, 'Thank you!'"

"Husbands who can't get it up around the house, can't get it up in bed either."

Housekeeping disagreements symbolize a good deal: All our old friends—guilt, dependency, impotence—come out to play. For men especially a transvaluation of all values is underway; there is evidence men are actually doing more about the house. But is there a country anywhere in the world where the working man comes home and cheerfully cleans out the oven? And is there a country in the world where working wives don't come home and throw themselves into household chores?

Unhappy is the husband who can't take care of himself; his self-esteem is going to take a licking. And central to sexual potency is self-esteem. Ergo, men who want to get it up in bed had best get it up around the house. And it is verifiable, men who get it up in bed have more gratified wives. Men who can't or don't have peevish wives.

The trouble begins with mom (See *Momism*). She took care of her sons and so *should* their wives. But wives who become bankers, cheerleaders, chauffeurs, secretaries, cooks, maids and child-care directors for their husbands make the poor dopes more dependent than ever. And the business of separating from mom is made more difficult than ever. At work, secretaries can do the same thing: Men who can't make their own phone calls, find anything in the files, make appointments or even decisions without consulting with their office wife, self-destruct on the home front, too.

Some wives encourage dependency in their husbands—they like, as we have seen, to be needed. Red-hot sexual passion vanishes in such a marriage: Husbands become incompetent in housekeeping and impotent in bed.

"Most of our fights are about some trivial housework responsibility."

No other subject in the money marriage—save sex and money—is so vexatious and confusing as the Great Housework Issue. My hunch is that husbands and wives who co-operate on the home front make mincemeat of the money issue and make out like minks in bed. Everything in a marriage is inter-related and everything that is related is important. Thus, there is no such thing as a trivial matter in marriage. Housework issues represent a good deal more than who cleans out the grease trap.

Thus, people who gladly play house together are likely to love each other—gladly. That's the key: Being glad to be together in the first place and take care of themselves in the second. The focus is on the self. But in housekeeping matters, if the focus shifts, be on guard against a nag attack.

Housekeeping is something we do for the self. It is not an act of accommodation nor appeasement. It's not something we do for our spouse; any more than going to work each morn is going to the salt mines for your family (See *Attitude Is Everything*).

"Working wives should domesticate the male animal."

Tame the beast in him; take care of him.

A man who can't take care of himself is bound to stay at home; he won't roam the reservation and consort with other women who make him feel like a man. Working wives, true, resent the docile, dull and dependent guy who shares their bed and come to believe, no matter how successful their husbands are on the job, they are failures at home.

Being married to a failure protects a woman from acknowledging her own failure. A woman who can't get it off in bed can blame the man in her bed (See *Sexual Politics*). The domesticated man is a eunuch; thus, the untamed man becomes the figment of an unsatisfied wife's imagination.

The message is taking responsibility: Men who care about their sex lives gladly vacuum the living room rug, stack the dishwasher, make their own breakfast. Wives who care about their sex lives gladly go to work, make a living, bring home a paycheck. Nobody is responsible for anyone but the self; no one is domesticated; she isn't on top; he isn't on the bottom, all of which is a working definition of *co-operation:* Two people operating together in housekeeping and coming together in bed.

"My big problem is doing more things around the house than he does."

So:

Become a "response-able" person.

Show your anger and be a bitch.

Stop doing things your husband can do himself.

Start doing things you can do without your husband.

Answer: All of the above.

Becoming "response-able" at home is far more difficult for working wives than their husbands. Wives feel in charge of the house; husbands feel in charge on the job. Thinking so makes it so: Working couples must eliminate their Conscience and raise their Consciousness (See *Conscience Doth Make Cowards*).

Becoming *responsible*, she to the home, he to his work, is a capitulation to custom; doing what we *should* and not what we *want*. Resentment is the result. Wives who work harder at home than their husbands, feel oppressed; husbands who work less at home than their wives, become dependent.

Potency, being happy in love and work, remember, is normal. Impotence, resenting our work and our home life, is abnormal. Potency is inside of us; impotency is imposed from the outside. Mom said, "Be a good wife and take care of your husband." Dad said, "Work hard and protect your wife and children." An example of how we are trained to become oppressed. Dependent. Inseparate.

"Every working couple needs a wife."

That's the spirit.

Plainly, if she has her career and he has his job, both need a wife. Surrogate wives are housekeepers, babysitters, caterers, a bevy of outsiders to take care of the home front while working couples work on the front lines.

Forget the cost; focus on the pleasure (See *Money [and Time] Management*). Sure, the price of outside help could *exceed* half the combined family income, but the payoff in freedom and self-expression is boundless. The point is that many hands make light work and the less work at home, the more time for the pleasure of each other's company.

"If one of us must stay at home and negotiate with the telephone repairman, it's always the wife."

Not always, but mostly.

Working wives, as we have seen, feel responsible for a smoothly running home front; working husbands for bringing home the bacon. But the work she does and the pleasure of her husband's company are more important than the clots of dust under the guest-room bed. The work he does and the pleasure of his working wife's company are more important than the running toilet in the downstairs bathroom.

Working couples *co-operate* best when neither thinks he (or she) is on top. A working husband gladly stays home and parlays with repairmen if he cares about and feels separate from his wife. A working wife gladly goes off to work and leaves her husband to househusband if she cares about her job and feels separate from her husband. But for either to do either each must raise his (or her) Consciousness and eliminate the Conscience.

"My wife does the housework; I do the yardwork."

Most men feel *responsible* waxing the car, cleaning out the garage, composting the vegetable garden; most working wives feel *responsible* waxing the kitchen floor, tidying up the utility closets, canning tomatoes. Home economists tell us the average full-time traditional wife is worth over $20,000 in terms of hourly wages paid chauffeurs, cooks, housecleaners and day-care workers; the traditional Mr. Fixit husband is worth many thousands of dollars, too, as a roofer, gardener, and plumber.

But many working wives complain about the division of labor: Yardwork, in their view, isn't as *important* as housework. Moreover, some men seem to *enjoy* it: Husbands are known to whistle while they work. Even worse, some men contract out chores to gardeners, carpenters and chimneysweepers. Working wives, however, labor joylessly, take housework *seriously,* and feel indispensable.

To make matters worse, many husbands complain about their working wives. The cheapest shot is that working wives oftentimes earn a lower income. "It costs me a bundle for my wife to work." Thus, many working wives think household tasks are what they should do to compensate. They feel they are on a payroll except they aren't paid for what they do. Attitude is everything and if we feel we are working *for someone*, it's going to cause resentment. The long and the short of it is that women feel responsible while they think their husbands are irresponsible: A formula for marital unhappiness (See *Attitude Is Everything*).

Responsible people, we have seen, feel resentment. Working wives feel guilty if the smallest household task goes unattended. To feel guilty is intolerable. So, punish yourself and be miserable. Many working wives are made miserable by their sense of responsibility and are accordingly no pleasure to themselves or their families. No wonder so many of their husbands are spending so much time on the job. Marriage to a miserable woman is a fate worse than celibacy; it might promote celibacy!

So keep in mind the following:

(1) Housekeeping matters are never fun if you think they are duties. True irresponsibility to the self is working at anything from a sense of duty rather than desire.

(2) In the money marriage, there is no such thing as women's work; a man's job. Forget the division of labor.

(3) No matter what a woman's income on the job, her "responsibility" for the home is no greater and no less than her husband's.

(4) The happily "remarried" enjoy housework; it's another thing they do together for the self.

"Housekeeping gives me a sense of accomplishment."

Cleaning out the clothes closet, polishing the furniture, and changing the linen makes some working wives mad; something their mothers no doubt did to them. To perform these tasks is to feel responsible; not to perform these tasks seems irresponsible; working wives catch it coming and going.

But think about it: House management is *doing something for the self*: Thinking we do the laundry for our family is our problem. Secondly, we *see* the product of our work: How many jobs do we initiate *and* conclude solely for ourselves? A tidy living room, a well-scrubbed kitchen floor, a polished samovar is something we see before us—a product of our own labor. An accomplishment. Plenty of working people throw themselves into homework projects— ceramicizing the bathroom, wallpapering the family room, repairing the hi-fi. These people often feel an enormous sense of accomplishment at home which they don't feel on the job.

The tricky thing is our attitude. Thinking, "That's her job." Saying, "That's my responsibility," is hardly feeling free: Nobody is responsible. To think your working wife is responsible for preparing the Thanksgiving Day dinner is to become dependent on her doing it. And to become dependent on anyone often makes us resentful as much as does being depended upon. Dependability is the ability to depend on our own free will. "Gee, I would just as soon forget Thanksgiving this year and take a four-day weekend in the Great Smokies," she says. A dependable wife is a woman who says what she wants; an undependable wife is a woman who does what she "ought." The first is a pleasure to live with; the second is a misery.

"My partner and I fight about what to keep and throw away."

People are divided into two groups: Those who *save* string and those who don't. It's likely string savers will marry people who throw it away; the rocks in his head fill the holes in hers. Arguments about whether to keep Aunt Tilly's antimacassars or put them in the Goodwill box vex most money marriages. Whether you are a string saver or a neatfreak, it's invariably compulsive conduct; we seemingly can't help being the way we are.

No person is quite like any other any more than one snowflake is exactly like another. In marriage, there are two sets of values on housekeeping matters which require reconciliation. How she toasts the bread isn't the way his mother toasted it.

A complete overlap in values isn't possible. And the difference between her values and his is the distance each must bridge if either is to effectively co-operate in house management. Hang tough. Being a neatfreak and living with a man who is a slob; being a slob and living with an anal retentive is an example of hanging tough in marriage.

"Whenever he does something around the house, I say, 'Thank you!'"

Why thank anyone for doing something for himself?

Grateful wives feel oppressed; husbands oppress them. Thanking a man for doing the laundry is as silly as a husband thanking his wife for going to work. But it's not husbands who oppress wives; it's their mothers. Mom brainwashed her daughter to be a good wife (not a working wife).

Every married person is enjoined to be polite. But the alternative isn't rudeness. There is a demonstrable middle ground. The truly courteous care about other people; they aren't grateful if that courtesy is returned. Discourteous people resent feeling oppressed (See *Caring Is Not to Worry*). Becoming separate is giving up being the grateful wife and becoming the courteous companion.

A working man can promote this sense of separation and common courtesy if he gives up expecting to be thanked for performing household tasks. Grateful wives resent feeling responsible for tasks men can perform perfectly well without their wives. A working wife isn't a traditional wife. And men who want both are doomed to be victimized by the sabotage of the truly grateful. Momism is alive and well in the daughters of gratitude.

One definition of a whore is a woman who gives pleasure but refuses to take it. Husbands and wives often prostitute themselves to each other; they please their mates (but take no pleasure themselves) and exact *payment!*

To pleasure someone without taking pleasure oneself is prostitution. Killjoys.

Killjoys insist we are responsible for their happiness. By denying the happiness only they can give themselves, they put the blame on others. And they exact payment: gratitude, money, services, favors.

In bed, at table, on the tennis court, it's our responsibility to the self to call this kind of bitchy conduct to account. Wives don't owe their husbands a good time in bed, a good meal at table or a good workout on the tennis court. They owe themselves the pleasures of a good time in bed, at table and on the tennis court! (See *Attitude Is Everything*).

As for gratitude, forget it! Each partner in a marriage gives the other the most precious possession each has: Time and the pleasure of our company. If in pleasing others, we don't please the self, who outside the Land of Nod should be grateful to us?

Finally, a few house-management insights shared with me by working couples:

Husbands aren't pulling their weight at home as much as they want because they feel incompetent; wives should show them *how* to baste a roast and use a colander.

Housework is great exercise; it beats jogging.

Working wives need to give up feeling in control (responsible) especially in the kitchen—the command post of the home front. Their husbands need to give up thinking their wives are in control.

Watch out for competition; plenty of wives are unconsciously jealous of husbands who are magicians with a Cuisinart. Plenty of husbands grow jealous of wives who bring home a fat pay raise. Clinical. Check with a psychiatrist: It has something to do with mom.

Interviewing
(Myth and Fact)

And God created the Organization and gave It dominion over man.

Genesis 1, 30A, Subparagraph VIII
BOB TOWNSEND, *Up The Organization*

"My problem is my wife knows what she wants to do, but I don't know what I want to do for a living."

"I need a job—any kind of job."

"The point in an interview is taking charge and doing the talking."

"I hate depending on my wife's salary when I go job hunting."

"Working couples should take into account what their partner does for a living."

"The aim of an interview is to get a job offer."

"Always try to please the interviewer."

"Try to control the interview."

"Never interrupt the interviewer."

"Don't disagree with the interviewer."

"Always let the interviewer terminate the interview."

"Never ask for the job; wait for it to be offered."

"Don't ask what you'll be paid."

"Always thank employers if you accept a job."

"Above all, avoid discussing what your spouse does for a living."

"Stop interviewing after you've accepted a job."

"Always put your best foot forward in an interview."

"My problem is my wife knows what she wants to do, but I don't know what I want to do for a living."

Those of you who are paying attention know working wives feel altogether too "responsible" for keeping the home fires burning. What's not so clear but just as true is that many men feel altogether too "responsible" in the world of work. Accordingly, working women are more inclined to buy the idea that they should work at what they want whereas their husbands are more likely to take a job, any job, because their families need the income. That way many working husbands avoid the guilt aroused by the pleasure of doing what they want. And like the working wife who is a misery around the house doing what she "should," her husband is a pain in the derriere going to a job every day he hates.

If you don't know what you want to do, for heaven's sake, don't interview for a job right now. Take two weeks or two months and schedule interviews with people who are working at jobs you might want. Apart from the information you obtain about yourself and the job market, interviewing for information about jobs (rather than asking for jobs you don't want and which might not be available) is a sure-fire way to become comfortable in the interviewing game. This strategy is a cinch to improve your ability to obtain interviews, takes pressure off the interviewer (he needn't offer a job he doesn't have), and improves your ability to interview the interviewer.

"I need a job—any kind of job."

Traditional wives, thus, inflict themselves on the job market because the family *needs* the income. Often they are underpaid because what they make is "pin money" whereas their husbands earn a "salary." Some traditional wives returning to the job market are so uptight thinking about the self (and all the pleasure and guilt such sinful thoughts entail) they are poor negotiators in obtaining the money they deserve.

So, traditional wives returning to the workforce need to put the self first and, like their husbands, interview for information about what they want. True, it might be necessary and desirable to accept a grunt job earning the cash to finance the job search for the job you want, not to mention the grocery bills which *need* to be paid. But the point is to keep your eye on the ball (the self) and use a stop-loss job (stopping the loss of income) as a base to find a job you do *so* want.

After interviewing for information, you'll probably know two or three kinds of jobs you'll want. And that's a major help in interviewing effectively. The most common complaint of employers is "These people don't know what they want." True. So knowing what you want gives you the edge on most of your competition who "need" a job, any job, but don't necessarily *want* it.

"The point in an interview is taking charge and doing the talking."
Oh, dear.

Everybody these days wants to take charge of their lives. Nobody's in charge! The way an interviewer will turn himself off with you is for you to try to take charge of him!

Interview the interviewer. If you are normally curious about people, this technique (which is not so much a gimmick as your natural style) is the single best strategy in creating a favorable impression. People love to hear the sound of their own voice, are eager to talk about what they know about (themselves, and their job), and look with favor on people who ask them effective questions.

"I hate depending on my wife's salary when I go job hunting."
Oh, there you go again, putting the self first. Irresponsible! In your mind, you think you are "using" your wife. It's a better than even chance, you often think she "uses" you. The feeling of dependency is a sure-fire way to feel resentment. Stop feeling dependent!

That way you will look for a job you want and be a pleasure to be with besides.

The payoff on the job and at home is a lessening of resentment. We don't mind being "used" by other people; that's because we are separate *from* them and involved *with* them. We don't mind "using" other people because we are separate *from* them and involved *with* them. But we feel resentment at being used or ashamed at using someone else if we sense we are a loyal subordinate (on the job) and a loyal helpmate at home.

It's much easier for working couples to launch self-directed job campaigns. Each uses the other's salary as a *base* to secure a job each wants.

But working couples in money marriages often don't act on the advantage. That's because men feel "responsible" for the workplace and their wives for the home front. Husbands, thus, work because they feel "obligated" to their wives and working wives feel "obligated" at home to their husbands. Money marriages which work represent two people doing what they want on the job and doing what they want at home.

The "her career, his job" thing causes conflict; but conflict *creates problems to be solved.* Some working couples *avoid* confrontation, conflict, and co-operation, and thus feel oppressed: They no longer take pleasure in each other. Divorce or an apathetic marriage is the outcome. Both parties blame it on conflicting careers. But the blame rests on each person's inability to focus on what each *wants*. Far better to marry a man or woman who knows what he/she wants; marriage to a person who doesn't means this person constantly feels compromised.

But worse is a money marriage where neither partner knows what he/she wants and constantly concedes to what each *thinks* the other *wants!* Another definition of hell.

"Working couples should take into account what their partner does for a living."

That's a great strategy for the merely married but won't work for couples who are "remarried." Remember, it's not the Marriage, it's not the job, and it's not my wife/husband which comes first.

When thinking through what you want to do, don't (repeat, don't) take your mate into account. Know thyself. And the same goes for the person you are living with. Each person must focus on his or her own *will*. Otherwise, working couples fall into the trap of accommodating each other's objectives and never their own. And job seekers in general are altogether too abject in accommodating employers. Therefore, accommodating everyone but the self eliminates yourself. No wonder you hate to work!

Don't think focusing on the self is selfish. Actually, two people in a money marriage who know what they want to do are in far better shape to co-operate with each other in doing it than two people who are merely married who don't know what they want to do.

What some men call a rat race, other men call a track meet. Attitude is everything. And other people's attitudes are less important than our own. Other people's attitudes can cause us to address what we want. But they can't be substituted for our *wants*.

And the abundance of options is often threatening: The younger we are, by definition, the richer in options. Younger people have more time to fulfill potential. But middle-aging people with restricted options (because they have less time) often find it easier to choose. To paraphrase Samuel Johnson, thinking about our demise powerfully concentrates the mind. So, while tradeoffs are tougher for the young rather than the aging, it's painful for both.

"The aim of an interview is to get a job offer."

Only half true. The real aim of an interview is to obtain the job you want. That often means rejecting job offers you don't want! Incompetent job seekers, however, become so used to accommodating employers' (and their spouses') expectations that they often easily qualify for jobs they don't want. So, before you do back-flips for an employer, be sure you want the job.

"Always try to please the interviewer."

Not true. Try to please yourself. Giving answers that you think will suit a potential employer, losing touch with your own feelings (in order to get in touch with some other person's feelings) and, in general, practicing an abject policy of appeasement are certain to get you nowhere. Of course, don't be hostile—nobody wants to hire someone disagreeable. But there is plainly a middle ground between being "nice" and being "nasty." An effective interview (whether you are offered the job or not) is like an exciting encounter in conversation with your seatmate on an airplane.

"Try to control the interview."

Nobody "controls" an interview—neither you nor the interviewer —although one or both parties often try. Then it becomes a phony exchange between two human beings; no business is likely to be transacted. When somebody tries to control us, we resent it. When we try to control somebody, they resent us. Remember, you can't control what an employer thinks of you, just as he can't control what you think of him. So hang loose when interviewing: Never dominate the interview. Compulsive behavior turns off your authenticity.

"Never interrupt the interviewer."

No dice. "Never talk when I'm interrupting," said McGeorge Bundy.

Good advice.

Study the style of an effective conversationalist: He interrupts and is interrupted! An exciting conversation always makes us feel free—free to interrupt, to disagree, to agree enthusiastically. We feel comfortable with people who allow us to be natural. So, when interviewing, half the responsibility lies with you. Do you seem uptight? Try being yourself for a change. Employers will either like or dislike you, but at least you'll have made an impression. Leaving an employer indifferent is the worst impression you can make. And the way to make an effective impression is to feel free to be yourself, which frees your interviewer to be himself!

"Don't disagree with the interviewer."

Another silly myth. If you don't disagree at times, you become, in effect, a "yes" man or woman. Don't be afraid to disagree with your interviewer—in an agreeable way. And don't hesitate to change your mind. The worst that could happen would be that the interviewer says to himself, "There's a person with an open mind!" The conventional wisdom says "be yourself," true enough. But how many people can be themselves if they don't feel free to disagree?

"Always let the interviewer terminate the interview."

Not necessarily. When interviewing for jobs you want, you'll inevitably be offered some you don't want. There's nothing wrong with courteously thanking the interviewer, explaining why you're not the right man or woman for that particular job and then explaining what kind of job you do want. That way, an interviewer never rejects you for a job you don't want or aren't able to perform (something interviewers hate to do—employers would rather say yes than no). And by taking the interviewer off the hook, you easily enlist his co-operation in finding the job you do want. And that's the main aim of interviewing. Thus, the trick is to terminate job interviews and convert them to information interviews.

"Never ask for the job; wait for it to be offered."

Another half-truth. Of course, it's easier to accept a job rather than ask for it. But it's also bad strategy to be an occupational wallflower. Ask for a job you want. Showing healthy assertiveness demonstrates a strong will and ambition, good qualifications for tough jobs. So don't crawfish: Be bold.

Of course, the bold, effective approach does mean that sometimes you'll have to cope with rejection and be turned down for a job you do want. But that's how you learn to be an effective job-hunter: You learn to bounce back from disappointment; you persist in looking for what you want. Drive and stamina are the hallmarks of people who get ahead.

Check yourself out; if you can handle disappointment, you have what it takes to find a good job.

"I have never been . . .

> *. . . turned down for a job I really wanted."* _____

> *. . . given my walking papers by a person I deeply loved."* _____

> *. . . disappointed in a vacation, a holiday or looked-forward-to event."* _____

. . . *unable to accomplish something I wanted to do."* _____

. . . *disappointed in my boss, mentor, teachers or parents."* _____

. . . *rejected by a school."* _____

"In like manner, I have never . . .

. . . *rejected an employee and fired him."* _____

. . . *given someone his walking papers."* _____

. . . *raised my hopes about a vacation, holiday or event."* _____

. . . *thwarted somebody and told them they had failed."* _____

. . . *disappointed my boss, mentor, teachers or parents."* _____

. . . *turned down a scholarship, a cool job offer and certain celebrity."* _____

. . . *backed off asking for a job I wanted because I might be rejected."* _____

"Don't ask what you'll be paid."

Nonsense. "By the way, what's your ballpark figure?" is a frequent question during an interview. Most job seekers fail to tell the interviewer what they want. But savvy job-hunters do just that (usually the maximum of what's realistic). And then add, "Of course, I'm flexible." Translation: I'm ready to listen to any reasonable offer.

The point in asking for the maximum amount is to set a figure high enough so that you can gracefully yield and negotiate downward. This shows you're a reasonable person. And this approach has the practical advantage of raising what the employer is willing to pay. Thus, both parties negotiate a midpoint salary (between what a job candidate wants and an employer wishes he would accept). That's a business transaction. But it won't work if a job candidate never says what she wants or else does it too late in the interviewing process. Otherwise, an employer might regard her maximum demands as unreasonable. Moreover, by putting too high a price on your services, you screen out employers who pay squat wages.

"Always thank employers if you accept a job."

Another myth. Thank employers for a job offer you turn down. Never thank employers for jobs you accept. Why? Accepting a job offer is concluding a business transaction: The employer has a job and pays a salary; you are selling her your valuable time. A fair exchange. Would you thank someone who bought your used Volkswagen? Would she thank you for selling it to her?

"Above all, avoid discussing what your spouse does for a living."

Actually, it's illegal to ask your marital status in many states. And some working women are convinced marriage and children are deficits. Accordingly, they bristle when an employer probes about their personal lives. Sometimes they should! There are plenty of rude rubes in the world of work who act like they just crawled out from under a rock. But what many working women fail to understand is that working men, too, are probed to find out about their personal lives. What employers are trying to do is figure out whether a candidate's personal situation meshes with on-the-job requirements. Any employer who doesn't satisfy himself that it's in a job candidate's interests to take a job isn't doing his job. So the point is to *volunteer* information about your personal life. That includes what your husband does. Being upfront and unthreatened by your personal situation is bound to impress employers.

"Stop interviewing after you've accepted a job."

Not true. You are never employed until you're on the payroll. Employers often make mistakes: They don't budget for jobs they offer, fail to convince their boss about the need for the job in the first place, don't clear it with the personnel department, and so forth—horror stories. Therefore, protect yourself and don't cancel appointments to interview, even after accepting a job offer you do want.

"Always put your best foot forward in an interview."

Why is it that whenever we try to please other people we often seem displeasing? Well, it's because we aren't pleasing the self. And that's the secret of interviewing well. At the same time, there are those who always succeed in putting their worst foot forward. That's because they hate pleasing other people! That's a certain formula to interview badly. In either case, "You First" interviewees and "Me

First" job-hunters aren't effective. Most people fall between both poles.

So check out how well you're interviewing these days for a job, of course(!), *you want:*

1. Do I always wait until an interviewer is seated before seating myself? (Answer: This is a business transaction, not a fraternal get-together. Don't *force* informality on an interviewer.)

2. Do I always write a nice, short thank-you letter to those who took the time to interview me? (Super! Employers are bound to remember and like you.)

3. Do I maintain good eye contact during an interview? (Swell. But a constant stare is too much of a good thing.)

4. Do I avoid being too cute, too clever, when interviewing? (Good humor is never forced; it's most effective when it's spontaneous and authentic.)

5. Do I dress for success? (Yes, but also dress to fit your craft, talent, profession, field—call it what you will. Obviously, you don't dress to interview as the business manager for a rock band the same way you would to face a Procter & Gamble campus recruiter.)

6. When an interviewer says, "Tell me something about yourself," do I stress abilities and accomplishments? (Right on! Don't build on college degrees or experience unless education and past jobs support the job you want.)

7. Do I show genuine curiosity about employers? (That is, do you ask the interviewer numerous questions? If an employer ends up doing most of the talking, it's clear he feels comfortable with you and you've made a favorable impression!)

8. Do I ask for advice in the job hunt? (Most people love giving advice and it's often useful.)

9. Do I avoid a too casual interviewing manner? (Phony sophistication is a real turn-off to employers.)

10. Do I have small talk ready to begin an interview? (Yesterday's Patriot-Redskins game, the devalued dollar, the wretched weather outside, all commonplace subjects that are natural items of discourse between strangers.)

11. Do I reveal strong feelings, values and convictions in the inter-

view? (Smart if you can persuasively backstop your opinions with examples in a logical and agreeable manner.)

12. Do I buckle under stress questions? (All of which are meant to see if you can be intimidated: Do you freeze, babble like a child, self-destruct?)

13. If I don't understand a question or why it's important, do I say so? ("Why is that question important, Ms. Employer?" An excellent way to find out what's really on the employer's mind.)

14. Am I able to say "I don't know" without embarrassment? (Who knows the answers to everything?)

15. Do I answer questions concisely? (Many long-winded job applicants answer questions that were never asked! Stick to the point and answer a question or say, "I don't know.")

16. Am I sensitive to an employer's being uninterested in my response? ("Am I giving you the information you want?" A good question to ask an interviewer when you note her eyes glazing over.)

17. Am I easily intimidated by authority? "Miss Intimidated meet Mr. Intimidator." The hidden attraction between these two is his obsession with always being right and hers with always being agreeable. It's no mystery why she got a job offer from him; no secret why he offered her the job. But is this situation what either party wants?

18. Am I being myself in a job interview? Being yourself is tough. Any place. Some people, however, naturally interview better than others. These lucky people are in touch with their feelings, know how to cope with authority, and are self-assured.

They're self-confident because they are authentic and never play a role. Moreover, they are excited about the prospect of finding a job.

Know Thyself

Everyone should investigate for himself. What you accept on faith you can also drop on faith.

A. A. BRILL

"Self-awareness is being selfish."

"Self-awareness is simple self-absorption."

"Self-awareness is feeling free."

"Self-awareness is feeling responsible."

"Self-awareness is real."

"Self-awareness is frustrating."

"Self-awareness is risky."

"Self-awareness is often a case of saying 'no' to the job."

"Self-awareness is being selfish."

The ancient injunction to "know thyself" is the modern equivalent of getting in touch with our own feelings. Looking outside ourselves for enlightenment, especially to the experts, belies our own expertise at self-analysis. The ability to love and work is inside everybody. And your*self* (not other people) is the focus. But many working couples eliminate the *self* in love and work and can't focus on themselves; they focus on other people. Self-sacrificial.

Self-awareness means putting yourself first. That means ignoring the State, the Church, the School, and the Family, all of which promote the alien idea that other people come first.

Looking out for Number 1?

Not quite.

Unfortunately, the "Me First" people took the golden rule and stood it on its head: Love thy neighbor as thyself became love thyself and screw thy neighbor. But neither philosophy works: (a) Living for others eliminates the self; (b) Living for the self eliminates reality.

The love thy neighbor crowd unwillingly does the will of others; the love thyself gang willfully takes advantage of them. Both types suffer from a wasted will; neither feels free to examine what they want. Each accepts on faith. But what you accept on faith you can also drop on faith. Disillusionment. The unexamined life isn't worth living: Look into yourself.

The human spirit thrives on self-awareness. Don't be put off: Self-awareness isn't selfishness. It's the beginning of wisdom without which we are weak vessels on stormy seas without a compass. To be aware of others and unaware of ourselves is alien to human nature. Organized religion is to blame for all of the confusion. To think we are here on earth to help others (work for others) is to prematurely emasculate.

Each partner in a money marriage has a room of *his* own and a view of *her* own. Both partners file a joint return but each brings more to the other than a separate income. Each invests another set of values, interests, habits, emotions: A separate body (and to get fancy a bit) a separate soul.

"Self-awareness is simple self-absorption."

To know thyself (write this on the blackboard a hundred times) is impossible alone. That's why marriage is so practical. There is always someone to talk to about the most important person in your life: You! People who live alone, or lonely people living together, are self-absorbed. They have no one to talk to about the self. Thus, the lonely reach out to other people to become self-aware. But people living alone together (the happily "remarried") have each other to talk to about Topic Number 1. The first want to break out of their solitary confinement; the second are neither confined nor solitary. For many people it's confusing: Plenty of people want us to be confused. Appealing to our Conscience ("Serve other people") is the way other people confuse and control us. We do their will by making ourselves feel guilty if we don't do it.

Living for others is unselfish and leads to self-contempt; living for the self is selfish and leads to self-love. Self-love and self-hate are the twin forces which defeat happiness. Both are alien to feeling free. People living for others eliminate the self and hate themselves. Accordingly, they turn their self-hatred outward onto other people. Contempt. But selfish people, living only for themselves, eliminate other people and are contemptible.

The unselfish are easily intimidated and vulnerable to other people; the selfish are unintimidated and invulnerable to other people. Neither kind of person is co-operating with reality.

Intimidated people will try to put other people down. Undermining another person's confidence, making fun of his/her prowess and subverting this person's strengths becomes a marital nightmare. Remember, the responsibility for intimidation lies with those intimidated.

Nobody feels free. "It's the nature of marriage," both say. But that's untrue: It's marriage's nature to help us become free. There is a big difference in merely being married and "remarried." It's the difference between taking a job and doing it. And acting freely, interestingly enough, reveals to authoritarians, our boss and our mates, that we don't *need* them.

How many times have we caught ourselves, when our boss gives us an order, finding some trivial task to perform *before* we accomplish what our boss wants? A sure sign we feel controlled, unfree. And how many times have we given instructions and noticed how our employees flinch, find some other task to do, before accomplishing what we want?

No, we can't control other people and we can't be controlled. But that doesn't mean as a manager we are forbidden to give orders, set goals and evaluate performance.

It doesn't mean, in marriage, we can't say what we want, ask our mates for help, and be dependent on their co-operation.

It doesn't mean with our children, we don't say what we want, establish limits, stand up for our rights.

Nobody is trying to control anybody; what we are doing is being an effective manager, mate and parent. Self-managers, thus, are authorities; "responsible" managers are authoritarian.

Our boss hires compliant people and is probably married to a compliant person. Obedience and loyalty are the two virtues he prizes the most. No wonder this person employed you; small wonder you married someone just like the boss!

To work is to be Somebody's Assistant; to be married is to be a Special Assistant. This situation works so long as it fills our *needs*. But the situation is intolerable if we begin to focus on what we *want*. And what everyone wants is to feel free. And nobody feels free working for or being married to a power-tripper.

Her responsibility to herself is to speak up in a staff meeting, point out his errors, and say what she feels. His responsibility to the self is to give up trying to manipulate, to welcome constructive criticism, and listen to what other people feel.

Result?

She might be cashiered. Sacked. Fired. He might think he's losing his grip, feel irresponsible, out of control. But her showing some spirit might make an impression on him. And he might enjoy his Conscience losing its grip, and being controlled by his feelings rather than trying to control them.

Responsible.

Whether either knows it, he has another employee and she has a different boss. She has been "re-employed." It's the same job but it won't seem the same since her attitude about it has changed and his attitude about work has, too. These two are bound to make music.

"Self-awareness is feeling free."

"Hooray, I'm free!"

But before the cheering starts, consider the following: (1) You can't be free alone; (2) nobody is too free (too happy); (3) thus, the self-aware are on a journey without end. Finally, (4) two self-aware people in a money marriage frustrate from time to time the other's self-awareness!

If two people know what they want (self-awareness) and it's what the other person wants, swell. But if two people (and their children) each know what they want and it isn't what the others want, trouble, trouble, trouble. Reality. There is no way, this side of Shangri-La, that that won't happen! Result: A squabble. Fighting fair, remember, involves revealing what you feel and what you *want* (your free will):

> I want to take in an ice hockey match tonight.
>
> My wife wants to go to her office Christmas party (and wants me to go with her).
>
> Our children want to go caroling at the community center (and want mommy and daddy to go with them).

There are three approaches to the problem: (1) The strategy of self-sacrifice ("You First!"); (b) the strategy of selfishness ("Me First!"); and (c) the strategy of self-awareness ("I and Thou First!"). In the first instance,

> I squelch going to Madison Square Garden, come home early, mix the drinks, eat dinner and do what the children want (sing Christmas carols).
>
> My wife backs off her office party, comes home early, fixes dinner, and does what the children want (goes Christmas caroling).
>
> Our children get what they want: a homecooked meal and a night out with their friends. But, somehow, it's no fun: Mom and dad both have the bag on. Spiteful.

How now, brown cow?

Well, at drinks before dinner, I pout over the *Wall Street Journal;* my wife burns the dinner; the children run amok. Spiteful conduct. Spiteful people injure other people after first wounding the self. Nobody except the kids did what they wanted and they feel—no surprise—unwanted.

Now, the second approach,

> I say, "To hell with her, I'm taking in the Rangers tonight."

My wife says, "To hell with him, I'm going to my party and drink a gallon of eggnog."

The children say, "To hell with them, let's go alone and raise a little Cain at the songfest."

So, neither approach works: Doing what we *should* causes resentment and spite. Doing what we want causes guilt and estrangement. In the first case, we do what somebody else wants and frustrate what we want; in the second, we do what we want and frustrate what other people want. We have done something we ought not to have done or we have not done something we ought to have done. Conscience doth make cowards of us all.

The third approach: The strategy, not of sacrifice nor selfishness, but of self-awareness: Everybody says what they want and we have another family squabble. It's understood quarreling causes pain but life is tough, always has been, always will be. And it's accepted that knowing what we want and revealing it doesn't mean we are going to get it. But that's better than not knowing what we want. And our exchange of emotion is normally conducted in a normal voice, but raising our voice isn't against the rules.

Results?

One outcome is each does his own thing. Not exactly the Christmas spirit, but doing unto others is why so many people flip out during the holiday season. And if we do our thing, it means forgetting what other people might think and feeling separate. Finally, it suggests our children are self-reliant, responsible, and dependable.

Another outcome is establishing other desirable objectives. So, I forget my ice hockey match, my wife exits early from her office party and we and the children meet downtown for drinks, dinner, a quick trip through Macy's toy department and a late movie everybody wants to see.

Still, another solution is to willingly concede to our wife, our husband, and our children: We do what someone else wants to do *more*. But that's because we want the pleasure of their company and not their goodwill.

"Self-awareness is feeling responsible."

Responsible to the self.

Ah, but there is a price! And for those of you who can read without moving your lips, you guessed it. The price is the prick of the Conscience. Why? Well, the pleasure of being yourself causes you to feel guilty: You might frustrate what other people want you to be.

Your children might want you to be like "other mommies"; your boss might want you to be like other "junior vice-presidents," your husband might want you to be the earth mother goddess one moment and Mary Magdalene the next; your wife might want you to be Sammy Glick on the job and Don Giovanni at home. Being unresponsive to what other people want makes you feel irresponsible.

But we all know by now what a responsible person is, don't we? And we know it's impossible being truly responsible to the self if you don't feel separate from others. But most working couples don't feel separate—they feel "married." Most working people don't feel separate—they feel in someone else's service. And children, remember, don't feel separate at all. That's the big difference between parents and their children: Children aren't separate; they are dependent. Grown-ups are able to become separate; they can be dependable.

"Self-awareness is real."

Self-awareness helps us co-operate with reality; part of reality is what we think of it. Attitude is everything. Knowing what we feel and expressing what we feel makes other people think we are responsible (response-able). But if we feel something and don't express it, how are other people to know what we are feeling? No wonder they think we are irresponsible.

In marriage, if neither partner reveals what he/she feels, it's unreal. Irresponsible. Neither is responsive to reality. Trained to conceal what we feel, we disguise our feelings entirely, accommodate other people's feelings and eventually cease to feel at all. Our will isn't free.

Happy marriages are "remarriages." Remarriage is a product of becoming separate. Becoming separate is a matter of self-awareness. Real. But focusing on others is merely being married and is unreal.

"Self-awareness is frustrating."

Whether you are a pessimist or an optimist, isn't necessarily realistic. A cheerful idiot is as out of touch with reality as a lugubrious crank. Life is tough. Becoming more aware of the self and reality is frustrating.

For example, a government contract is canceled and you lose your job. Reality. But part of reality is finding another (and better) job. Losing our job is real; thinking we can't find another job is unreal. Life is tough (you lose your job); life is a joy (you find a better job). It's unreal being the Compleat Pessimist or the Cheerful Idiot.

Coping with the frustration of life and taking pleasure in it is cooperating with reality. That means using your freedom. But feeling unfree, feeling you are shaped by your environment, and judging yourself by what other people think of you, is self-sacrificial. Eliminating the self obviously makes self-awareness impossible.

But self-awareness is frustrating. You resist. Your obsolete defenses (an acquired and "used up" character) stand between the unreal you and the real you. Even if you eliminated your inner resistance to change, reality would still be the same. No job you hold or person you marry will be frustration-free unless it's a nonjob or a nonperson in which case it's neither work nor love.

In money marriages, the opportunities for frustration and pleasure are greater; more money, less time, greater demands, more options. Taking pleasure and hanging tough in love and work requires self-awareness. Sure, we are often our own worst enemy but we can be our own best friend.

"Self-awareness is risky."

The risk is discovering unpleasant but important truths about the self. Mothers discover they sometimes dislike their children; husbands are sometimes sexually incompetent; wives are unresponsive; managers have enormous control problems; working people have problems with authority.

But the truth does make us free. Self-awareness is self-knowledge, our strengths and our weaknesses. How can we correct weaknesses if we aren't aware of them? How can we build on our strengths if we don't know what they are?

The best way to become self-aware is to cultivate desire: In desire begins responsibility.

The message for working wives is to give up worrying about threatening your husbands; the message for working men with working wives is to give up feeling you are in control. Wives are not responsible for their husbands' feelings; husbands are not responsible for their wives' security. Attitude is everything.

The non-intimate marriage, where two people turn themselves off to the pleasure of each other's company, is disillusioning. The conjugal contract is an agreement between impotents. And the marriage "works"—they stay together—so long as they remain impotent with each other. Let a woman reach out and find a potent man (Lady Chatterley's Lover) and, woe, her husband could go into a murderous rage. Let a man sweetheart his secretary, feeling potent at last, and, lo, his wife could become a murderous harridan.

"Self-awareness is often a case of saying 'no' to the job."

Saying "no" to the job and saying "yes" to the self often means rejecting promotions and reassignments. The dues are steep, the price high, the consequences painful: Hang tough. But hanging tough is like a kite which flies highest against the wind. The trade-off is a happier home life.

Such decisions cause pain. The cop-out is avoiding the pain by following through on other people's expectations. The knack is *feeling* through these decisions. And being married helps; major decisions can't be made alone. Marriage helps you touch base with what you are feeling. So, facing up to an unwanted promotion causes pain. But not facing up to it causes more pain. The pain is self-inflicted: That's why you suffer from insomnia, migraines, and lower lumbar strain. If you turn down an unwanted promotion, refuse an important transfer, back off a desirable assignment, you feel irresponsible to your employer. But if you accept an unwanted promotion you feel irresponsible to the self.

Let's suppose you've a shot at the executive vice-presidency where you work. So do three of your associates. You hesitate telling your husband about this opportunity; you don't want him to be disappointed (and don't want him to know you're disappointed) if you don't grab the golden ring. And let's suppose your best womanfriend on the job lands the job. What do you feel?

Well, disappointed (first), dejected (second), acutely depressed (third). Your husband thinks you need a physical exam. It's another example of how we beat ourselves at our own confidence game. Protecting yourself from the disappointment of not bagging a cool promotion and your husband from the knowledge of such a possibility fences off "reality." But the only "defense" in emotional matters is a good offense: Sure, you would *still* be disappointed if you shared your prospects at work with your husband; and, for a day or two, even dejected. But acute depression? No, indeed.

And it's easy understanding why. You have confessed your real feelings. But let's turn the same situation inside out; let's suppose you do get that promotion and feel depressed.

A big part of the problem is other people. "What a swell deal," your best friend says. "You're just the woman for the job," you are told. "My Gawd, but your family will be proud," says another.

There are abundant reasons for your depression: (a) A great opportunity at work can radically change your life at home; (b) what our employers want for us isn't really what *we* want; (c) our circumstances (pay, location, status, power) change but we ourselves—our old disappointing identity—stay the same; (d) what we always *thought* we wanted (a vice-presidency, a foreign assignment, a huge income, a shot at top management) aren't what we wanted. In a word, everything in the world carries its price. The sudden realization of "success" makes us aware of the consequences. There are dues to be paid.

Still another less examined reason is that a promotion, a transfer, a new job is often a reward we secretly believe other people deserve. Moreover, a new job often removes us from our field of force. Our skills, so easily demonstrated on this job, don't apply to that job. And exercising our skills on a job is a definition of job satisfaction; being unable to exercise our talent on a job is a definition of job dissatisfaction. I'm a superb piccolo player, but I've no talent conducting the orchestra.

Free decisions are made independent of employers and spouses, "I and Thou." Separation. It's imperative to focus on your will—what you *want*—before taking into consideration the claims of "other people." Focus on the pleasure an opportunity brings; put "other people" second.

The way to get off the horns of a dilemma is to transcend the problem, not hang on one of its horns. What's important is neither to compromise "career" nor "marriage." That means focusing on the self first.

"Cruel Choices."

But the fact we can *choose* shows our freedom. Far, far worse to have a life where cruel (and delightful) dilemmas didn't exist! And transcending a dilemma is possible so long as both parties keep their eye on the bouncing ball which is the self.

The extraordinary outcome of focusing on the self first is that the conflict between what he wants (the job in N.Y.C.) and what she wants (a chance to be self-employed in Des Moines) causes them to address third objectives (finding jobs in the Thousand Islands) where they both want to live.

Alternative outcomes are not necessarily compromises. Because you knew what you wanted (self-awareness), revealed what you wanted (confrontation), argued for what you wanted (conflict), established what you wanted most (which was your partner), you discover new goals: Circumferential marriage is the creation of a third collateral circle of mutual involvement (See *Ethics, Work and Worth*).

Marriage Half-Truths (and Hard Truths)

> We cannot live in the afternoon of life according to the program of life's morning. . . .
>
> CARL JUNG

"Marriage is maturity."

"Marriage is tolerance."

"Marriage is commitment."

"Marriage is obedience."

"Marriage is loyalty."

"Marriage is trust."

"Marriage is compromise."

"Marriage is self-sacrifice."

"Marriage is fidelity."

"A midmarriage crisis is inevitable."

"Her career is my happiness/his happiness is my job."

"Two-paycheck marriages work if both partners are in a similar field."

"Marriage is maturity."

The trouble with mature people is that they never seem to be having any fun. The facts are that the only people we can expect to act in a mature manner from time to time are certain five- and six-year-olds. Past is prologue: So don't expect to act "grown-up" while married. Marriage, after all, is simply another stage, as we are about to see, in growing up. "Remarriage" is still another. Thus, don't expect to grow up in marriage more rapidly than you have grown up apart.

The ages of man begin with baby safe at mother's teat. That's Stage One. The day baby says "No!" is Stage Two. Stage Three is childhood: No normal child worries about his/her free will. Kids know what they want: A good time. Thus, Stage Three is an age of wonder, innocence and growth. Alas, all of this changes at adolescence—Stage Four. Something about sex, of course. Sex, that most desirable of all pastimes, confuses people; suddenly, stickball and hopscotch lose their fascination. Teenagers start groping after, hang tough, *the self!*

Well, Stage Five is young man- and womanhood: Children are no longer young, but still dependent, all the while loving independence. It's in this stage that we generally marry. But we aren't "grown-up." Many people never leave Stage Five: They never successfully cope with frustration, excellence and, above all, other people. Marriage is Stage Six but many people haven't left Stage Five.

Not to worry.

Being married isn't being "remarried." That's Stage Seven. Remarriage, remember, is living alone together, co-operating with reality, growing in our ability to be response-able, coping with frustration, excellence and "other people." Stage Eight is parenthood which, as we have seen, is particularly rough on those still in a holding pattern in Stage Five. Stage Nine, we kick our brood out of the nest. The last stages of life are often the happiest. We have succeeded in being responsible to the self, grown-up, mature.

We don't go from one stage into the next as through Passport Control: We carry the luggage of our experience—luggage we no longer need (our unreal character)—from one stage to the next. For example, Stage One we *needed* our mother's teat; plenty of people can't give up looking for someone to take care of them! Employers.

Lovers. Spouses. Friends. But the point in going from one stage into the next is to learn how to take care of the self.

Each stage shapes us: But everyone possesses a free will. People are not the sum of their conditioned reflexes; puppets on a string manipulated by experience. In money marriage, there are two free wills in collision and in collusion; two people growing up together.

The most difficult aspect to grasp is that while she might be in Stage Eight, her husband is still in Stage Five. Hanging tough in love is understanding that two separate people don't "grow up" at the same rate of speed. Divorced people often put it another way, "We simply grew apart." But people growing apart aren't growing up. Immature.

"Marriage is tolerance."

Be mature. Show respect. Button your lip. Don't complain. Do your duty.

That was a definition of marriage, but no more. It didn't work, doesn't work, won't work. Tolerance, like humility and gratitude, are much over-rated. If I'm a boozer (and my wife doesn't complain), if my wife's a compulsive spender (and I don't complain), if we tolerate each other's weaknesses, it's self-defeating. The "marriage" survives, but we are miserable.

Of course, complaining won't help my wife give up her charge-account way of life, nagging won't make me stop hitting the bottle, but nobody should back off saying what they feel (See *Fighting Fair*). And you keen students of the subject know nobody can change anybody else. That's not the point: Saving others from themselves. The point is saving your own life.

Mutual toleration of the other's weaknesses is a mutual self-elimination society. Each partner has been brainwashed to think he/she must overlook and tolerate the unacceptable conduct and unreal characteristics every person brings into marriage. Eliminating our own feelings eliminates the self and makes us boring companions indeed. So every act of commission and omission which bugs you in your partner deserves comment. Every man has a right to be an angry bastard from time to time; every woman, a right to be an angry bitch. Intolerable!

Feeling free to express resentment, oddly enough, frees people to show love. Good sex often follows a free expression of hostility. Bad or no sex follows a poor or no expression of anger. This is difficult to understand. But not too difficult: Feeling free to say what we feel is feeling free.

Hubby leaves a dirty ring in the bathtub, smokes his cigars in the bedroom, and bites his nails during an anxiety attack. Nasty habits, no? But his wife leaves her wet pantyhose on the shower rack, forgets to fill the car with gas, and becomes hysterical when things go bump in the night. Gross, *nicht wahr?*

The conventional wisdom about marriage is to overlook tiresome features in our mates. Thus, we avoid a fight and the clash of gears. But self-awareness is the clutching mechanism to mesh gears. If we are not aware of our own feelings or fail to express them, we fail at becoming separate; we don't feel separated from the source of our complaint.

Complaining, therefore, isn't always nagging. Each partner has a responsibility to the self to say what bugs her. That *won't* change him into who she wants him to be. Remember, we can't change anyone but ourselves! But the ventilation of real feeling is a sign we feel separate and promotes similar conduct in one's partner.

Now, there is no right or wrong about it, no good or bad about it, no rhyme or reason to it: We are either furious about a dirty bathtub or an empty gas tank or we come to accept it. If we tolerate it, it doesn't necessarily mean personal capitulation. And if we can't stand it (and say so), it doesn't make us an inveterate nag. Moreover, we often complain about something one day and don't notice it the next. Some of the time we cherish the curious habits of the person we sleep with: She misses her husband's snoring (when he is on the road); he misses her harum-scarum ways (when she is away). Having someone to *resent* sure is an improvement on resenting the self. And two people hanging tough together are going to resent each other from time to time.

What follows is a fragment of a fragment of the complaints we hear the harried married make:

She never answers a question directly.

He cools his soup by blowing on it.

He can't talk to the children without first mixing a martini.

She repeats the same three jokes at every party.

He is crazy about buying stocks on margin.

She never lets me forget my father never graduated from high school.

He can't keep a secret.

All of which drive us up the wall, off our feed, and into our cups and at the same time triggers similar behavior in our spouse. It's "marriage" with all its warts and without its halo.

That's why being responsible to the self is such good strategy. Having an experience which makes us feel good about the self frees the self to bitch about matters that makes us feel bad about the self. That's "remarriage" with all its dimples and care-worn creases.

"Marriage is commitment."

Sweet Jesus.

A lifelong sentence without probation for *good* behavior is no way to feel free. Thus, a lifelong sentence with probation for bad behavior encourages divorce. We act irresponsibly, self-destructively and spitefully in order to get off the hook. And believing marriage is a hook—a commitment, a responsibility, a lifetime of "sharing and giving"—hooks us on divorce.

To think that when you marry that you are no longer free, that it's no longer *me* but *us* is crackers. The sheer strain of playing on a team destroys the pleasure each would take in the other's company. "What am I getting out of this marriage?" is the question we ask and are asked every day in marriage. The commitment is not to marriage. The commitment is not to another person. The commitment is to the self.

People "committed" to marriage are uninvolved with each other; people involved with each other don't give two figs for the marriage. And being committed to another person is possible so long as we realize we can break commitments (See *Conscience Doth Make Cowards*). Otherwise to be committed is to feel locked-in. Response-able people feel free; they *freely* make commitments. But the point is *they can break commitments*. And feeling free to break commitments, especially with the person we live with, is an aspect of pleasing the self. This is a fact conveniently overlooked by moralists: To feel free to break up our marriage if it no longer gives pleasure is a precondition to feeling separate while married.

"Marriage is obedience."

"Husbands, love your wives . . . wives, submit yourselves to your own husbands" (St. Paul).

Husbands don't *unwillingly* love their wives; wives don't *unwillingly* obey their husbands. Acting against our will is a violation of the free will; we hate it. And the hate is turned on ourselves. Self-contempt. That's unbearable, too. So, we turn it outward and hate the person we live with. The story of the merely married is entitled "Contempt."

Feeling free to say "yes" and "no" is central to two people co-operating. What was the first word we learned as children? Well, it was "Mommy!" The second word we learned was "No!" Every mother knows children say no all the time. It's a declaration of independence. But declaring our independence doesn't make us free. It is, however, a start.

Saying "no"—being disobedient—is vital in a child's development. After we "grow up," it's still important. Otherwise, we don't become separate and feel free: "Remarriage." Perfect obedience and perfect love are illusions in marriage. But co-operation and tough love are not illusions. Many married people are disillusioned. A few married people are normal: They co-operate together, feel love and hate, and have hope. Feeling free to give orders or to take orders is what's wanted. "Now you lead, now I follow; Now I lead, now you follow."

In working couple marriages, love is constantly being *tested* by opportunities to go other places, do other things. The price is our separation from the person we are married to. Two-career couples don't break up because of the conflict between careers; their love for each other is no longer strong enough to keep them together. They blame it on their conflicting jobs. But it's their self-sacrifice which is to blame.

You love whom you feel free with; you are loved by those who feel free with you. And an aspect of freedom is feeling free to become angry with the person we love (See *Fighting Fair*). Otherwise we murder what we love; we don't feel free to hate so we kill what we love. And what we murder is the love we felt.

Love is perfect freedom: Love doesn't so much solve problems between people as dissolve them. If you give up a great job to follow your wife to her job in Boca Raton, it might be love; if she gives up a great job in Bloomington, Illinois, to follow you to Puget Sound, it might be love.

But it might not, too!

Who is aroused most in love, the lover or the loved?

Who experiences the greatest pleasure, the gift giver or the gift taker?

My bet is on the lover and the gift giver. It is the passion we arouse in the self, not in others, that is central in being intimate at home (and effective on the job).

"Marriage is loyalty."

True loyalty is a question of feeling free. We are loyal to people we feel free with; and people who feel free with us are loyal to us.

People are disloyal to people with whom they feel unfree. Trapped. And people who are trapped—helpless people—lash out like caged animals. So, if you are trapped in a job you hate or are married to a person you despise, you may sabotage both.

But people are not really trapped unless they think so. We can find another job (and another boss); we can divorce and remarry. Our helplessness, our oppression, our unhappiness is our responsibility. And our responsibility is to respond to what we are feeling. Oppressed on the job? Well, then speak up! Oppressed in marriage? Well, stand up and sound off.

The expression of feeling relieves (but does not eliminate) what's causing us to feel so badly. But without an outlet, feelings are turned inward and cause depression as surely as the sun will rise in the East tomorrow. And in protecting your husband from your feelings, you show a great disrespect for him and yourself. Protecting other people's feelings reveals a barely concealed contempt for them and the self. And contempt between working couples destroys the pleasure of each other's company.

Of course, there are dues to pay: Every action has its consequences. Your boss might fire you and your spouse might divorce you. Well, good riddance to bad rubbish. To be *ordered* to be loyal is intolerable.

At the same time, a show of spirit on your own behalf might pleasantly surprise your boss and give pleasure to your spouse. People who feel free—no surprise—are simply better workers on the job and a pleasure to be with at home. And you would be crazy, indeed, to be disloyal to those with whom you feel free. That wouldn't be loyal to the self.

"Marriage is trust."

A lot of people think so.

This old chestnut is responsible for the demoralized state of "marriage." We trust those with whom we feel free; we distrust those with whom we don't feel free. To demand trust and to command it of others doesn't work: Nobody feels free to protect his own interests. Protecting our own interests in marriage is tough. But the myth-makers want us to think other people can be trusted to protect our interests.

You live in this world to fulfill other people's expectations and other people are here to live up to yours: No wonder you don't feel separate. Free.

Chances are you show your dissatisfaction indirectly. Silently. The intimidated back off direct confrontation, are often apologetic and grateful and are most at home asking permission. The intimidated live in the Land of the Bland: They are shaped by their environment since they don't feel separated from it. Thus, the frightened folk need to learn some new moves.

The intimidated hate to answer telephones; someone on the other end of the line might challenge them. The worst thing that can happen to a nervous Nellie is to have her weaknesses revealed. "Don't make any demands on me!" is what they seem to be saying.

Plenty of people hire the intimidated: The employer who wins through intimidation hires people who lose through intimidation. It would upset the applecart on the job if she suddenly became potent and effective. And at home, her husband, accustomed to protecting her feelings, might not feel needed.

The unintimidated do not live to fulfill other people's expectations. So, if she learns some new moves, her boss and her husband are going to learn some new moves, too. Her boss might fire her and her husband might divorce her. But her boss might also admire her and promote her and her husband might come to enjoy the pleasure of her company.

To blindly trust other people is to encourage untrustworthy conduct. We feel exploited. Oppressed. But the responsibility for our oppression lies more with us than our exploiters. Protect thine own interests. Feeling free is taking responsibility for your own happiness.

Happiness thrives on freedom, and we trust those we feel free with and are trusted by those who feel free with us. Feeling a sense of accomplishment in our work, pleasure with our mates, and freedom with other people *attracts* others to us. They trust us. And we are attracted to other people. They are to be trusted. But blindly trusting our jobs (to our employers), our happiness (to our spouse) and our freedom (to other people's opinion of us) isn't feeling free.

A trustworthy person is someone we can trust to reveal what he feels. An untrustworthy person is someone who doesn't trust his own feelings with other people. The untrustworthies reveal their feelings about us to everyone but us. Sneaky people. So, learning to trust our own feelings and saying what we feel is a potent act and threatens the impotent. Moreover, by showing anger at what we hate, we preserve what we love. But not trusting ourselves to show anger at what we hate, is to murder what we love.

So, marriages are composed of four kinds of people: The *Intimidated*—people who are involved with their partners but who don't feel separate with them; the *Unintimidated*—people who are uninvolved with their partners but can't feel separated from them; the *Intimidators*—people who are so uninvolved and unseparated from their partners they try to control them; the *Intimate*—people who are sometimes involved, sometimes separated with their partners: Trustworthy people.

"Marriage is compromise."
Half true.

But the whole truth is that we can't compromise—co-operate—if we don't know what we are compromising. To concede without knowing what we are conceding isn't compromise, it's capitulation. Surrender! Thus, many co-operative people simply reveal a weak will when what is wanted are strong convictions. At the same time, never compromising—co-operating—reveals the same thing. Willful people, "Me first" types, know what they *want* but don't know how to get it!

Strong convictions indicate a great strategist; the ability to compromise indicates a great tactician. Conviction flows from a free will. Thus, "Give a little to get a little" doesn't work unless you know what you want to get. Knowing what we want means taking a chance. We risk frustrating what our mate wants. That means confrontation: Conflict. Conviction, confrontation and conflict lead to compromise and co-operation.

"Marriage is self-sacrifice."

That's the major reason singles are so scared of marriage: To sacrifice the self means to commit suicide. If marriage is self-sacrifice, no wonder people are forgoing marriage.

Marriage isn't self-sacrifice. Marriage is *co*-operation. The emphasis is on the *co*: Coalesce, co-ordinate, co-operate. It takes two to tango. But each must *want to* dance. There can be no co-operation if there is self-sacrifice. Otherwise he co-operates with her while she "co-opts him"; she manages while he is managed; wifey maneuvers and hubby is maneuvered.

People each have interests to protect. But we can't co-operate if we don't know what our interests are or if we can't protect them. Negotiating interests is why marriage is tough and why a strong ego is necessary.

Feeling free.

Free people say, "I love you." They never say, "Do you love me?" Free people say, "I want lasagna and a tossed green salad for dinner." They don't say, "What do you want for dinner?" They say, "I want that job in Chicago." They don't say, "What do you think about my job offer in Chicago?"

Strong, declarative expressions which express our free will promotes the same on the part of our partner. "No, dammit, I *don't* love you." Or, "Let's go to an Italian restaurant." Or, "I hate those Chicago winters." Nobody can negotiate (much less co-operate) unless we establish what we feel (know thyself), reveal it (confrontation) and resolve it (co-operation).

"Marriage is fidelity."

"Thou shalt not commit adultery." But fornicating outside of marriage has been an ongoing custom since 36,000 B.C. Married folk step out on their partners when they don't get at home what they want: a good lay in the hay.

But there is a price. The price is the end of your marriage. Divorce. Don't expect married partners, no matter how unfulfilling in bed, not to resent—deeply resent—play-around husbands and wives. But don't expect unfulfilled spouses not to think about and many times do something about their need for sexual expression.

The Credo:

Any married man sexually satisfied and sexually fulfilling is lunatic to step out on his wife. Irresponsible! Why wreck a great and constant thing (a durable engagement) by a short and sometime thing (a brief encounter).

Any married man sexually unsatisfied but who is sexually fulfilling should see a psychiatrist, pronto. A great pleasure of sex is in the pleasure we give, and not taking pleasure in it is a problem clearly for the people in the white coats.

Any married man unsatisfied sexually and sexually unfulfilling besides should talk it out with his wife and with her seek out therapeutic help.

Any working wife sexually satisfied and sexually fulfilling is bonkers to cheat on her husband. That's cheating herself. Irresponsible!

Any working wife sexually unsatisfied and sexually fulfilling should want to know why she can give but can't get. She should see a shrink.

Any working wife sexually unsatisfied and sexually unfulfilling as well should talk it out with her husband and with him get a psychiatrist on the case.

If both partners are unable to get it on after therapeutic help then surely still more therapy or a divorce are considerations. But if both partners are too threatened by sexual fulfillment and otherwise take pleasure in each other's company, why end a marriage or even have an affair? The same condition will follow you into both.

Partners who step out on each other show neither consideration nor respect. But it's more complicated than that. Many "married" people are undeserving of consideration and respect; especially pleasure-hating types who try to command fidelity.

Marriage can survive adultery. But that's because each partner sees it for the crisis it is and does something about it. Sex is a basic human need. We are either fulfilled and fulfilling in marriage or we aren't. Fidelity cannot be commanded; the unfulfilled and the unfulfilling aren't faithful to the self (See *Sexual Politics*).

"A midmarriage crisis is inevitable."
Piffle!
A midcareer marriage crisis is no more "inevitable" than a midcareer crisis. Thinking otherwise is to think "society" is responsible for all our problems. Believing we are determined by circumstances, mere products of class, education, and income level, sexual preference and all the rest is life-denying. Unfree. Even adolescence is far more a culturally induced crisis than personal. Programming yourself for the Seven-Year Itch or a post-married depression is putting yourself in the hands of experts and soothsayers, all of whom explain our lives in terms of economics, life styles and trends without taking into account everybody's free will.

My point is simple:
It isn't inevitable your husband will play around after marriage because most husbands do.

It isn't unavoidable that your children will smoke marijuana because most young people do.

It isn't ordained you will burn out on the job after five years because many people do.

Fight the tendency to fit the Procrustean categories shaped by other people. Disobey! Trend-bucking is a sign of great spirit and a tough ego.

Love's not an easy thing (Society wants you impotent); it's not an irresponsible thing (loving responsibility—tough love/tough jobs is how to be intimate at home and effective on the job); it's not a some-time thing (becoming the person the self wants to be takes a lifetime and that's not enough time). The qualification needed to be a loving and effective person is courage. The courage to resist the appeals of Conscience, other people, and "Society." And loving means cultivating the capacity to disobey. What we disobey is the Conscience.

Know thyself and look into your own self and "if by chance we find each other, it's beautiful; *if not, it can't be helped*" (Frederick S. Perls). That's what we forget: Some things can't be helped.

"Her career is my happiness/his happiness is my job."

Charles de Gaulle was married to France. Madame de Gaulle was married to Charles. Therefore, Madame was married to fighting France.

Madame de Staël was married to European Civilization. She had husbands and lovers. Therefore, they were married to Civilization.

Ike was married to the Army. Mamie was married to Ike. Therefore, Mamie was an Army wife.

The two-person career.

It worked, it works, it will work; so long as what he wants is what she wants and vice versa. The operational word is want. The free will. The fusion of personal and professional objectives represents the two-person career.

Such a marriage is as close to the romantic as realism allows. But the two-person career is anti-modern.

"Two-paycheck marriages work if both partners are in a similar field."

This may be desirable but not essential. Opposites attract. A working wife who is an investment banker finds refreshment in a husband who is a ceramics dealer.

Believing so doesn't take into account that a money marriage is a "Career," that many men and women are making two and three "career" changes in their lives, that younger and middle-aging people are "dropping out" into alternative occupations, that the quality of life is more important than its quantity.

Married, to Be or Not to Be

Is not marriage an open question, when it is alleged, from the beginning of the world, that such as are in the institution wish to get out, and such as are out wish to get in?

EMERSON

"I can't be sure I want to get married."

"But I have promises to keep,/and miles to go before I sleep" (Frost).

"My work requires all my emotion, lots of travel and horrendous hours."

"Children, debts, property and marriage are burdens."

"I'm constantly hassled by on-the-job problems, have trouble knowing what I want to do, and can't be sure I'm able to make a living doing it."

"I'm never less alone than with myself."

"I'm never less alone than with my partner."

"The lonely are the brave."

"I hate being alone with myself."

"Say it with flowers but put it in writing."

"I can't be sure I want to get married."

Well, relax, drink a Dr. Pepper and don't take life so seriously. Everyone, especially those who are married, have doubts. Doubt is true of every important decision we make. An article of faith in feeling free is the accompanying doubt and hesitation. "Is this what I really want?" we ask.

A tough ego lives with the doubt. This person knows we finally can't be *sure*, that living is a dubious proposition. And that making a mistake in love, as in everything else, isn't blame-worthy. So, to answer your question, ask yourself a question: "What's wrong with making a mistake?" And if your answer is, "Nothing," the odds are better than even you want to get married. But if your answer is, "Everything!" chances are better than even you have some growing up to do: The guilt of mistake-making is preventing you from growing up.

A word about men and marriage: Many have a two-tier conception of it: Younger men are all caught up in the notion that marriage is option-closing. Thus, younger men think freedom is being free *from* responsibility. Younger men are quite high on "personal growth," "being a loving person," and "working loose." Older men, on the other hand, are confused in different ways: They are all caught up with "growing with the Company," "being a responsible person," and "staying the course." Thus, older men think freedom is doing their duty. Each attitude is the reverse side of the same false coin: Many young men are laid back, drift from job to job, bed to bed without joy or sorrow; many older men are uptight, rigid, and stick to jobs they hate and stay in marriages they despise. Neither generation is right: Marriage must stage a comeback with the young and "remarriage" with older men if the men of either generation want to be free.

Oh, since I've put the knock on men *in general*, let me do a favor for the ladies, too. Many women thirty years ago dreamed about "catching" a man and having a passel of kids. A generation later their daughters are hell-bent on landing a good job: "Fie on marriage! Up my career! Children? Well, maybe *one* child when I'm thirty-five and a senior law partner." My hope is women won't become as disillusioned with the world of work as many profess to be with the world of men. Everybody reads about the "new woman." But I'm interviewing a lot of women who would gladly trade their jobs for a happy marriage. So would plenty of men. Why not have both?

So, the need for a redefinition of marriage seems clear:

Marriage counselors, psychologists, and people in the "helping" professions (me included) report that younger people are troubled by the random and declining quality of boy/girl stuff. The sleep-around generation may find joy in sex but only sorrow in love. Thus:

Chastity is staging a comeback.

Divorces, given current trends, will exceed marriages within a decade.

Nearly fifty percent of all remarriages fail.

In California, younger people "living together" exceed those couples who are married.

Younger men are postponing marriage entirely, working loose at alternate employment while younger women are moving in to take their place at the entrance and middle levels of industry, government, and academia.

Adolescence is painfully prolonged through years of unnecessary schooling, on-the-job training, and "living-with-somebody" arrangements. It appears harder and harder for younger people, particularly young men, to cope with frustration.

Marriage counseling is booming; more and more married couples are at least trying marriage before divorce.

Among the older generation, everyone knows at least one couple who split the day their last child finished college.

The runaway wife signals our interesting times. (Runaway husbands, of course, have been a sign of every time.)

Children are running away in numbers ten times greater than twenty years ago. The American family is in big trouble.

All of the theories advanced to diagnose our interesting age put the blame on society. Tom tit. Some people feel out of synch if they don't conform to this year's up-to-date "role model." They blame society, the "rules." Yesterday they complained about the stifling effects of the extended family; today they complain about the breakdown of the nuclear family; yesterday they resented their mother-in-law living next door; today they grope to find a built-in baby sitter; yesterday they gloried in the arrival of their first born; today they are overpopulating the planet; yesterday they introduced their wives as Mrs.; today they drop the title entirely.

No, sorry, marriage isn't about romance. Besides, everybody knows about *that!* If we are in love, it's surely the best thing since Hepburn met Tracy; if we have fallen out of love, it's surely the worst thing since Liz left Richard. Marriage isn't about *first* scenes (it's about next scenes), not about romance (it's about what follows), not about brief encounters (but durable engagements).

Facts, paraphrasing Winston Churchill, are so much more comforting than dreams. And whatever the facts of our marriage, they represent the truth. For those who ask, "Whatever happened to Romance?" my answer is that romance after marriage is in the dustbin where it belongs. Romance served its purpose, weaving its illusions about the altar-bound lovers. Trying to keep it alive in marriage is to live in a world of illusion. And since that's impossible, married folk become disillusioned. But tough love endures. Tough love is for those who have hope: Romantic love is for the wishful who are without hope.

"But I have promises to keep,/and miles to go before I sleep" (Frost).

Our partner must cosign the promissory note.

The politician dedicated to public service; the dancer married to her craft; the ambitious business person consumed in making his first million before age thirty—all examples of people "married" to a goal. Goal-oriented people ought to marry persons with the *same* goal: The congruence of goals means compatibility; goal discongruence is incompatibility.

My main point is *feeling free.* Free to love; free to work. It sounds easy enough and it's a cinch to read about. But feeling free is tough. We weren't born free and everywhere people are in chains. Our human bondage makes up a good part of our unreal character. Feeling free means first breaking free of our unreal character and finding our real selves. Tough. Breaking free of our unreal identity, as we have seen, means constant self-awareness. And becoming self-aware

—repeat after me three times—*can't be done alone.* That's why marriage and living with someone won't go out of style. And feeling free isn't half the fun; it's all the fun.

Freedom is the message. It's facing up to the hard truths that happiness (and unhappiness) is our own responsibility, that becoming the person we want to be (and not trying to change our mate into what we want him to be) and co-operating with reality is tough. Life is tough, always has been, always will be. But, if we believe, as so many do, that we are responsible for other people's happiness then it's but a short step to believing other people are responsible for our happiness. And married people are unhappy in direct proportion to how responsible they feel for the happiness of the person they live with.

So, whether yours is a traditional marriage or a money marriage or whether you are simply living together, there is pleasure and pain:

Going on your first vacation in three years and having your husband come down with the Asian flu.

Taking enormous joy as you nail in the last cedar shingle in your vacation cottage and then developing lower cervical pain.

Feeling great pride as your oldest son becomes an altar boy and despair when he spills the communion wine on the priest's chasuble.

Trying to make monthly payments on a house mortgage rivaling the national debt and watching your equity quadruple.

Reality. Co-operating with reality, the pain *and* pleasure of it, requires spirit. And part of reality is our attitude. A great spirit is the gift we bring to tough jobs and tough love.

So two-person careers work so long as both partners keep their eye on the goal. But if partners to a two-person career change their minds about the goal, if one or the other can't reach the goal, or if either loses interest in the goal, then that's a crisis. Many crises are commitments we make to the *self* we feel we can't break. But any commitment is breakable, especially to the *self*, all of which is another definition of flexibility.

But feeling free means being free to break commitments. People who can't, can't manage the guilt. But everyone needs to change with changing times. Any commitment can be broken.

So, if you have some promises to keep before you sleep, it could be circumstances will force you to break those commitments. The point is not to have fixed objectives; the moral is to feel free to *change* those objectives. And "remarriage" often means agreeing on *new* goals. Being able to flexibly readjust goals, personal and vocational, is a qualification for those who would be happily "remarried."

"My work requires all my emotion, lots of travel and horrendous hours."

And you sincerely want to get married? No way. Politicians, entertainers and sixteen-hour-a-day corporate stemwinders pursuing power, celebrity and money are no more qualified to be married (much less "remarried") than they are free to read *Remembrance of Things Past.*

People married to work, who can't say *no* to it, aren't qualified to marry until they can. The reasons might be mental or environmental: Either they see a therapist and change their character or they radically readjust their work habits: The second outcome might be a consequence of the first.

To feel *who* you are is *what* you do is hardly feeling separate from work. And the inability to separate from work means an inability to be involved in love (See *Burnout*). And becoming separate—feeling free—is essential to being "normal" in love and work.

"Children, debts, property and marriage are burdens."

Chances are you have no promises to keep, have troubles thinking through what you want, and as a child suffered from having all the "advantages." The best way to protect yourself from frustration is *not to want anything*: Squelch desire, especially desire for another person.

Fortunately, most people are not permanently crazy. In our sane moments, we recognize that in desires begin responsibilities. And as we grow more responsible, as our desire increases, and as our will grows stronger we become more potent. "Working loose" and "living free" of other people becomes a drag. Children, debts, property, and other people no longer seem like burdens but challenges. A test of our potency; our sense of responsibility to the self.

For people protected from reality, given the "advantages," and having every reason to have a head start in life, this problem of "what is it I want" is more insidious. Necessity is not the mother of invention but circumstances do promote co-operating with reality. If, as children, we were given opportunities (and didn't earn them) our character is correspondingly weak. Desire is often rooted in deprivation: Slake a man's thirst and he won't want to drink.

"I'm constantly hassled by on-the-job problems, have trouble knowing what I want to do, and can't be sure I'm able to make a living doing it."

So, before you marry, you want to find yourself. But the problem is you need someone else now: Human needs don't go on vacation while you look for the real me. And plenty of people will marry you because they love to be needed!

Thus, first marriages are a risky proposition: A younger person by definition hasn't the time to "know himself"; it's a bitch. All the more reason for younger marrieds in entry level jobs, getting started, to hang tough with each other: Being married isn't "remarriage." That takes a lifetime.

When should you get married?

Well, no one is ever "old" enough! But you sincerely want to marry when you are tired of *only* being your best friend, able to make a living doing what you want, are learning to feel separate from "other people" and are challenged by responsibilities and not found wanting. That's a big order for anyone and especially younger people who are rich in options but weak in spirit.

Another and second priority: Do you have the scratch to marry? Most people don't and most younger people especially. Unfair. We lack money most when we are young; we usually have it when we are older.

Two working people bring to money marriage two incomes. And if we can make a living doing what we want (and our partner can, too), then we are able to marry. Knowing your skills, marketing those skills,* becoming more competent (and compensated) in the exercise of our abilities is having a vocation (as the Victorians say). We feel free on the job (we sense we can find other jobs) and feel free at home (we don't depend on our spouse to support us).

Money marriages require partners able to launch self-directed job campaigns. A self-managed job search means putting yourself first and finding work which meshes hours, income and quality of work with the work of thy mate* (See *Organizations [and the Working Couple]*).

Sure, it's tough. And you often don't both ring that old bell the first or even the second job out of school. But you keep your eye on the ball, continue to think about what job you want *next* and hang tough with your partner who does the same. So, to avoid a post-married depression, forget the "marriage" and focus on the self in love and work. That means feeling separate (and involved) with both your job and your partner.

"I'm never less alone than with myself."

The reason people marry is that single types are lonely guys and gals. No put-down intended. A spell of living alone is a qualification for living with someone.

Some do better than others and those that do cultivate an inner life which isn't a bad life: Being happy with the self is the single most important quality in being married. We aren't necessarily lonely when we are alone but we are lonely if we no longer *want to be* alone!

"Great," we say, "I'll marry and never be lonely again." But, as we have seen, plenty of married folk are lonely: They don't feel free; they don't feel separate. They are lonely *with* someone. Lonely marrieds, thus, think single people are free. Ha! And single people think married folk aren't lonely. Ho!

Message? Don't *stop* being your own best friend while married. Don't expect you won't want to be alone. Don't expect your partner not to want to be alone. Younger types call it "space." But it's free-

* See *Go Hire Yourself an Employer* for a book-length treatment of this important subject.

dom. And we feel free with a partner with whom we are—at varying times—both separate and then involved.

"I'm never less alone than with my partner."
Ah, love! Perfect freedom.

That's why lovers are envied: Uncrowned royalty. Most of us make way for them; a few malcontents, however, charge lovers with being "irresponsible." Ignore them.

Lovers aren't separate: They are heavily involved with each other. But, lovers, too, must separate—they go to work, carry out the trash, walk the dog, take business trips. Separation is intolerable for lovers. A certain way to cope with separation anxiety is to become angry with the beloved, wash that man or woman out of your hair. Thus, separation is accomplished. All of which is by way of explaining the inevitability of lovers' quarrels.

Before marriage, the serpentine back-and-forth of two people in love is dramatic. "Settling down" seems like a silly way to sow wild oats. Sowing a few oats is how people break free of family. Declaring our independence ("I'm liberated!") and being independent ("I'm free!") is finally realized in a I/thou "remarriage," not a Me/Me affair, or an I/It marriage.

After marriage, the complicated catch-as-catch-can of being both separate and involved becomes melodrama. The crazy nature of marriage (and all boy/girl stuff) is caught up in the never-ending dependency/independency dynamic. That's why in money marriages quarrels are inevitable: People need to separate. And it's also why married partners come back together: People need to be involved. In love, the partners to it are constantly weaving in-and-out of each other. Stormy. Passionate. Fun. But if you lack imagination and believe marriage is sugar and spice and everything nice, marriage is bound to be neither passionate nor fun. Love is drama; marriage is melodrama; "remarriage" is high drama.

"The lonely are the brave."
Captains Courageous.

Nobody can be anybody without somebody (Forbes). "My defenses are down," we say before we fall off the wagon. Independ-

ent people, remember, aren't self-sufficient. Read Aristotle. Martin
Buber. Ann Landers.

While it's half true that the lonely are the brave, it's the whole
truth that more courage is required to love. Happiness is a consequence of feeling free; marriage augments our freedom. But if we
feel responsible for each other's happiness or if both partners regress
into Kings- and Queens-In-Exile neither will feel separate or involved with the other.

So, if you are about to get married, fasten your seat belts and
prepare for a rocky ride. Turbulent conditions are forecast. But trouble strengthens character and qualifies us for tough love.

"I hate being alone with myself."

This guy or gal is the opposite of the person who is never less
alone than with him/herself. They are certain to find each other in
the lonely crowd.

People who hate being alone enjoy the passing parade and particularly enjoy fulfilling other people's needs. They often marry people
who *need* other people to do their social downfield blocking: Two
cripples in love.

Both are happy so long as each fulfills the other's needs. Trouble
begins when either resents his dependence on the other. So if you
hate being alone with yourself, you have some growing up to do.
We are born *alone* and die *alone* and come together to take pleasure
in each other's company. And we can no more take pleasure in another's company if we can't separate from that person than we can
take pleasure in another's company without being involved.

Growing up is tough. And we know nobody is fully grown any
more than someone is completely free. Thus, marriage is simply another stage in life following adolescence and preceding parenthood.

*"Say it with flowers but put it in writing."**

Pre-nuptial contracting.

This makes a lot of sense if one of you brings substantial mone-
tary assets (don't you wish!) to the other. Property you earn or in-

---

* See Paul Ashley's book *Oh Promise Me but Put it in Writing* for a com-
prehensive legal overview of living-together agreements.

herit before you marry is yours; property you earn or inherit after you marry is ours.

Fortune-seekers and gold diggers are still with us. And someone with substantial property who marries someone without ·it should protect his/her own interests. That's best done with a pre-nuptial contract. And it tests the reasons your intended wants to share your bed. If it's clear you are loved for your gilt-edged securities and you sense this *after* marriage, you haven't protected your interests. You might make your mate earn every penny of your money ("I have the money and I'm in charge") or be exploited ("I have the money but you're in charge"). So, if you are in the chips, see a lawyer before you see the preacher.

Finally, to marry or not to marry, is a question of your *wants*. Remember, the old vaudeville gag made popular by Woody Allen: The joke about our brother who thought he was a chicken. "Why don't you have him put away," said the psychiatrist. "Well," is the reply, "I need the eggs!" Same on the job, we want to work; same at home, we want the pleasure of someone's company.

Now, of course, some people object. They say, "I work to make money. Now I have enough; I don't *have to* work." Or they say, "I've learned to live alone; now I don't *need* anyone." Well, it doesn't work!

Money (and Time) Management

Let us roll all our strength and all
Our sweetness up into one ball,
And tear our pleasures with rough strife
Through the iron gates of life:
Thus, though we cannot make our sun
Stand still, yet we will make him run.

ANDREW MARVELL

"Money is time."

"We've gotta have fun!"

"Having fun seems like a waste of time."

"I spend all my time helping other people."

"My problem is spending all my time involved on the job."

"I never accept invitations without checking first with my partner."

"I want my wife to attend all social functions which are part of my career."

"Doing things fast is saving time."

"Finding time for pleasure means saying 'no' to other people's pleasure."

"Time waiteth for no man."

"Money is the root of all evil."

"A million dollars would make me happy."

"I consider price first, pleasure second."

"Pleasure, yes, price, no."

"I hate spending money on myself."

"I love spending money on other people."

"I let my mate make up my mind about what to spend and what to save."

"I always (never) pay my bills on time."

"Moonlighting is essential to keep us afloat."

"A recession is when my best friend loses his job, a depression is when I lose mine, and panic is when my wife loses hers."

"Money is time."

In money marriages, time management causes as many conflicts as sexual misfires, money matters and house management. Many working couples are scheduled like airliners with specific destinations on airtight schedules.* Time becomes a commodity, like money, which must be spent and conserved wisely.

Time for the self; time with your family; time with your work. It's a commonplace that time is money; what's not so clear is that money is time. Small wonder working couples fight for free time. It's a crock.

Anthropologists tell us that we are a time-bound culture. Everybody is using time "constructively." But is anyone having any fun? We dress up to go to a party, throw a banquet and plan a vacation. But we vaccinate ourselves against the *pleasure*. The "working vaca-

* The October, 1979 issue of *Harper's* contains the funniest and single best put-down of time management amongst working couples. The title of the article is "Fastfolk" and it's by a superb writer named Louis Grant. Page 106.

tion" is an example; entertaining people *we work with* is another; planning a trip for its "educational value" is still another.

Other people have turned the Puritan ethic inside out; they abandon the ceremony of party-giving entirely, eat on the run and drift rather than travel. If an activity is "constructive," these people think, it must be bad!

What's missing is an appreciation of how to savor time. The ability to savor time in America is an acquired characteristic. It should be a required course in schools of business administration. Often our best ideas about "work" we have off the job when we "play."

"We've gotta have fun!"

Well, if you *gotta* do anything, happiness goes AWOL.

Attitude is everything. The greatest challenge in marriage is to be happy. Eighty-seven percent of the public, according to a recent poll, said a happy home life was preferable to more money, success and celebrity. The other thirteen percent are either happy or are lying.

Happiness has her enemy: Guilt. And for those of you who have been taking notes, you know that guilt is a result of feeling responsible for the feelings of others. That's the way to be unhappy. But, of course, the problem of guilt is more complicated. To take responsibility for the self means giving up our innocence. The innocent are those who think they are the passive product of their environment. Determinists. Thus, the modern notion that unhappiness is outside of us.

"We've gotta have fun," is the motto of every working couple. But it's truer that we *want to* have fun. And to do that we've gotta get organized!

So the next step is learning how to be response-able, self-aware, focused. Focus requires us to "Be alert!" Being alert to our own feelings is a start. And no one in a working couple's marriage is going to be able to *focus* and *concentrate* without being *flexible*.

A tall order; it sounds like a job description for a tight-rope artist. But every money marriage is a high-wire act: You need a safety net. The safety net is self-awareness (See *Know Thyself*).

Self-awareness means postponing less important items and rescheduling or "saying no" to them. That could be cooking breakfast, drawing up an agenda for tomorrow morning's staff meeting, or diapering baby. But try thinking about tomorrow's meeting, planning breakfast, talking with a neighbor on the phone and diapering baby *at the same time*. To be self-aware means "saying no"—breaking off our phone conversation, putting off 'til this afternoon Monday morning's agenda, and focusing on baby!

Effective executives know how to do it; they know how to manage time, money, data, and people on an orderly basis.

Actually, they *appear* to do it but no manager admits doing it with ease! The point is to shift from one subject to the next as smoothly as possible. Feeling free is feeling separate from *other people*, other things, other problems, saying "no" to this and "yes" to that.

"Having fun seems like a waste of time."

She's a full-time travel agent with annual earnings of $35,000 (salary plus commissions). He's an orthopedic surgeon at $100,000 per year. It's clear why these people only meet over Sunday brunch. Both are in a time-bind, focused entirely on other people's needs (low cervical back strain, on the one hand, and packaged Club Med tours, on the other). There is no time to have a fight, make love, repair the garbage disposal or scout-out some interesting country property.

A combined income of $135,000 has bought these folks a tennis club membership, two Mercedes, a winter vacation (five days!) in St. Croix, five Russian wolfhounds and a partridge in a pear tree. But what income can't buy, is pleasure itself.

What would "other people think," what about the children's education, what about a hundred other "extras"? Yeah, but what about pleasure? Is it really worth working three days out of five for the government? (Taxes take a major part of people's earned income.)

To give up a new Mercedes in order to really pull your rock garden together, to spend some time at the ball park, to pursue that mad hang-gliding pastime is neither madness nor destructive. "Wasting time" is taking pleasure in life.

"I spend all my time helping other people."

To proficiently fulfill other people's needs and fail to concentrate on our own leads to feeling no longer loved nor loving but like an overworked computer service representative. Is mankind worth it?

People might admire you for keeping four oranges in the air at the same time. It excites envy in friends and the congrats of time-management "experts." But the problem is, while your marriage is working, you're miserable!

Concentrating, focusing, balancing and being flexible—all characteristics of the effective time manager—are for nought if you never have time for the self. Spending ninety-nine percent of every waking hour helping junior with his algebra, holding a subordinate's hand, counseling a friend on a tax problem, explains why life is no fun anymore.

"My problem is spending all my time involved on the job."

The result is both burnout on the job and in marriage. You botch love and work. Inseparate from work; uninvolved in marriage. Parallel lines don't meet: Real talk is minimal, sex is grabbed on the run, and time together, much less with the self, is scarce.

In time-rich marriages, partners say "no" to work and "yes" to themselves. They are *willing* to love and work. A free will is the key to time management. People who don't know what they want never have enough time. They are suckers to fill other people's needs. People who know what they want find time.

"I never accept invitations without checking first with my partner."

That's hardly feeling separate.

Why can't you accept (or decline) on your own behalf and agree to check with your mate? To become the social secretary of your spouse and to treat yourself as part of a "unit" makes marriage bondage.

And that goes for *inviting* people. Treat everyone *separately*. To accept (or invite) people on the basis of membership on a "team" is not the way you want to be treated nor the way you want to treat other people.

"I want my wife to attend all social functions which are part of my career."

Well, it's certainly OK for you *to want* her by your side. And it's OK for her *to want* you by her side.

The operating word is *want;* where both parties "expect" the other to fulfill their "responsibilities" and/or when either party "obliges" the other, nobody feels free. So, a politician who expects his wife to be on the campaign trail, a college president who expects her husband to attend alumni meetings, a company officer who expects his mate at the boss's Christmas party are trying to control other people.

Conversely, if you follow through and do what is expected (not what you want), you "function" as a family unit. Oh, boy! Who wants to be part of a unit? A team? And if you are "expected" to attend your wife's induction as President of the PTA, chances are you would rather be in Philadelphia.

The use of time is all bound up in the human will. "What do I want to do?" is at bottom the question you ask the self. What you *want to do* is connected with *disobedience:* You must disobey maxims carefully learned at mother's knee, "A stitch in time saves nine," "Time waiteth for no man," and "The race is to the swift."

"Doing things fast is saving time."

Our love affair with speed is a national character flaw. Doing something fast often inoculates us against pleasure and usually isn't efficient. Taking pains in what we do means we don't redo sloppy work. Speed reading, fast food, quick fixes: Much motion but no progress; activity but no action; much ado about nothing.

The hyperthyroid life is hell on wheels—chauffeuring, chaperoning and consuming—running ever faster to keep in place.

Plenty of people can do only what they *want* after doing what they *should.* It's why weekends are so looked forward to in our lives, "I've worked all week and done what I should, now I'm free to do what I want." It's also why we are bored on Sunday.

Irresponsible.

Irresponsible people can't cope with too much pleasure: Pleasure causes guilt, raises the anxiety quotient, and paralyzes the free will.

Doing what we should eliminates the guilt, reduces anxiety, and eliminates desire. Thus do working couples become disillusioned.

Effective time managers manage time for pleasure's sake.

"Finding time for pleasure means saying 'no' to other people's pleasure."

Yes and no. It depends on our free will.

But some people, as we have seen, can no more say "no" than some people can resist hard drink. Other people can no more say "yes" than they can drop a bad habit. Neither feels free.

"I'm forbidden to break commitments," she thinks.

"I always feel bad when I say 'no,'" he thinks.

Attitude is everything.

On the one hand we feel trapped (committed); on the other hand, we feel irresponsible (guilty). No commitment is unbreakable. Especially commitments working couples make with each other. The business of feeling responsible causes the unhappiness, and makes us ineffective time managers. We don't feel free of other people's needs. Saying "no" to them is thwarting their pleasure. But if you know how to say no, you have a shot at being an effective time manager.

"Time waiteth for no man."

What follows are some useful suggestions on how to find time to "savor." That's the major reason to be an effective time manager. Working couples:

> With excellent incomes become part-time professionals all of which doubles the time for pleasure.
>
> With lots of children welcome congenial live-in in-laws to help with child-care.
>
> Contract out services: Housekeeping, catering, child-care, lawn work, and employ investment advisors, tennis coaches, and bottle washers.
>
> Seek out jobs with flex-time hours of work and negotiate assignments which can be done at home: Every home can become an office: Typewriters, dictaphones, telephones and Xerox machines often make "going to work" unnecessary.

Use the phone (weekend rates are incredibly low) and forget writing Christmas cards.

Find time for sleep and exercise. Without your health nothing is possible.

Throw one big catered bash a year and touch base with everyone they don't see enough of. They also come to their own party and hire a professional to do the bartending.

Lock up the television room and keep the tube on tap, never on top. TV narcoleptics never have time for real talk, good sex, or fine music.

Eschew the squirrel mentality; they throw away what they don't want even though some day they might *need* it. That way they don't file it, insure it, forget where it is, lend it or wonder if it should be replaced.

Aren't well informed on *everything*. They don't read the Sunday New York *Times* and thus find time to have a good time.

Patronize fast-food franchises which deliver *to* your door, use mail-order catalogs to shop and skip the suburban Saturday shopping trip.

Use dry cleaners. No working woman should have to fret about ring-around-the-collar.

Hire the neighbor's teenage son to feed their pets, wax the car, clean out the basement, and paint the rumpus room.

Keep a common calendar of events in the kitchen and by the phone.

Send the pets to kennels and cat-houses. Besides, it does them good to get away from home.

Insist employers put their vacation plans in *writing* and delicately threaten to resign if the boss dreams up a sudden assignment.

Spend on their own pleasure. The better you feel about yourself the more competent you become.

"Money is the root of all evil."

But evil is the absence of good. And an absence of money is no good thing. Money isn't the most important thing; it's the second most important thing. In money marriages, there are as many fights about money as there are about housekeeping. Thus, the publisher has agreed to send any reader of this book a silver St. Francis of Assisi medal if money is never important to him.

Working couples earn big bucks. But prosperity accompanies as many broken marriages as adversity. Money of itself won't "save" you in a money marriage. But being able to earn it (and spend it) augments self-esteem and is another means, like sex and housekeeping, of becoming involved with your partner.

Money isn't evil; money is power. And using power either makes or breaks you; it either gives you power over your own life or it (or the lack of it) breaks you. The money question is the eternal back-and-forth of two strong wills answering the question, "What do I want?"

"A million dollars would make me happy."

But happiness is feeling free. A million dollars changes our circumstances ("Now I never *have to* work again") but our character remains the same. The externals have changed but the internals remain. And that's the rub about lots of money (or sudden success, celebrity, travel): Nothing inside has changed although everything outwardly has. Feeling free can't be bought.

Interviews with young men and women entering into the world of work reveal an interesting pattern. As they climb the organizational ladder they often become less happy with their lives; what they thought they wanted isn't what they wanted at all. And what they thought they wanted was success when what they really wanted was to feel free. Circumstances change ($45,000 per annum, assistant vice-president, a reserved seat on the company's Learjet, and membership in the Racquet Club) but the worn-out character stays the same.

Some few people are made so miserable they put an end to their lives: Success hasn't brought them what they wanted. But what they want to put an end to is certain unreal characteristics which Success(!), Power(!), and Money(!) can't change.

"I consider price first, pleasure second."

Most people, married or not, do. But most people are unhappy.

Unfree. A way to make the self unhappy is by never separating the pleasure of something from its price. Self-awareness (Know Thyself) is focusing on pleasure independent of price. Tough.

I take pleasure in considering a round-the-world cruise first-class on the *Queen Elizabeth II;* my wife takes pleasure in thinking about a ski chalet in St. Moritz: Pleasure before price.

Everyone knows someone in the flush of retirement who fell to pieces. Many retired people have the money and the time to do what they want. But many working couples are so habituated to delayed gratification ("Tomorrow, we'll have fun"), they wake up twenty years later unable to pursue Pleasure because of Price.

The knack of feeling free about money is a steady-state focus on pleasure *first* and price *second*. A winter vacation is a norm, household help pro forma, dining out a sine qua non without which a marriage becomes a business partnership. Spending money on the self makes you feel better about yourself and self-esteem is the root of effectiveness on the job, pleasure at home and performance in bed.

"Pleasure, yes, price, no."
Whoa!
Price isn't the most important thing. It's the second most important thing! Paying the price is the dues we pay. To spend without a thought to reality is being an infant: Children accept pleasure but fail to understand reality; grown-ups accept pleasure and co-operate with reality. Failing to co-operate with reality is being irresponsible. People who spend money heedlessly ("There is no tomorrow") are as trapped as people who can't spend money on the self at all.

Spending money on the self increases self-esteem. It also pricks the Conscience. That's the price of increased self-esteem: Guilt. Scan a menu in a three-star restaurant and some people go from left (the boiled lobster) to right (the price). Rather than satisfy the inner man or woman, many people choose the blue plate special. Self-defeating. Other people, fewer people, scan a menu and never go from left to right. Irresponsible.

It could be the rocks in his head fill the holes in hers: You save money, but can't spend it; your wife spends it, but can't save it. She focuses on pleasure to the exclusion of price; he focuses on price to the exclusion of pleasure.

"I hate spending money on myself."

Pleasure causes guilt. The way, thus, to avoid guilt is to forgo pleasure.

Nice going.

So, change your mind! A good start is recognizing guilt in the first place, laughing at it in the second, and learning to live with it in the third. And finally eliminating it.

What could be more natural than spending money on your own pleasure? Feeling free: Buying that blue blazer on impulse while buying your children their back-to-school togs. Shopping for the self, like working and fornicating—acting on your pleasure—raises self-esteem, routs resentment, and vanquishes self-pity.

"I love spending money on other people."

Well, so be it!

It's clear you are a giving person: You take pleasure in giving pleasure. Pleasing other people pleases you.

Attitude is everything.

But if you save money to put your children through a school of chiropractic, give to the United Fund, and buy an expensive anniversary gift *because it's your duty,* watch out! Nobody enjoys *doing his duty.*

Many men forget wedding anniversaries. Well, it's understandable: They consider an obligation, any duty, a burden. Beasts of burden are forgetful, stubborn and surly. Anniversaries, Christmas, birthdays—gift-giving days. We are expected to give and be given to . . . We are *obliged.* That's the trouble; we don't feel free.

If we act out of a sense of obligation, we are certain to displease. We might buy a gift certain to displease. Or "forget" our anniversary. Giving other people pleasure because it's our duty is displeasing.

So, if we give a gift to our wife because we want to (it also could be "expected"), it could please us. It depends on our attitude. It's the same if we receive gifts: If we expect it (it's someone's duty to give) this could be displeasing. We don't feel free to take pleasure in receiving because the giver felt unfree in the giving/the receiver in the receiving! But spontaneous gift giving on days of the year it's *not* expected is feeling free. A dozen roses for his lady, a bushel of golf balls for her man, surprise gifts, are sure to warm their hearts (and yours).

So, the subject is roses: Working couples in working marriages, acting on whim, will please each other and themselves if they catch themselves feeling free to extend the pleasure they feel about themselves to partners. Gift giving isn't the only way; but it's a certain way.

"I let my mate make up my mind about what to spend and what to save."

That's putting the self second. Sucking hind tit. So say what you want and consider price later: Have a fight and establish other things you might *both* want. Sure, he wants to buy a new Maserati and she wants to remodel the kitchen. A productive fight demonstrates that, yes, your kitchen is good for two more years and the family car is worth tuning up. Why not a vacation on Aruba for two?

In some money marriages, husbands hand over the keys to the family treasury (and its jewels) to working wives; something about the way their dads kept the peace with their moms. But anyone who wants to keep his self-esteem intact won't delegate the spending power in the name of domestic harmony. In other money marriages, wives leave all the big decisions to Daddy Warbucks. No wonder they are Little Orphan Annies. Probably their fathers bore any burden, paid any price and kept their mothers on a short leash. That's no reason why working wives should give up the spending power in their marriages.

"I always (never) pay my bills on time."

If you pay bills thirty days before the due date, it's due to your inability to feel obligated to others. If you can't pay bills until thirty days after they are due, it's because you resent being obligated to others.

If you can't go into debt, borrow money for a business venture, and spend money on the self, the condition is rooted in childhood. Mom said, "Don't be a deadbeat" and you never feel an upbeat. No separation. In like manner, people who evade paying bills can't face up to reality. As children, mom and dad no doubt paid their way, protected them from the consequences of pleasure and provided all the advantages. Some kind of upbringing: Protecting children from the facts of life! Again, a separation problem.

Most people avoid both extremes. But if they can't, they need to change. That means giving up your compulsion to be debt-free or always in debt. In small matters first—the dry cleaning bill, for example—try paying it *on* time or (if you hate feeling responsible) try waiting ten days. Change—any kind of personal change—will cause anxiety. That's normal; it's nature's way of signaling you your progress report.

"Moonlighting is essential to keep us afloat."

Five kids college-bound? And your husband wants to buy a seashore cottage at Bar Harbor? And you are keen to enroll in an expensive French cookery course? And everything costs money, right? So, you punch another ticket, take a second job: Another TV sitcom, "The Moonlighting Marrieds."

To take on a second job (added to your full-time occupation) is a *last* resort. Having no choice doesn't mean you aren't free. Alexander Solzhenitsyn had no choice but the Gulag. But his spirit was free.

A monumental family crisis might justify moonlighting. But there are other resorts: Debt, for example. A better strategy would be to think through whether your children can't work their way through college (an honorable American tradition), whether your husband can't build his own cabin, and whether you can't learn French cookery on your own.

Money management and time management are indissoluably linked. If our time here on earth is like the days of the week, for plenty of us it's Friday afternoon! To spend the time remaining working at a *second* job, is no way to take pleasure in life.

"A recession is when my best friend loses his job, a depression is when I lose mine, and panic is when my wife loses hers!"

Working couples are spending up to fifty percent of combined income to meet mortgage payments. No two-paycheck couple should spend more than twenty-five percent. Otherwise both partners become so dependent on their jobs they can't help but resent work; the anxiety of meeting monthly payments paralyzes free behavior—we are in effect part-time employees of Uncle Sam and the mortgage company. A money marriage without discretionary scratch isn't any fun. Remember, the point of marriage is to have fun!

An excruciating bind: Working couples can't amass the down payment for a house if they are paying huge rent; owning an expensive house (there are no inexpensive houses) requires even greater monthly payments. Solution? Inherit money. Moonlight at a second job. Defer children indefinitely. Move in with your mother-in-law. Emigrate.

Here are some of the ways working couples are managing the money crisis:

> Securing low-interest loans from rich relatives for a house down payment.
>
> Buying cheap inner-city property and restoring it.
>
> Going for broke, buying an apartment house, becoming property managers, and living in a "rent-free" apartment.
>
> Moving to the North Woods and becoming self-employed.
>
> Forgetting equity ownership entirely and sticking strictly to rental property.
>
> Working for organizations which provide housing as part of compensation.
>
> Going into the home-buying business full time, living in one house, turning over a second house, restoring a third, and renting out the fourth.
>
> Going into debt on an indexed salary in a steady job paying off housing loans with increasingly cheaper dollars.
>
> Buying second homes—vacation cottages—in combination with other money marrieds.
>
> Hiring investment advisors to manage joint income, pay the bills and invest joint income for maximum return.

OK. Life is tough: Inflation, deflation, rising (and lowering) expectations and changing times make the money marriage necessary. But back to basics: The plain facts are that marriages are tough today (as they were yesterday) for reasons that have nothing to do with money.

They have everything to do with our being human: Weak vessels in stormy seas.

So, if you have a tough job and are happy with someone who does, too, the spirit moves you. Working at *what* we love and living with *whom* we love is happiness. It's the major theme in this book. Sure, many money marriages fail; so do many traditional marriages. But, the stress of both tough jobs and tough love ("Married love") enlarges the spirit. So, again, the focus is on oneself on the job and in marriage. The human spirit is central in qualifying for a tough job or taking pleasure in tough love.

erything wrong about me is my mother's fault."

Poor old mom, we blame her for everything these days. Unhappy the job? Blame it on mom. No confidence with other people? Blame it on mom. Can't learn foreign languages? Obviously, it's mom's fault.

A generation ago it was called momism. In my business—job counseling—we call it mother-smother. Mother-loving. Houdini, MacArthur, Sigmund Freud, yes, Siggie himself, all had a dose. According to Carl Jung, Americans have the worst case of any nationality in the Western World.

There is a good deal of evidence that if mom thought you "special," you will be: You have no choice. Successful. Outstanding. A mother's special love is more applicable to sons than daughters. Some evidence suggests "successful" women are extremely close to their fathers. But the theme of this book is freedom. Plenty of successful people aren't free.

If to be especially blessed by mom is to gain a head start in the world, do we have any choice but to be successful? Are we *free* to fail? All of which is reminiscent of the soldier bleeding to death in his fox hole in no-man's-land. "All I want to do is die," he thinks. Then he thinks of mom! "My Gawd, if I die like a rat, my mom will feel terrible!" So he hauls himself back to friendly lines and lives happily ever after.

Moral?

A grand story of mother-love? Hardly. The moral of this tale, as my sixth grade teacher was wont to say, is not mother-love. To save his life to protect his mom is crazy! In the name of his free will, he would want to save his own life!

Look at it another way: Suppose our soldier boy was unloved by his mother. And pulled himself together and saved his life. His free will saves him. This guy has a chance to be happy.

No matter if your connection with mommy was mostly loving or unloving, the point is feeling free. To blame everything wrong with us on mom is a cop-out; mom had a mom, too. To credit everything right about us to mom is a cop-out; people are free to keep and discard what mothers give them.

One of the things mothers give us is a model of marriage. We are

Momism

The greatest harm that man does to man is the damage to
esteem, particularly in the relative helpless dependency of
child's development by overstrictness or overindulgence or oth
deprivations of self-esteem.

EDITH WEIGERT, *The Courage to Love*

"Everything wrong about me is my mother's fault."

"I talk to my mom every day."

"I never talk with my mother."

"I've completely rejected my mom."

"If my husband screws up, I fly into a rage."

"My wife is just like my mom."

"My husband often acts just like his mother."

"I married him because he was like my mom."

*"While I was studying for my law boards, my mother came for the
weekend and stayed for six months."*

"I hate it when my husband puts the knock on my mother."

"Honor thy father and mother."

free to copy it, change it, or reject it. But if we don't feel free, we put ourselves in her control for the rest of our life.

"I talk to my mom every day."

No other human connection is as profound or so confused as the mother-thing. *My Mother/My Self* is just as true for men as for women. Except men are more fortunate. Thanks to their greater sexual freedom, men have more power to break free of mom. Women have a tougher time of it.

So, if you're in daily touch with your mother, stop, look, and listen: You won't feel separate in marriage if you're still uptight with mom. Marriage is the most important stage in helping people break free of her. Traditionally, men and women use other men and women to help break free. And increasingly, women are pursuing careers to do it.

Men and women often transfer feelings toward mom (love, hate, affection, anger) to spouses. Many men, it's no secret, unconsciously want a mother; many women do, too! In a word, people often *replace* mothers with a wife or husband. But mom can't be replaced! And as for sex—good sex—forget it! Who has good sex who mentally goes to bed with his mother?

Single people generally scoff at the mother-connection. But after people marry, many notice repeated patterns of behavior in spouses similar to that of their mothers-in-law. And, being self-aware, they spot similar signs in their own character. Marriage might physically separate us from mom, but being married often re-establishes her dominion in our heads.

"I never talk with my mother."

Thus, you have broken free of her?

Not very bloody likely! People uninvolved with mom are often as inseparate as those who can't make a move without her. It depends: An orphan might be as caught up in momism as anyone else and spend his whole life looking for mother-love.

People with unloving mothers often have enormous difficulty feeling close to other people; people with smother-mothers often can't feel separate: The unintimidated are likely to have unloving mothers; the intimidated are likely to have too "loving" mothers. And those of us, most of us, with "good enough" mothers—mothers who were both loving and unloving—have trouble sometimes feeling separate, sometimes feeling close.

Dad? Well, his job is helping his kids break free of mom. Dads that don't, fail. As for dads who try to make their children into their own image, the intimidators, they are no help at all. His sons try to live up to Himself's expectations and his daughters spend a lifetime trying to find a man just like daddy. And as for unfeeling and/or absent fathers, they often contribute to the general contempt women have for men and can be responsible for their sons' homosexuality.

Dad's main emotional investment is his wife; his wife's primary connection is him. If dad and mom have a good thing, the mommy-thing for their children won't be the most important thing.

"I've completely rejected my mom."

"She was a heavy drinker (I'm a social drinker)."

"She was an oppressed hausfrau (I'm a liberated woman)."

"She voted the straight Republican ticket (I'm a good Democrat)."

"She liked stable men (I like crazy guys)."

"She goes along to get along (I'm pretty bitchy)."

The daughter's drift is definitely against the current. But is she free? There is no right or wrong about it: Completely rejecting mom is as unseparated as blindly accepting her. Either way she doesn't feel free. But if she becomes free, it's through her own self-awareness: Talking about the self with her husband (and he with her) is the way both get some purchase on the mommy-thing.

Message?

Talk a lot (See *Real Talk*). Plenty of disagreeable mutual assessments, to be sure. But good talk, talking about the self, frees people up from momism. People come to understand they might be just like mom and completely inseparate or just like her and separate; completely unlike her and inseparate or unlike her and separate.

"If my husband screws up, I fly into a rage."

Deep down in our psyche, mom is alive and well. No matter that she lives next door or is long dead: Flying into a rage with your husband (like she did with your father) is momism. You are reading aloud the lines written for you fifty years ago. Heck, you might look like your mother in high dudgeon!

Why do we swallow indigestible characteristics of our parents? Our unreal self? Well, if you despised your mother's tantrums as a child, you can keep her alive and well in your heart by acting in a way you deeply disapproved of her acting. Clinicians call it introjection. And if you keep in your stomach what she forced down your gullet as a child, that way you need never separate from mom.

To give up an unhappy characteristic of your mom is upchucking it. And you can't do that unless you feel the nausea. You've got to hate the unreal you. But once you've put your mommy's temper tantrums behind you, you'll feel a lot better. That's why every marriage that works is a "remarriage." Your husband helps you discard the indigestible part of your mother's character that you don't want. Feeling alone together, being happily "remarried," is feeling separate from mom in the first place and thus feeling happy with your husband in the second. And what working wife who is suffering from momism can do that?

"My wife is just like my mom."

Still another reason many working wives have difficulty integrating the executive suite. Most working men had mothers who stayed home and sewed the bearskins their fathers captured on the hunt. Thus, many working men these days are uncomfortable with working women who not only join the hunt but bring home the pelf as well. So, a guy who marries a gal just like dear old mom goes comatose when his wife becomes the working woman. That means wifey can no longer be his mommy.

Well, the message to the working wife is: Don't worry about the *man*. That's not her problem; it's his. Working wives are now in the business of bringing home the bacon, just like their husbands, and both need to shape up and manage the home front. Tough on men who married their mothers. But that's the only way a money marriage can work.

Mothers-in-law might not approve. "She's not taking care of my little boy." But any working wife bringing home a paycheck is helping her little boy.

So, it's a male problem: Men and momism. The great challenge to modern men is deprogramming themselves of dependent needs and learning to take care of themselves. A working man should give up feeling dependent ("I need her") and start feeling independent ("I want her"). Independent people, like independent nations, make alliances, work as allies, co-operate as equals. Dependent people, like colonies to nation-states, charge imperialism, profess gratitude, but show resentment. The first is tough love and remarriage; the second is marriage and momism.

"My husband often acts just like his mother."

Does he act in ways he secretly condemned in his mom?

Did she forbid him to go into debt? (It follows he won't let you own a charge card.) Did his mom heap contempt on his dad? (I bet he loses no opportunity to put the knock on you.) Compulsive: Unwilling behavior; he can't help what he does.

As a matter of fact, he can help himself. But you've got to make him aware of his mother/himself. Once he becomes more self-aware, he can (a) stop and reflect before he acts; (b) ask himself whether this is how mom acted with dad; (c) hate her for it; and (d) substitute another action in its place. It's scary: He thinks he is losing his identity. But, in truth, he is finding his real self.

"I married him because he was like my mom."

Many men marry women like their mothers. What's not so clear is that many women do, too. This is not as silly as it seems. In fact, it's not silly at all: Many women marry men with a personality, values, and interests similar to mom. Conversely, many women marry men with a personality, values and interests dissimilar to their mothers. Neither type is free: Separate from mom.

We "remarry" when we deprogram ourselves (and our mates are debugged) of unreal characteristics of mom. This doesn't mean we throw out everything mom gave us: People pick and choose. But it's tough. It's not unlike going through mother's possessions, keeping *this* and giving away *that*. And if it's too difficult, hire a therapist (See *Therapy, the Uses of*). Therapists have the same problem, too, and having found their way to the well, they can show others how to, too.

"While I was studying for my law boards, my mother came for the weekend and stayed for six months."

The greatest part of the problem isn't your mother at all; it's you! Why don't you have it out with your husband (and her) and put your cards on the table? "I'm going to my room for six months and study Blackstone; you two may keep house, cook, and birdwatch together. I've got other fish to fry!"

Result? Well, your mother might leave in a huff, throw her shoulder to the wheel—do the cooking, cleaning and baking, or go into a corner and cry softly. Almost anything. And, husband, well he might file for divorce, pitch in and do the cooking, cleaning and baking, or go pout in the corner. Point? You pass your law boards despite hell and high water; you have become a *responsible* person.

"I hate it when my husband puts the knock on my mother."

And your first husband, best friend, second cousins, and the boss: Married types counter-attack when friends and family—especially mom—are criticized. An attack on mom is an attack on them. Defensive. But if you feel separate from mom, an attack on her isn't an attack on the self. So, when he says, "You're a slowpoke and your mom was no ball of fire, either," it's understandable why you take umbrage. You are cut to the quick when hit at home. And home for the merely married is where mom and pop live.

So, if she's a slowpoke, maybe her mother was, too. If hubby puts the knock on her mother, he could be helping his wife give up her unreal self. And our unreal selves are simply characteristics of our parents we were forced to swallow when as children we were too weak to resist. Introjection: Trying to digest what we despise in our parents is a way we force ourselves to stay "close to home." But grown-ups are strong enough to "leave home" and that means putting on the shelf what we don't want to keep of our parents.

People in second marriages, in like manner, report that second spouses don't like to discuss their mate's first wife or husband. Another protection racket: Don't rake up the past. Protection rackets are the pastime of poor spirits and weak egos. It's no definition of tough love. To be forbidden (or to forbid the self) to talk about the past (our first wife/husband) is a violation of everyone's freedom. We can't protect our second spouses from reality and part of reality is what we feel about first mates. That includes both the happy and the unhappy times. Feeling separate is feeling free to talk about both.

Tough love is characterized by a responsibility to our own feelings; nobody backs off from what they feel. Protective love is characterized by what our mate might feel; everybody evades showing what they are feeling. A policy of "no comment" is part of protective lovers' marriage contracts: "Don't tread on me, and I won't tread on you." And protection rackets are as common as the common cold.

So, if you and your mate have an unwritten protective clause in your marriage contract, it could be because you can't be critical (or hate being criticized). That's a problem that goes back to mom: Feeling inseparate from her isn't helping you become separate with your spouse. No wonder you have problems with intimacy: You imitate your parents! You don't feel separate from them. And that's no way to honor thy father, thy mother, or thyself.

"Honor thy father and mother."
The famous last words of countless celebrated people lying on their deathbed is, "Mother." Dying soldiers on the battlefields of the world cry for their mothers. The first word we learn in this world is "Mommy!" (The second word we learn is "No!") And 'twixt crying for mom and saying "no" to her is the dramatic battleground of growing up. Fighting free. Becoming separate.

The battle of feeling *separate* is the healthy product of human aggression, the darker, creative and more interesting aspect of the human spirit. Becoming separate of mom (peers, employers, husbands, wives) is life-long. We carry this fighting spirit into marriage (spouses are mother-surrogates), through middle age and into the grave. It's a tug-of-war: On the one hand, we want to break free of mom; on the other hand, we want mom to take care of us. And through life, the self-same drama is taking place between liberty and order, adventure and security, myself/my mother.

Honor thy father and mother. But there is another, higher honor: The honor to God. God is freedom. If we become the person we want to be, we honor God *and* our mother and father. If we have no choice *but* to be what our mom and dad wants us to be, we aren't free. And we dishonor ourselves, our parents, *and* God.

Options, Keeping Open

Youth is the proper time to find the human race false and hopeless, a theory that is neither arrogant nor inaccurate. Its only flaw is that it's useless.

WILLIAM SAROYAN

"Happiness is a contract marriage."

"Liberation is being free of responsibility."

"I stay single to keep my options open."

"He travels fastest who travels alone."

" 'Working loose' keeps my options open."

"Single people invest more time on the job."

"If I had a million dollars, I would at last feel free."

"All my sorority sisters are going back to work."

"The aim of living is personal growth."

"Marriage means I'm home free."

"Happiness is a contract marriage."

Pre-nuptial agreements (See *Married, to Be or Not to Be*) which a lawyer can draw up on your behalf aren't the same as contract marriages which each party agrees in writing to:

Prepare no more than three evening meals per week.

Spend no more than one week away each year with mother.

Insist on conjugal relations no more than three times a week.

Spend no more than fifty dollars per month on booze.

Well, you get the idea!

Throw out post-nuptial contracts, written or unwritten. Contract marriages are no way to protect your interests *after* marriage: A hilarious example of the pragmatic tradition eating its own tail. Contract marriages don't work.

Marriage contracting belies your spontaneity and capacity for change. Moreover, contract marriages fly in the face of a healthy trend among people who are suspicious of "vows" and "obligations." To canonize Commitments and Duties as a certificate of marriage is like certifying love of country by filing an income tax return.

Contract marriages are attractive to people with weak egos and tepid spirits. Becoming separate is constant negotiation between strong egos and great spirits. But contract marriages rob people of the opportunity for confrontation.

"Liberation is being free of responsibility."

It's now official in the state of California; more people are in unholy wedlock than are joined in holy matrimony. My grandfather called this common-law marriage; my father called it shacking up; I call it having an affair; younger people call it living together. A rose, however, by any other name, is still a rose. The more things change, the more they stay the same.

We aren't liberated because we say so; we are free because we are so! Liberation lingo serves to confuse rather than clarify: freedom yes, involvement no; sex yes, love no; independence yes, interdependence no.

People are avoiding marriage, believing it an irrevocable commitment. So they live together uncommitted. Millions bed-hop and—on the job—job-hop.

Liberation isn't being free of responsibility; liberation is feeling strong enough to accept responsibility. And listlessly going from bed to bed, job to job doesn't work. It's destructive to self-esteem. No wonder chastity is staging a comeback.

Is the modern rage to "live together" the real cause behind the plunging birth rate? Are children, like marriage itself, seen as a burden, another option to keep open?

"I stay single to keep my options open."
It doesn't work.

Nobody feels free alone. The confusion about liberation rests in the word self-sufficiency. No nation, for example, is self-sufficient, and no human being is either.

If people think to marry is to give up freedom, it's understandable why they delay getting married. How can anyone feel happy who isn't free? Marriage isn't an eternal vow, an irrevocable contract, an unbreakable commitment: Knowing we can exit from marriage, break commitments, is a precondition to feeling separate while married.

"Closing options"—getting married—constitutes the major reason young men are in a mid-adolescent holding pattern. "Don't tie me down" is more than a rock music theme: It's the motto of the new pragmatism. But it's not pragmatic since it doesn't work. To indefinitely keep options open is to miss the bus. "I want a job, an apartment, and an independent life style, and then I want to get married," a young woman once said to me. ". . . and then I want to get married." What's implied is that after marriage, she's no longer free. After tasting an "independent life style," she gives it up and takes on the responsibility of marriage.

Crazy.

Marriage enhances our freedom because it shapes it. If what I write must be no more than 200 words, this doesn't limit my freedom so much as shape it. And if I marry, it doesn't mean I give up my freedom so much as I take it.

"He travels fastest who travels alone."
If companionate relationships are random and unsatisfying (and marriage obsolete) and children a burden to bear rather than a joy to have, our age of liberation is a bondage. "Working loose," making no commitments, and keeping options open locks us in a jailhouse of our own making.

To be unmarried is to lead a hassle-free life. But people who hate a hassle aren't strong enough to be responsible. They especially loathe taking responsibility for the self. They confuse movement with change, self-sufficiency with independence, free speech with feeling free.

And working couples cultivate private fantasies about the single life. "If I were single again, I would be free from all these nitpicking responsibilities," they say. But feeling free doesn't mean freedom from responsibility; feeling free means being willing to be responsible: Responsible to the self. But most people think responsibility to others is what is meant. No wonder they hate being married—even the idea of being married!

"Take care of me and I'll take care of you" is the commonplace definition of responsibility. That means nobody is going to be a grown-up. Nobody feels free: People feel dependent and resentful. "Feeling needed" and "needing someone" is the pits.

" 'Working loose' keeps my options open."

Drifting from one job to the next, putting off "career" commitments, being cool is working loose. It's a pastime for the very young and innocent. It finally palls. Working loose simply provides the means to avoid commitments. As if any kind of commitment was irrevocable. Thinking so reveals a wasted will. If we can't do anything except loosely, it means we can't take pains and be excellent doing what we want. To feel locked-in, typecast and predetermined by commitments isn't feeling free.

But the world of work is nowhere near as complicated as people make it. Most people today have three or four "careers." What they were trained to do they aren't doing: More than half the lawyers in this country don't practice law; many doctors don't practice hands-on medicine; working people are not the sum of their education and experience unless thinking so makes it so. What's most important is neither education nor experience but our ability. But people who believe education and experience shape them and not their own native ability and free will hesitate about making "career" commitments believing they will choose the "wrong" road.

Nobody wastes his education or experience: It's the property we carry around in our heads which nobody can steal. People unable to determine what they want and consequently working loose must give up thinking about "fields," and "professions," and "disciplines," and focus on skills and abilities instead. Form follows function. And skills are transferable from one "field" to another.*

Life for people who work and love "loose," drifting from one job to the next, from one bedroom to another, the cool and laid-back—sophisticated and non-committed—are miserable advertisements of the new liberation. "Life is meaningless," they say. And, of course, it's meaningless. The pain of isolation is self-inflicted; the self-sufficiency sought is won consuming the victor in his triumph. Pyrrhic.

"Single people invest more time on the job."

But it's not the amount of time we invest on a job so much as *how* we invest it that counts in so far as both productivity and job satisfaction are concerned: A student can study nine hours for a calculus exam and do worse than a student who *truly studies* for an hour and a half; it's the same on the job.

Countless studies have shown that married men are more stable, focused and responsible in the world of work. There are surprisingly few divorced presidents of *Fortune* 500 corporations, university presidents, foundation chiefs, or small business managers. A stabilized home front is the best security if we work at tough jobs on organizational front lines.

The qualification for tough jobs (judgment jobs, knowledge jobs, growth jobs—take your pick) is dependability. Effective managers are accustomed to being depended upon. They have strong egos. And strength of character, being able to assume lots of responsibility, is what organizational leadership requires. At bottom, the leadership crisis in America is the increasing incapacity of Americans to be responsible.

"If I had a million dollars, I would at last feel free."

That goes for anything we might want: Celebrity, a vacation cot-

* See *Go Hire Yourself an Employer* if you are still confused.

tage, a trip to mainland China. But it doesn't work (See *Money [and Time] Management*).

Indeed, money, lots of it, means we no longer have the excuse for not feeling free. A lot of us thought we would at last be happy when we married. And we *were* but *are* we? Our circumstances changed but we didn't. And the disappointment of discovering that our environment—events, money, other people—can't make us happy is the beginning of wisdom. Happiness is inside us. With a million dollars in our back pocket, we can change our circumstances. But have we changed our character?

"All my sorority sisters are going back to work."

Traditional wives must be on guard against working wives. Sure, it's statistically true most wives work; twenty years ago most wives stayed home. But neither way is right or wrong: A traditional wife goes back to work because she wants to, not because her best friend wants her to.

Following the crowd is bad judgment. Great spirits feel separated from the crowd. If they follow the crowd, it's because the crowd is going where they want. Know thyself: "Am I going back to work to please my neighbor?" she asks. It's not much different than the college senior who asks himself whether he is going to Law School so much to please himself as his father who wants him to go. Or the wife who wants a child because her mother wants a grandchild.

"The aim of living is personal growth."

Personal growth.

Flexibility.

Keeping options open.

Tradeoffs.

The expressions used by younger people who want it all—money, fame, self-fulfillment and a home in the country—now. The great fear is that younger men, like their fathers, will be caught up living for work rather than working for a living. And younger women are frightened of Kinder, Küche, and Kirche.

Love and work are *traps*, another expression we hear a lot. But flexibility is itself a trap: Elasticity of choice is so stretched there is no tension nor shape to people's lives. Postponing responsibilities postpones gratification.

"Marriage means I'm home free."

That's not marriage, that's death!

Marriage is the next stage in most single people's lives but they often act as if it were the last act. Marriage is thus boring.

Thinking marriage is necessarily settling is a myth. Marriage conceals seething melodramas under the surface. Living closely with another person reveals, as nothing else, our basic infancy. Marriage is building in an effective b.s. detector. And that's threatening to the weak-spirited. Marriage is sometimes, yes, a safe harbor. But often it's a high-seas adventure.

Organizations
(and the Working Couple)

People are always blaming their circumstances for what they are. I don't believe in circumstances. The people who get on in this world are the people who get up and look for the circumstances they want, and if they can't find them—make them.

GEORGE BERNARD SHAW, *Mrs. Warren's Profession*

"Mesh personal goals with organizational goals."

"Working couples should focus on skills first, pay second."

"The aim in a money marriage is to make more money."

"My greatest satisfaction is being accomplished at what I do."

"Imagination is the secret in meshing personal with organizational goals."

"My wife is interviewing the IBM people in Westchester and I'm talking to Honeywell in Boston."

"Think twice about working for the same organization."

"Conflict of interest issues are each working person's responsibility."

"Working couples should negotiate sharing the same job with the organization."

"Organizations aren't helping working mothers."

"Organizations should take into account the dual-career marriage."

"Mesh personal goals with organizational goals."

The money marriage has caught organizations by surprise: government, business and academia are just beginning to adjust. The problems are acutely complex for individuals, as we have seen, and for institutions, as you are about to see.

For younger working couples just starting out the gate, a piece of my mind: Forget the mammoth organizations. For both of you to hassle separate negotiations with two different conglomerates certain to relocate one of you within twenty-four months shows no imagination.

As for the middle-aging in midcareer, weary of quarreling about whose job comes *first*, go back and read *Attitude Is Everything* and think through launching a self-directed job search. Self-managed job campaigns take into account personal and professional goals. An obvious personal objective in marriage is living together; replace the work ethic with the worth ethic.

A self-directed job search is pro-active. But most job seekers are passive. The self-managed job hunt puts you first; most job seekers put organizations first. The difference is attitude: The first are responsible to the self; the second are responsible to others. Feeling free to find the job you want is central to the self-directed job search; feeling you must accept what an organization offers is the conventional attitude. So do what *you want* for an employer who needs it done.

A successful self-directed job search guarantees a mesh between your personal goals and organizational objectives: a definition of job satisfaction. But there is a price: It takes time, money, and imagination. And caring about the self in finding the job you want—no surprise—often causes guilt.

"Working couples should focus on skills first, pay second."

So, yes, finding an employer who puts us to work doing what we want is the secret of job satisfaction. It's also the basis, turned inside out (finding the most *able and willing* people), of sound participation (i.e., "personnel") policy in an organization.*

* See *If Things Don't Improve Soon, I May Ask You To Fire Me!*

Having established your skills means going the final lap and finding somebody to pay you (and pay you very well) for the exercise of those skills. All of which means eliminating most employers and focusing on organizations which can foot your bill. Tough.

But nowhere as difficult as dispersing yourself in every direction and shooting for a job *any place*. Passive. Dependent. Accommodating. Skill-oriented, charged-up people with a series of job goals (all of which relate to their generic skills) motivate themselves: They know what they want, where, for how much. Pro-active. Dependable. Responsible. Setting a price on your skills (your "salary requirements") is essential.

Putting a high price on your skills impresses next employers. How can you be worthwhile if you don't think so! Finding work you want and do very well which pays well is a great confidence-builder. But the basis of self-confidence is ability: Know thyself. Know thy abilities. Ask and it shall be given. People who don't know themselves think they have no abilities—skills. They think they are worthless. Therefore, they accept lousy salaries at jobs they *don't* want.

"The aim in a money marriage is to make more money."

Half true.

The whole truth is that people want to make money doing what they want and doing what they want very well.

The key to satisfaction in the workplace—at every age, income, level of responsibility—is neither compensation nor prestige. What everybody *wants* is a chance to *excel* in his work; we want to put *our mark* on what we do; we want to say, "I did that!"

The eerie nature of organizational environments, the increasing blue- and white-collar alienation from work itself, and the difficulty of feeling a sense of real achievement on the job has caused people to focus on Success(!) and Power(!) on the job and to forget the inner man or woman; corny but true.

The decline in the achievement ethic and the other directed nature of work ("It's not what you do but how you play the boss") destroys the spirit of younger people. It literally kills the older ones. So, working couples looking for work, ought to ask how a job *tests* them: Strengthens and pushes them. The key is how accomplished we are on the job. Am I effective and am I becoming better and better every day in every way?

"My greatest satisfaction is being accomplished at what I do."

The increasing dissatisfaction with work is the result of organizational dynamics which remove people from the source of their satisfaction: The exercise of their skills. Exercising skills brings the feeling of accomplishment, without it no job, no matter how prestigious, well paid or important, pays the job holder off.

ITEM: A professor of English is nominated to be his college's president. In his new job, he feels strangely dissatisfied and unfulfilled despite an increase in income, power and visibility.

ITEM: A crackerjack production whiz is promoted to a group vice-presidency. He works on government relations and is unhappy despite an enormous increase in pay and privileges.

ITEM: An expert family counselor accepts an important policy-making job in the government. She much prefers the satisfaction of her lively private practice.

Working couples need to guard against unwanted promotions: Teachers who become administrators, consultants who become managers, craftsmen who become directors, are players who become spectators: All complain inwardly about their jobs. They "should" like their jobs but they don't.

To separate people from their skills, to promote them to a job where they can't exercise their abilities, to reassign the competent to areas where they feel incompetent is no uncommon thing. Something does die in them. What they were "meant" to do isn't what they are doing!

"Imagination is the secret in meshing personal with organizational goals."

The responsibility for meshing personal with organizational goals rests with each individual. To think that Bell Telephone Labs can take into account the job objectives of the six hundred electrical engineers it hires each year *and* the career plans of their spouses is absurd. But every Spring, thousands of eager MBAs passively accept

jobs with *Fortune* 500 firms and marry other MBAs with jobs with
other industrial giants.

Well, it won't work. The design of the linear career is faulty. And
the blame lies with people, not organizations. What's lacking is
imagination: Each partner to a money marriage feels dependent on
prospective employers. Result? Working couples accept jobs based
on whether (a) a job is offered and (b) whether it's "professional."
The consequence is that many people in money marriages forget personal considerations, minor details like the quality of their marriage.

Another result, of course, is that one partner or the other (usually
the wife) sucks hind tit. And the inevitable quarrels, "My turn now,
your turn later," erupt.

The biggest obstacle to overcome in mounting a self-directed job
campaign is thinking Big Organizations have all the jobs. Remember, more than half the employed people in the country work in
organizations with fifty or fewer employees. Select-out organizations
which can't provide what you want; for many working couples,
those are the biggest but not the best.

*"My wife is interviewing the IBM people in Westchester and I'm
talking to Honeywell in Boston."*

No imagination.

Seeking out the biggest companies and forgetting the smallest isn't
taking into account that you and yours would like to live *and* work
in the same place! Sleeping together is a strong argument for employment in the same place. "Another reason I want to work for you
guys is that my wife has bagged a great job with the Pittsfield
School system."

Knowing what you want, knowing what you can do, knowing
where you and your wife want to live are the three questions both
must answer before launching self-directed job campaigns. That
way, the first to get a job supports the other.

Give up thinking like your grandfather: Nobody in a money marriage—except under unusual circumstances—can have a linear career
(See *Ethics, Work and Worth*). Give up thinking being married is a
constraint on your freedom: Constraints more often shape our freedom than eliminate it. Give up trying to compromise ("My turn

now, your turn next time"); give up trying to accommodate your partner's career goals—that's putting the self second; give up the work ethic and get with the worth ethic; give up thinking you can't have what you want—one thing you both *want* is each other!

So, clearly she can't work in Westchester with IBM and live with her husband who works with Honeywell in Boston. But why can't both focus on jobs with Digital Equipment in New England. That way they work together and don't sleep alone.

"Think twice about working for the same organization."

Suppose he is hired by Digital in Operations Research but she is turned away for a similar job? Rough. All the more reason to think twice about interviewing the same organization. Remember, think about skills and how they transfer from one organization to the next: She might find work in computer programming with the city government, a university, or another firm. Conversely, she might do something she hasn't been trained to do but does very well: Stop thinking people can only do what they have been trained to do.* Don't count on the organization taking care of you! The aim of sound organizational development is encouraging everyone to take care of themselves.**

Here are some considerations working couples should think through:

1. In interviewing for similar or different jobs in the same organization, inevitably one of you is going to be considered the "stronger" candidate. It takes an unusually strong ego to handle being Number 2 or the guilt of being Number 1.

2. It's unrealistic to think both partners will advance in the organization at the same rate of speed. If you jog while your partner dashes, you need a heroic ego.

3. Both partners might be overlooked for significant reassignments and enviable relocations because the organization refuses to separate married couples.

* See *Go Hire Yourself an Employer.* (Chapter Three)
** See *If Things Don't Improve Soon, I May Ask You To Fire Me!* (Chapter Nine)

4. If both partners work in different departments which are adversarial (the business versus the editorial department, the marketing versus the production department), tensions on the job overflow into the home, and conflict of interest issues raise their ugly heads.

5. Working wives, increasingly sensitive to discrimination on the job, must cultivate tough egos to cope with male preferment. Men with working wives must do the same; they might be victims of "Affirmative Action" discrimination.

"Conflict of interest issues are each working person's responsibility."

Increasingly in the world of work, there are conflicts of interest between what she *does* for a living and what he *does*. Conflicts of interest are resolved only if people know what their interests *are*. But plenty of working couples heedlessly put themselves in harm's way. Everyone has egg on his face.

Moreover, working couples must avoid not only a *real* conflict of interest but must conduct themselves so as to avoid the *appearance* of a conflict. The way to protect your own interests and not be in conflict with your partner's is to master the art of anticipatory problem-solving: Working couples anticipate potential problems between organizational interests and self-interests and lance the boil before it does its mischief; it's individuals (not organizations) which must take the initiative. Who is the best judge of my interests and whether they conflict with my wife's: Anaconda Copper? HUD? Princeton University? Monogram Industries?

Let's look at some examples:

ITEM: She works as a technical proposal development writer for an aircraft manufacturer which does extensive business with the Defense Department. Her job is to win contracts put out for bid by Uncle Sam. Her husband works as a contracts negotiator for the Defense Department. His job is to put contracts out for bid. Her company bids on a proposal she writes which her husband is responsible for awarding. Conflict of Interest.

ITEM: She's an editor for a major New York publishing house. The man she is living with handles screen rights for a California movie company. Her job is to auction hot literary properties to Hollywood. Each talks to the other about his/her job. She tells him about a sleeper book certain to be a blockbuster movie. His company moves quickly and buys the screen rights from her firm without competitive bidding. Conflict of Interest.

ITEM: He's a professor of Babylonian history at a huge midwestern university. She's a special assistant to the Chancellor in charge of administrating faculty salaries and fringes. Her husband is awarded an unscheduled sabbatical. Conflict of Interest.

ITEM: He's a new-product attorney for a major pharmaceutical company responsible for representing and winning the approval of new Brand drugs before the Federal Drug Administration. She's a program officer for the FDA responsible for co-ordinating the evaluation of potential new drug issues. His company is never overruled by the government. Conflict of Interest.

In every case, these people are in professional peril: Set-ups for "Gotcha." Transparently—no matter how innocent each person might be—both are in a position where there is an *appearance* of wrong doing. And as the French say, appearance is everything.

Item (1): Our lady who sells to the "public sector" while her man buys from the "private sector" is a juicy tidbit for a newspaper gossip columnist. Item (2): The editor with the hot book in bed with a man who buys hot books is in jeopardy: Her boss, learning of her liaison, is likely to sack her. Item (3): The special assistant and her college professor husband are certain to provoke arched eyebrows in the faculty club. Item (4): The attorney and the program review officer are both expendable if word leaks out.

The message?

Anticipate: Each partner must discuss with the other whether the jobs they have or jobs they want, are likely to conflict. Nobody who knows his own interests is going to willingly—no matter how desirable the job—put himself in an ethical bind.

So, if in a conflict of interest dilemma, take employers into your confidence: Let them know the facts. Reason together. Result? Probably a transfer, reassignment, a reclassification of responsibilities. Protective reaction. It's tough making the painful tradeoffs between your personal life and your occupational interests. But it's much tougher finding yourself in the middle of a scandal that simple self-awareness could have prevented.

"Working couples should negotiate sharing the same job with the organization."

Job-sharing, as you would expect, is vastly more popular with job candidates than employers. Employers worry about (1) the expense of two people on the payroll, and (2) who's in charge? Organizations which hire two people to do one job pay out only one salary but *two* fringe benefit packages. But worse, employers fret about the job falling between two stools: What happens if the couple divorces?

Some employers are discovering if you hire a part-timer, you lock him in full-time: People don't stop thinking about work when they walk onto the employee parking lot (See *Burnout*). Hiring a working couple to do one job is securing a 300 percent effort. The difficulty is convincing an employer.

Message to employers: Job-sharing often works better than filling the job full-time with one person; it depends on the quality of the people and how well they work together. Message to job-sharers: It's your job to convince employers job-sharing works. Message to both: Job-sharing works *least* well with people unequal in ability, motivation and dependability or those infected with control problems. Control problems are difficult enough to resolve in marriage without compounding them on the same job.

Take the proposal approach if you both want to negotiate sharing a job with an organization or anything else. Make a proposition to your next or current employer. Write it up: A concept paper. Cost it out. Show employers why you need help in educating your kids, relocating to Seattle, taking time off for an educational sabbatical. Show employers how much more effective and productive you will be if they (a) provide a company-owned car to drive to work, (b) pay for a full-time housekeeper while you cover a three-month assignment in Birmingham, (c) reassign you on a half-time basis to Quality Control, and (d) loan you money at no interest to put your oldest through law school.

"Organizations aren't helping working mothers."

Nor working wives, single parents or for that matter working couples: But being a working mother is hardest of all. The exponential increase in money marriages with or without children is causing changes in the way we work. But organizations lag behind working mothers' needs and must be changed. The point is that a tough ego —a great spirit—is what everyone needs in any age. Organizations aren't helping working mothers. That doesn't mean they won't.

The demands people make on organizations and the response employers make is one way society changes. So, don't stop trying to shape up organizations. That means joining with other working mothers with similar demands and together reasonably making your case to the people who need to know it. Above all, it's knowing what you want from an organization (a well-paid, part-time job, for example) and persuading an employer of the sweet reason of your demands.

Changing organizational employment patterns through flex-time hours, job-sharing, and part-time jobs is tough. Don't expect organizations to change without you and your allies helping it to happen. Personal change, we have seen, is tough work. If *you* have trouble changing, think about organizations! And, remember, it's easier changing organizations when you are on a payroll: Coming in from the outside and pushing for a corporate day-care center is much, much tougher.*

"Organizations should take into account the dual-career marriage."

Actually, it's working couples who should take into account the organization in showing employers how imaginative working arrangements make them more effective.

A children's garden of delights: Organizations, as if they weren't already drowning their people in barrels of maple syrup, now are being asked to classify and assign people on a family-based strategy. It won't be long before every company, like the Armed Forces, has its own corporate cemetery.

My advice to employers is to keep your eye on the ball: Find the most effective people to fill the tough jobs. To take into consideration other matters before the main matter, the job, is bound to hamstring sound man and woman power development: Fix on that guy or gal in the organization who can do the job better than any-

* This point is made well by Bob Townsend in *Up The Organization!*

one else. Offer this person the job. Then, discuss how this promotion, reassignment, or relocation meshes with his/her self-interest. Is there a mesh?

My advice to *people* is to focus on the job independent of spouse, children, boss, organizational objectives, and your pension plan *first*. Focus on pleasure first, price second: The truth is you want *that* job. Great! Now face up to the consequences: (1) Taking your children out of school in midterm; (2) Hazarding a downturning real estate market; (3) Confronting your husband about the Big Promotion; (4) Having a fight.

So, get off the horns of a dilemma and discuss your self-interests with the boss. Confess what you want: "I don't want the Western Region until my husband passes his law boards."

Now that's the kind of information organizations need. Lots of solutions recommend themselves: (a) Appointing an acting director; (b) putting you on a commuter basis for nine months; (c) flying your family once a month to Denver; (d) offering your husband a job in its Legal Counsel Division in Denver; or (e) saying, "Tough, we needed someone yesterday."

The last is a cruel decision. But painful choices are the stuff of management, including self-management. Unhappily, many organizations make decisions about people based, not on the most effective person to fill a job, but from mere convenience: "Jake is available, and he doesn't have to sell his house. Let's send him to the Arabian Gulf." And working couples—no different than organizations—make decisions dependent on convenience; i.e., the working wife with a shot at the Western Region who turned it down for the sake of her husband and his law boards. If she turned down the job because she *should* stay with her husband, big trouble; if she accepted the job because she wanted to flee her husband, bigger trouble. What's important is whether her decision was free-formed!

Any decision we don't freely make is irresponsible! Irresponsible people put the self second and everyone (including the organization) comes in third.

Organizations are trying harder to accommodate working couples. But don't depend on it. Depend on the self. The key to helping organizations change lies with the people who work for them. Work-

ing couples must establish what each wants from an employer besides a paycheck: Company transport, short-term travel, no lengthy
reassignments and so forth. For example:

My firm, an international management consulting firm, now offers maternity and *paternity leave.*

Many organizations when relocating key people buy the family
home, provide an upfront cash down payment on another
house at the next assignment, and escrow the whole messy
real estate thing.

Some public accounting firms with traveling auditors fly spouses
around the country for weekend marriages on any assignment
which exceeds a fortnight in duration.

Another firm, a defense contractor, flies a working mother's children to her every weekend she is on the road.

Winds of change. But it's working couples who must press for
these changes.

Real Talk

" 'Real talk between a man and a woman offers the supreme privilege of keeping the other sane and being kept sane by the other. As we look about us, it is obvious this privilege is not often fulfilled, and I suspect this has always been true. Nor is it the only way of staying sane. But it will remain, I believe, one of our best hopes.' "*

LESLIE FARBER

"Real talk often precedes or follows good sex."

"After work, all my husband wants to do is read the paper, watch TV or work in his hobby shop."

"My husband and I never discuss general issues but talk about co-ordinating our schedules, fat-free diets and faster commute routes to the city."

"Our talk is mostly shop talk."

"I find talking to perfect strangers easier than to my wife."

"I hate interrupting people and I hate being interrupted."

"I always think about what I'm going to say next rather than listening to my feelings about what is being said."

* "Lying, Despair, Jealousy, Envy, Sex, Suicide, Drugs, and the Good Life." Leslie Farber, Basic Books, page 179.

"My husband is as shy as a titmouse and I run on like a babbling brook."

"My husband and I often have long conversations in bed before going to sleep."

"I insist my family talk at mealtime."

"Real talk often precedes or follows good sex."

If and when the world ends, we can be sure a few survivors with doctorates in the social sciences will blame the end of the world on a "breakdown in communication." But bad communication is a *consequence,* not a cause, of marital breakdowns.

There is no way two people can live together without communicating. As everywhere else, one way we talk to each other is silently. Every husband, every wife has a *look:* This "look" communicates much more than words. But in marriage, as in statecraft, *words are deeds.* Explaining in words what we mean with "looks" is good communication policy. It starts us talking about the self.

Good conversation precedes good sex as surely as good writing follows clear thinking. Harried working couples caught up in a vortex of activities, leading lives of "ought" and not "want," focused on duty, never desire, always complain about "communication" problems. "We had a communication barrier," they say after the divorce.

Bad sex or no sex follows no talk or shop talk. Winston Churchill, in another context, once said to jaw-jaw is better than to war-war. And jawboning, like sex, is what every working couple can never do too much.

"After work, all my husband wants to do is read the paper, watch TV or work in his hobby shop."

Most people stress the importance of being *tolerant.* "Wives, let thy husband rest in peace. Husbands, listen, truly listen to and love thy wife." It doesn't work. No man or woman in marriage can *tolerate* it: Women go into a purple funk; men into a purple passion.

Working men have inherited a malignant attitude toward "Work" which is destructive to happiness. Men are altogether too serious about what they *do*: Every work day, trudging off to work with lunch pail, brief case or sample box in tow, men earn the money to protect their families from the wolf at the door. Working men of the world are "responsible." Even thieves, crooks, and scalawags are often good "family men."

Thus, of an evening—after work and especially before dinner— men think, "I've done my job, earned my pay, kept big bad wolf from the door, done what *they* (employers) want, now it's my turn to do what I want." Working wives don't feel this acute sense of responsibility.

Working wives simply don't take work as seriously as men. Oh, sure, single working women might show the same symptoms as men as well as "displaced homemakers." But in the main, men are so caught up in work—even those in "alternative work"—that *what* they do is *who* they are.

A comparable state of mind for most working women—especially working women—is the "seriousness" with which they approach the home. Try as they will, women feel the home is their "responsibility." Working women anguish about matters at home, the grocery shopping, the flaking bathroom wallpaper, the children's tattered wardrobe—responsibilities their husbands never "see." A man doesn't "see" these things because he doesn't feel responsible. And a woman doesn't "see" how important the world of work is to her husband.

So, men, don't take Work so seriously. Women, don't start taking Work too seriously. In fact, quit taking life seriously. This is a really "serious" proposition!

"My husband and I never discuss general issues but talk about co-ordinating our schedules, fat-free diets and faster commute routes to the city."

Another aspect of working couples is what they talk about. "Before we married, we discussed the Restoration Comedies, now we quarrel about who stacks the dishwasher. Either that or it's job *this* and job *that*."

Reality.

Exit romance, enter reality.

But marriage helps us cope with reality. Remember, if I live alone, there is nobody with whom to discuss the job or the Restoration Comedies and no choice but stacking the dishwasher myself. Nobody to enjoy life with; nobody to *resent*.

Stacking the dishwasher and discussing the poems of John Donne and the job are all real. But if working couples feel the dishes and job are *real* and the Elizabethan sonnets *unreal* then neither partner is co-operating with reality. Part of reality is a clean dish; part of reality is great literature.

The solution? Stack the dishwasher while reciting Shakespeare's sonnets.

The worst disillusionment to the newly married is the evaporation of the Great Conversation. Modern men and women are starved for good conversation. And good conversation is all about us, laid out like a banquet. But as Auntie Mame says, "The dumb bastards can't bring themselves to eat."

A recent study of the length of time married folks typically talk to each other in any given day is less, repeat *less*, than five minutes. Hell's bells, we talk to our plants longer than that!

People bored by marriage invariably stop talking about Great Issues and can scarcely think, much less talk, about anything except chicken issues. But both the Great and the Small are enduring aspects of the Great Conversation.

"Our talk is mostly shop talk."

Learning how to become separate with our partners (which takes a lifetime) carries over on the job. Happy people leave the office at the office: Good insurance sales types don't discuss new rate schedules over morning coffee with their spouses; lawyers don't make their briefs after making love; cops don't talk about robbers after their tour is up.

Most of us fall halfway between full disclosure and complete silence about our job. "He comes home, opens a Bud, and reads the paper," complains the martyred wife. "She jabbers away like a bluejay about her job," complains the long-suffering husband. To feel self-pity, to be long-suffering, is self-defeating. "Oh, if I had only married a man who talked to me," says the wife; "Oh, if I had only married a serene and silent woman," says the husband.

Illusions.

What both partners really feel is anger. Not expressing this anger leads to self-contempt and contempt for our partner. Anger makes us feel better about ourselves (and the person we live with). Feeling free is a question of feeling free to express emotion (See *Fighting Fair*).

"I find talking to perfect strangers easier than to my wife."

You feel free with strangers; a prisoner at home.

Crazy.

Knowing you are crazy, helps. And hating feeling alone in marriage helps, too. Finally, knowing you are partly responsible for your loneliness helps most of all.

Real talk is a result of becoming separate. Real talk is saying what you feel. If real talk is to happen between a husband and his wife, men—more so than women—must begin it. And the best way is to start talking about the self.

Self-awareness.

The disagreeable aspect of being self-aware, revealing your own feelings, and feeling what you say is shedding the notion that you must protect your wife from your feelings. This is tricky for men who learned early in life to spare their mothers (See *Momism*).

Real talk is honest. Authentic. The real thing.

No talk or unreal talk is pussyfooting. Feelings are avoided to keep the peace. Women, thus, are starved of emotion, feel unloved and scream, "Why don't you ever talk to me!" And the peace is broken; war is declared.

Real talk is revealed emotion. Remember, there is nothing "wrong" about negative feelings unless you think there is. So stop thinking your wife isn't strong enough to handle your feelings. That's self-defeating: Protecting others eliminates the self.

To start "communicating" in your marriage, you gotta feel free! That's why talk with strangers is often more invigorating. You feel separate; but you don't feel free at home because dull and docile partners are easier to control.

The secret of real talk amounts to revealing what we are feeling; poor communication policy is telling our spouses what *they* are feeling. That's trying to *control* another person. And when somebody tries to tell you what you are feeling you resent it.

"I hate interrupting people and I hate being interrupted."
If married types interrupt each other, it's an indication both feel separate. Real talk is spontaneous, a free interplay of persons with self-aware minds. A bad conversation is being acutely aware of each other: No one *feels free.* Conversation is controlled, deliberate and dull; no one feels free to interrupt. Docile folk never interrupt.

Among working couples real talk is a pleasure, interrupting and being interrupted is a part of tough love; both in public and in private. Don't try to protect your wife from your feelings. Don't expect her to protect you.

If I'm on the telephone and my wife hears me make an engagement for next Saturday P.M., she isn't helping herself by not interrupting and telling me I've promised to umpire a Little League game. I'm not helping myself when she confuses the date of the outbreak of the First World War with the date of its ending. In the first instance, it's important to her to make me *aware* of a previous commitment; in the second, it's important to me to make her *aware* of her confusion.

"I always think about what I'm going to say next rather than listening to my feelings about what is being said."
Self-consciousness.
The opposite of self-awareness.
Self-conscious people are not active listeners; they don't listen to their own feelings. And thus don't "listen"* to what other people are saying. Thus, they eliminate the self from real talk.

Active listening isn't a passive exercise, any more than close reading is passive. But if we aren't listening to what is being said (i.e., we aren't listening to our feelings about what is being said), it's ex-

* To "listen to your feelings" means *thinking* about what is being said and asking the self what you *feel* about it.

actly like reading without understanding. We are insensible. Dumb.

To listen effectively and to talk effectively means being self-aware. "I'm sorry dear, fly that by me one more time," is what we say when we catch ourselves acting dumb. An important part of real talk is talking about why we are having trouble listening or talking. Something causes us to block out our consciousness.

So, if my wife wants to talk about the climbing price of chicken giblets, maybe I'm having trouble listening to her. My own anxiety about missing out on a sure sale that afternoon might be the reason. Rather than feign interest in the price of giblets, I should confess my real anxiety. Real talk is about the self.

Before real talk can take place you must feel free. Anxiety paralyzes free thinking. Eliminate the anxiety by talking about it. So, ask out loud, "What am I afraid of?" the next time you go into a asphasic coma. Your baby crying in the next room is real; your wife's fears that the child is dying are probably imaginary. But for her not to express her anxiety out of consideration for her husband's feelings is unreal. An IRS audit is real; your husband's fears are probably imaginary. But for him to try to accommodate his wife by not expressing his own feelings is unreal. Her promotion at work causes her inexplicable misery; her anxiety is probably imaginary. But for her to clam-up out of sensitivity to her husband is unreal.

So, a lot of unreal talk is simple worrywarting. Anxiety is believing the worst will happen, never the best. Anxious people are full-time fault-finders: They especially fault themselves. They hate having things on their Conscience; their talk is all about what is "right" and what is "wrong." The conversation hour is a recitation of every snafu, disappointment, misfire which occurred that day. No wonder husbands hide behind the paper, wives turn to the stove.

The way working couples foster real talk is hearing out each other's anxieties and helping them separate out what is real from what is unreal. Therapeutic. Be alert. Self-aware. Every anxiety is the tip of an emotional iceberg. Letting our partners see our view of the iceberg helps clarify the confusion in their minds. And letting our spouses draw their view of our anxieties helps us to see the forest as well as the trees in our own mind.

"My husband is as shy as a titmouse and I run on like a babbling brook."

She depends on his being a good listener; he depends on her to do his social downfield blocking.

But they hate being dependent; he's frightened of going to a party without her; she's at a loss without her in-house sounding board. They hate their need for each other; they begin to hate each other.

Dependency isn't the issue. There is no way in God's green earth we don't depend on other people. Being dependent needn't cause resentment. The trick is being able to do what others normally do for us.

So if he can learn to talk it up at social gatherings and if she can learn to live with her own thoughts, who is to say they won't *want* the companionship of each other quite apart from their need for it?

No, the issue isn't dependency: It's freedom. Learning to live in marriage without need is feeling free to want. And the people who do this best are those who feel separate from other people. Thus, he shouldn't feel responsible for his wife's needs and she needn't feel responsible for his. Once partners start taking responsibility for their own needs and stop taking responsibility for other people's needs, they feel separate with other people.

"My husband and I often have long conversations in bed before going to sleep."

Another thing about good talk is where we do it. And bed is as good a place as any. The phone has stopped ringing, the kids are asleep, the next day is eight hours away. No more dumb chores and mindless activity. Maybe it's the physical proximity, the intimacy of the bedchamber, the privacy—whatever it is—you feel free.

But, of course, you want to feel free everyplace: In the car, on an airplane, at a dinner party. If you don't, it's because you turn yourself off to having fun of which real talk is central. Anxiety and obligation—in equal measures—blocks out real feeling. And expressing feeling is the secret in feeling free.

Real talk is for grown-ups. Thus, children who can listen in might (or might not) join in. Kids love to see their folks enjoying each other.

But no or unreal talk anyplace (much less the bedroom) isn't feeling free. Unfeeling. Boring.

"I insist my family talk at mealtime."

That's how to kill conversation. You can no more order up real talk—like an order of french fries—than you can insist on your children's "respect." What you can do is simply start talking. Table talk is happy talk. So, why not postpone talk about death and taxes and focus on pleasurable things.

Confrontations—tough talk—are best saved until after dinner. Everyone is more agreeable: Our felt needs are satisfied. And eating is satisfying to the inner man and woman.

Mealtimes are when families celebrate together. They might be the major sacrament in marriage. Children don't have to be called twice to eat if it's fun being with mom and dad. But if mom and dad don't feel good about themselves, children themselves might feel responsible.

Finally, real talk is simply the expression of feelings. But most men feel feelings are nowhere near as important as action. But real action grows out of passion. Men who put self-control ahead of real talk eliminate the self. And people praised for their remarkable self-control are often depressed (and depressing).

Sexual Politics

Such music in a skin.

THEODORE ROETHKE

(a) "I feel awful if my wife doesn't make it."
(b) "My husband is responsible for my making it."

(a) "My partner turns me off."
(b) "My partner turns me on."

(a) "There are no clumsy lovers, simply frigid women."
(b) "There are no frigid women, simply clumsy lovers."

(a) "Good sex is simply a question of good technique."
(b) "Bad sex is simply a question of bad technique."

(a) "My sexual unhappiness is my partner's fault."
(b) "My sexual happiness is my responsibility."

(a) "I care about pleasing myself in bed."
(b) "I'm concerned about pleasing my mate in bed."

(a) "Good sex is characteristic of happiness."
(b) "The sex is great but the marriage is terrible."

(a) "Working wives make sexy women."
(b) "Working couples are too tired for good sex."

(a) "I hate it if my wife shows sexual interest in other men."
(b) "I hate it if my husband is attracted to another woman."

(a) *"Working couples are likely to play around on the job."*
(b) *"Don't dip your quill in the company ink."*

(a) *"Sexual infidelity is less likely among working couples."*
(b) *"Sexual infidelity is more likely among working couples."*

(a) *"Working wives are subject to sexual harassment on the job."*
(b) *"Working husbands are subject to sexual entrapment."*

(a) *"My husband often thinks sex is his doing me a favor."*
(b) *"My wife often makes sex conditional on something else."*

(a) *"I feel awful if my wife doesn't make it."*
(b) *"My husband is responsible for my making it."*

HUSBAND: "Did you?"

WIFE: "Did you, you did, didn't you?"

HUSBAND: "Yes, I'm afraid I—Oh, I'm sorry. I am sorry. I know how it makes you feel."

WIFE: "Oh, don't worry about it. I'm sure I'll quiet down after a while."

HUSBAND: "I'm so sorry, dearest. Let me help you."

WIFE: "I rather you didn't."

HUSBAND: "But I. . . ."

WIFE: "What good is it when you've just—when you don't really want to? You know perfectly well, if you don't really want to, it doesn't work."

HUSBAND: "But I do really want to! Believe me. It will work, you'll see. Only let me!"

WIFE: "Please, couldn't we just forget it? For now the thing is done, finished. Besides, it's not really that important. My tension always wears off eventually. And anyhow . . . maybe next time it'll be different."

HUSBAND: "Oh, it will, I know it will. Next time I won't be so tired or eager. I'll make sure of that. Next time it's going to be fine—but about tonight—I'm sorry, dear."*

Now in this classic conversation which takes place every night in

---

* "I'm Sorry, Dear," a dialogue from a paper by Leslie Farber, M.D.

a million bedrooms, each person is deceiving the other. She believes he is impotent and *doesn't say so;* he believes she is frigid and *doesn't say so.* Each is secretly contemptuous of the other. Each is disillusioned. Neither expects anything *real* in love. Nobody is disappointed.

(a) *"My partner turns me off."*
(b) *"My partner turns me on."*

Nobody turns me on; nobody turns me off.

Nobody changes me; I can't change anybody.

Nobody makes me happy; I can't make anyone happy.

Nobody motivates me; I can't motivate anybody.

All of the above are half true. But, of course, it isn't the whole truth. The point to keep in mind—so important to good sex—is our sense of separation and self in sexual expression. If I believe my wife can turn me on, I'll believe she can turn me off. That's not feeling separate. Free. And if I believe I can turn her on and off—like a light switch—she feels in my control. Unfree.

The message is that we turn the self on. Believing otherwise is to feel *responsible for other people's happiness.* And feeling responsible turns us off. Though we blame the turn-off on our partner, it's really our sense of responsibility which turns us off.

Grasp this concept in your brain and live it in your gut, and your sex life will improve overnight. But don't count on it. Substituting a sense of separation for your sense of responsibility takes a lifetime. At the same time, while we are not responsible for other people's happiness, we can contribute, stimulate, promote other people's happiness. But we can't cause it. We cultivate our garden; we don't "make" the plants grow.

(a) *"There are no clumsy lovers, simply frigid women."*
(b) *"There are no frigid women, simply clumsy lovers."*

Thus, wives are "ballbreakers"; but working wives don't rob men of the family jewels—they do that to the self. Wives don't turn men off; men turn the self off. That's when men start thinking about technique and try fornicating hanging by their ankles from the bedroom beam!

Deprogram the self from thinking that sexual fulfillment is simply a question of good technique. Pornography is the last refuge of the romantic imagination. Irresponsible. Good sex is rooted in feeling and you can no more replace feelings with technique than you can replace the idea of the thing for the thing.

Sure, wives often discourage potency in their husbands; husbands show no consideration and encourage incompetency in their wives. But nobody causes sexual misfires except the self. So blaming your wife, blaming your husband isn't taking responsibility for the self. That's due to the inability of the self to be *at blame* (See *Conscience Doth Make Cowards*). Thus, people shift the responsibility. "My wife is frigid" and "My husband's a lousy lover." Irresponsible.

Feeling responsible for other people's happiness causes accommodation anxiety. Focusing on the pleasure of our partner switches us off: Men go limp and women go dry. And impotent men and incompetent women soon conclude sex isn't much fun anymore. But the need for sex is constant.

Good sex won't bring romance back into your marriage. God helps us. Good sex brings back something much better. Passion. If people go to the altar believing from this time forward life is a dialogue between beautiful souls, there are some married people who believe there is romantic fire in the ashes. Hmm. This is a touching tribute to the Romantic Movement. Don't knock it; romance is part of reality. But romantic love is blind. Blind as a walleyed old bat. But tough lovers—married types—see things wholly and clearly. Foxy.

(a) *"Good sex is simply a question of good technique."*
(b) *"Bad sex is simply a question of bad technique."*

For women and men alike to focus on "performance" technique and pleasing one's partner (and being pleased) causes both men and women to lose touch with their own feelings. How can anyone enjoy sex without feeling?

Accommodating the pleasure of our partner in bed, putting technique before passion, feeling responsible, and being depended on to "perform" is a prescription for sexual misfire. We fail in feeling free.

Taking sex seriously, like your job, is the reason neither is any fun anymore. Our attitude to both wants changing. How can some-

thing so serious be any fun? Important, yes; serious, no. Start playing around at work/playing around in bed, and work and sex are
fun again. But if you think bad sex is the end of the world, a termi-
nal condition, a catastrophe: Well, you've missed the streetcar
named desire.

In bed, make the distinction between accommodating your partner's needs (which doesn't work) and show consideration instead.
This means you are free to accommodate your own needs and feel
free to show consideration to your partner. Feeling responsible kills
desire.

Giving pleasure is not more important than taking it: The anxiety
of feeling responsible kills the pleasure. At the same time, to take
pleasure and not give pleasure (showing no consideration) is being
irresponsible to the self.

Good sex is an act between two people taking and giving pleasure.
But the focus is on the taking. *Care* about your own pleasure and
show consideration to your partner. That's being responsible.

Good sex is like launching a rocket to the moon. An achievement.
But to "work" at it, won't "make it"; play at it. And if you make it,
the whole act is as natural as sneezing; if you don't, it's as complex
as a moon shot.

(a) *"My sexual unhappiness is my partner's fault."*
(b) *"My sexual happiness is my responsibility."*
Square #1: Somebody's "right"; somebody's "wrong." Nobody
wants to take the *blame*. Both people hate being responsible. Therefore, our partners are to blame for our unhappiness in bed.

This is true in the bedroom, the dining room, the children's room
—every room in the house: Happiness is outside of us—it's *his* responsibility to make me happy, she thinks; it's *her* responsibility to
make me happy, he thinks. And this kind of thinking, we have seen,
is irresponsible.

Irresponsible people don't feel separate. People living together a
long time are, therefore, less likely than strangers, who have just met,
to feel sexy. That's the quintessential attraction between people:
Feeling separate. Feeling free.

The truth of this proposition is graphically revealed in bad sex.

Each party feels responsible for the other; each experiences paralyzing accommodation anxiety; each hates the blame of sexual failure. And yet both solemnly attest to the good neighbor policy of doing unto others as they would have them do unto you. It doesn't work since other people's happiness isn't your responsibility.

Fortunately, most everyone has experienced good sex. If God has anything better to offer, He kept it for Himself. But God, of course, simply gives us the means to be happy. And since feeling free is at the bottom of being happy, anyone who wants to be happy in bed, feels free to focus on his own happiness in the sack.

Bad sex is the best example of the "irresponsibility" of feeling responsible for others: Good sex is where your pleasure is mine and mine is yours. It's the fusion of two separate personalities and the sole event in life when people feel *complete*.

(a) *"I care about pleasing myself in bed."*
(b) *"I'm concerned about pleasing my mate in bed."*
     Remember, caring is not to worry:

CARING	CONCERN
"I care about pleasing myself."	"I'm concerned my mate have a good time."
"I want to make love."	"I need to make love."
"Good sex is a question of losing control of myself."	"I'm concerned I'll lose control of my feelings."
"I care about 'making it.'"	"I worry I won't."
"I care about showing consideration."	"I'm concerned I'm not considerate."
"I show my feelings about bad sex."	"I worry about showing my feelings about bad sex."
"Sex is necessary and nice."	"Sex is neither nice nor necessary."
"Sex is the most important thing in life."	"Sex is number fourteen on my list."

Men rank sex Number 1; most women rank it in the midteens somewhere after leisure reading and before needlepointing. Clearly women, in the main, are more concerned than caring if they rank sex so low.

The key to this massive discrepancy between the sexes about sex is the inability of either gender to come to terms with pleasure. People are confused: Men focus on performance and giving pleasure; women focus on being pleasured and being overcome. A man "feels responsible" to "make" his wife; a wife "feels responsible" being made. To a great extent, women must feel "forced" to consummate in sex. Thus, men feel responsible for forcing them, being the performer while women are performed upon: Neither approach is being responsible to the self. Wives: Let go and take responsibility for your own feelings! Husbands: Wake up and quit taking responsibility for your wives' feelings! That's the sexual revolution of the future.

(a) *"Good sex is characteristic of happiness."*
(b) *"The sex is great but the marriage is terrible."*
    Answers: (a) True
                (b) False

Good sex is a consequence of becoming separate. Bad sex or no sex is associated with the merely married. Now, true, married folk function within marriages where there is no sex or bad sex. But happiness? No way. Happiness is feeling free and separate with whom we live. But in sexual congress, as our forefathers said, the pleasure is in feeling transfigured and inseparate. It's the supreme activity in life which allows us to give up the burden of selfhood; the only time men and women feel complete.

The loss of self, "the small death," is the whole point. And it's precisely those who feel separate who are likely to experience the best sex. Inseparated and unfree people have no "self" to give up!

There is no way to have good sex and a "bad" marriage; no way to have "bad" sex or no sex and be happy.

(a) *"Working wives make sexy women."*
(b) *"Working couples are too tired for good sex."*
Self-esteem is the root of sexual potency. Two people in bed to-

gether who like themselves and each other could learn to have good sex; two people in bed together who don't like themselves or each other are bound to have bad sex.

Thus, if a working wife increases her self-esteem by having a job, it follows her good opinion of the self could spill over into bed. But if she dislikes her job, needs to work rather than wants to, and feels work is a burden, it's bound to have an effect in the bedroom: The same with working men.

Working people make money; sometimes lots of money. Money is power and people who feel they have power over their own lives, as we said in the late, unlamented sixties, might feel empowered to take responsibility for their own sexual pleasure.

The good news about working couples is that they make more money. Making money at work we like is certain to increase our self-esteem. It might improve our sex life. But the bad news is that it works in reverse, too: a bad job (or no job) and scut wages (or unearned earnings) often destroy self-esteem. And that might money-wrench our sex life.

Fatigue isn't the issue. Working wives too tired for good sex, working husbands too tired to have sex, are the excuses working couples use to back off sex with each other. Dog-tired partners who burn out in the sack, burn out not because they are both working, but because they have stopped *feeling*.

Working couples spread themselves mighty thin (See *Money [and Time] Management*). Having sex is "wasting time." But finding time to diaper baby, meet weekly production deadlines, and go to Grandma's for Sunday supper and not find time for a good lay in the hay is absurd. To be too tired for pleasure is a violation of human nature.

Another reason the husbands of working wives who properly put good sex Number 1, want to pitch in and keep house. And frequent travel, separation, and obverse working hours don't destroy sex between working couples. (Indeed, crazy hours can contribute.) Regularity of sexual expression (anathema to free spirits) is a bore. Regularized sexual expression vaccinates people against pleasure: They don't feel separate. And feeling free is quintessential. This means playing at sex and not taking it seriously: Don't perceive it as an obligation to fulfill (men) or endure (women) but as the apex of human involvement: The activity you most want to do.

(a) *"I hate it if my wife shows sexual interest in other men."*
(b) *"I hate it if my husband is attracted to another woman."*

Husbands hate play-around wives. A working wife who finds sexual happiness with another man reveals—as nothing else—her husband's impotence. Lady Chatterley found in the arms of the gamekeeper a lot more than in the arms of her husband. Why wouldn't any healthy woman who cares about the self grab for happiness elsewhere?

Irresponsible?

Hardly. Every man and woman must take responsibility for his or her own sexual happiness. It takes two to have sex: A major reason why so many people unfulfilled in marriage play around outside of it.

Jealousy is your early warning system, your emotional radar which reveals your own impotence. It's nature's clever way of telling you to shape up. Ah, but it's more complicated (everything is much more complex).

Question: Why does Jack feel potent with Jill and impotent with his wife, Jane?

Question: Why does Jane feel competent with Jake but not her husband, Jack?

Answer: Neither feels free. Separate. Each feels responsible for the other. Another reason infidelity causes so much guilt. It gives so much pleasure feeling separate and free with another.

Solution: Give up feeling responsible for your partner's pleasure. Focus on your own.

Most married men step out on their wives because they can't get it up at home and/or their wives can't get it off. They feel impotent. Any man who cares about the self is going to look around; any wife who cares about herself is going to ask herself why he is looking around. Both are going to talk about it (See *Real Talk*). And if they value the pleasure of each other's company, they see a therapist. And if they don't, they file for divorce.

The changing sexual ethic makes married people especially attractive to single people who hate the "hassle" of emotional affairs. Married people have mates to go home to; the hairy involvement between a man and a woman is avoided. And plenty of single people have the attitude that the opposite sex is good for only one thing. Sex, yes; involvement, no. Thus, the opportunities for extramarital high jinks are immeasurably augmented by the "times." Another reason no man or woman is safely married.

(a) *"Working couples are likely to play around on the job."*
(b) *"Don't dip your quill in the company ink."*

The late Margaret Mead observed that the destructive politics of on-the-job sex makes the incest taboo in the work place all the more important. "Thou shalt not play around with thy working brethren" is good advice.

Organizations can't regulate sexual activity; but working people can regulate themselves. The sexual integration of the work force makes the incest taboo all the more important. Sex rears its head wherever men and women meet: But working couples are often confused about the consequences of sexual expression associated with the job and the steep price people pay who play sexual politics.

Working people perform a task; they are a task force. Task forces are like families. Brother and sister go *outside* the family to find sex; working couples leave the organizational perimeter and go home to do the same.

To ignore the incest taboo, accounts for the outcry among working women (sexual harassment), the working man's lament (sexual entrapment), and general grumbling from working stiffs on the line (sexual politics). So it's high time to take into account the price of double-crossing Mother Nature.

An aspect of tough jobs is how emotionally involved we often become in doing the job. Often on the job we invest the self while at home, we hold back. The consequence is that at work we are open, vulnerable and effective, and at home, we are closed, defensive and unintimate. Accordingly, our defenses being down at work, a colleague easily captures the castle. He falls in love with his secretary; she falls in love with her special assistant.

So, yes, working couples are more susceptible in some ways to sexual politics on the job. All the more reason to remember the incest taboo.

(a) *"Sexual infidelity is less likely among working couples."*
(b) *"Sexual infidelity is more likely among working couples."*

Many working men cheat on their wives; increasingly, working wives are stepping out on their husbands: It's the unadmitted reason lots of men don't want their wives to work.

Double-income marriages undermine the double standard. Fair is fair: If Jack takes up with Jill, why shouldn't his wife, Jane, take up with Jake? The motto of the sexual revolution is, "If it feels good, *do* it!" All of which is a far cry from the Seventh Commandment.

Sexual expression is natural. Marriage is the normal means to satisfy sexual appetite. But marriage no more guarantees a good sex life than taking a job guarantees job satisfaction. So, if you aren't getting any love at home, it's natural to look for it on the job.

Dilemma: If sexual expression is normal but sexual infidelity wrong, how can a frustrated wife or husband be happy? The way to break dilemmas is to transcend them: Rise above what is right or wrong. Focus on the *consequences* of your actions or inactions.

Plainly, working couples who play around outside marriage feel impotent inside it. Even couples who think about it and don't do anything about it are saying to themselves, "I'm not getting what I want out of this marriage." But if we say this *only* to ourselves and not the person we live with, we are being irresponsible to the self. An important consequence of playing around is the enormous resentment it causes in our mates.

Sexual exclusivity is a condition of married life. Working couples who loathe their feelings of jealousy toward the "other" man or woman, are crazy, but this craziness is natural. To feel otherwise ("He is free," or "She can see who she wants.") destroys our sense of self-esteem. We think we are being tolerant, open, sensible, and modern when we are really being self-defeating. Married types who are not sexually exclusive eliminate the self from the sexual equation.

The point is to expect feelings of jealousy in your marriage, and arouse it in your mate. But to *deliberately* try to raise your spouse's envy quotient is unacceptable. To insist your spouse conduct himself so he won't feel jealous is absurd. So, if we conduct ourselves with opposite-sex members so *as not* to arouse the jealousy of our mates (or flaunt our sexuality in order to arouse it), neither action is free.

Free is the state of mind which says, "My wife attracts men like honey does bees"; "My husband is the sexiest dude in town." No wonder other men and women envy you. You live dangerously! But catch your mate stepping out on you, then raise the roof.

Does anyone over the age of thirteen believe we can possess some-one sexually and not arouse jealousy? Well, you probably believe the moon is made of green cheese. And does anyone think—still, in the eighties—that attractive, self-possessed, and successful people won't attract opposite-sex admirers? Well, if so, we believe there are politicians who never told a lie.

Facts are facts. To be married to someone who neither attracts (nor is attracted to) the opposite sex is a fantastic assumption.

We hang on one horn of the dilemma: For her to say to her husband, "It's wrong of you to sit under the apple tree with anyone but me," and for him to say to her, "Wife, obey thy husband," is crazy if neither is putting out in bed. If he can't get it up and she get it on —if both play sexual politics rather than play at sex with each other —it's a malfunction. And it's normal to look elsewhere for our pleasure.

Two people leading full lives outside the home are going to have arithmetically more contacts with attractive men and women than traditional marriages. But infidelity is a product not of a working couple's marriage but something dysfunctional in each partner.

(a) *"Working wives are subject to sexual harassment on the job."*
(b) *"Working husbands are subject to sexual entrapment."*

ITEM: His company wants him to represent it at the annual conference in San Juan. He invites his attractive special assistant to accompany him at the organization's expense. It's made clear her nominal function (conference delegate) disguises her real role (prostitute). And if she doesn't take a dive—good jobs are hard to find—her last duty (working for him) is finding her replacement. Sexual harassment.

Such a proposition is an intolerable violation of her freedom and the incest taboo. It's simple coercion. And her options: (a) Going to *his* boss and charging sexual harassment; (b) refusing his proposal; and (c) reasoning with the dummy—could lead in the end to her exiting from the organization and scouting up another job. A fourth option, a law suit, is expensive, time-consuming and requires proof.

Oh yes, there is another possibility; she genuinely digs the guy and considers a Puerto Rican trip and the pleasure of his company another company perk.

So there might be more at stake here than coercion and play-for-pay. But even if she's his *willing* tool, it's still prostitution. And even platonic relationships give the *appearance* of sexual complicity. No working person can forget that appearances are everything; smart politicians don't travel *alone* with opposite-sex assistants; savvy managers sexually recreate off the company turf.

ITEM: His attractive Special Assistant makes a down payment on an ocean-front condominium and is having difficulty making the mortgage. He hand-carries her new position description (Executive Special Assistant) through Personnel, establishing a substantial raise in pay. It's understood her boss is the only overnight guest at the upcoming housewarming. Sexual entrapment.

Sexually *macha* conduct is confusing the bedroom with the board room. Macha women dress to seduce in order to succeed. And when her working sisters become aware that the way to the top in this place is on their backs, there's hell to pay. Sexual entrapment, like sexual harassment, is simple coercion. It's an unacceptable violation of the incest taboo. Both actions are blackmail. And it wrecks people's sex lives: If we must pay for sex (or make people pay) it destroys self-esteem, which is the essence of sexual potency.

A much more common (very *common*) violation of the incest taboo is the mindless mashing working wives suffer at the hands of *macho* associates. Every woman needs to cultivate one doggone, knock-out obscenity to upgrade her second strike capability. The instant after a clumsy forward pass, a verbal karate-chop delivered in the company of other males, powerfully concentrates a man's focus on his work rather than his workmate.

Observing the incest taboo is avoiding Big Trouble. Making

others aware of it, too, is every working person's responsibility
trick is avoiding not only the act of sexual complicity but its app
ance.

(a) *"My husband often thinks sex is his doing me a favor."*
(b) *"My wife often makes sex conditional on something else."*

Conditional sex is bound to be bad; unconditional sex is likely to
be good! In the first, people's attitude is absurd. Engaging in sex is
never extending someone else a favor; it's something people do for
the self. Otherwise, sexual involvement between marrieds is prostitution.

A whore is a person who allows you to take your pleasure after ex-
acting payment but takes no pleasure in you. To hold the self back
from taking pleasure in sex is being irresponsible to the self and
shows no consideration to your partner.

There are no happy men in whorehouses: They have taken *their*
pleasure but are denied the joy of sharing it.

Therapy, the Uses of

"What has confession taught you about men?" "Oh, confession teaches nothing, you know, because when a priest goes into the confessional, he becomes another person—grace and all that. And yet. . . . First of all, people are much more unhappy than one thinks . . . and then. . . ."
"And then, the fundamental fact is that there's no such thing as a grown-up person."

ANDRÉ MALRAUX, *Anti-Memoirs*

"I think anyone who sees a therapist is crazy."

"The object of therapy is to help me grow up."

"The object of therapy is to save the marriage."

"The best therapy is simply to choose another life style."

"God is my therapist."

"The rocks in his head fill the holes in hers."

"My father's an alcoholic and so's my husband."

"My mother's a hypochondriac and so's my wife."

"Therapy is useful to divorced people who want to try a second time."

"Therapy will make me hate myself."

"I shopped around until I found the help I wanted."

"Therapy is too tough."

"I think anyone who sees a therapist is crazy."

Crazy people don't ask for help: Therapists can't help them. That's why they dose them with Thorazine. Working couples who aren't crazy but simply unhappy are crazy not to hire a therapist to figure out what's wrong. See a therapist before you get a divorce; especially if you decide to divorce.

"The object of therapy is to help me grow up."

That's right. And that means you want to change.

Personal change is tough. But being miserable is worse. And everyone needs courage: The courage to love. So a therapist will:

Help you want to change (in desire begins responsibility).

Help you find the courage (nobody can change alone).

Help you cope with the guilt of changing (remember, as we become free, we feel pleasure).

Help you redefine responsibility (to yourself, not to others).

Help you co-operate with reality (therapy establishes reality and how you can shape it).

Help you recognize that part of reality is inside your own head (attitude is everything).

"The object of therapy is to save the marriage."

The object of therapy is to save yourself. That might mean filing for divorce. Marriage is abstract; people are real. The point in therapy is to help you change and learn to co-operate with reality. Its main object is the self. So, forget your responsibility to the Marriage; (it might be your sense of responsibility to it which is causing you to turn off). The way to measure how well you are doing in therapy is evaluating how much more effective you are on the job, in bed, and with other people.

One of therapy's purposes is to help you talk with your partner. Real talk. And married types can't talk too much with each other.

Therapy simply improves the view from the room which is your own. Thus, many marriages needn't end in divorce. But if only one partner uses a therapist, it could end the marriage. When marriages crumble, it's rarely one person's fault. Believing we are *not* at fault is another reason marriages crumble!

Nagging your husband to see a therapist doesn't work. Men often dig in their heels! Therapists are seen as rivals. Husbands become quite nasty about it. His jealousy might be a sign of impotence. "Why does she love him and not me?" an irate husband roars.

Impotence—our inability to feel—is as common to women as men. And impotence isn't just sexual. But if a marriage isn't working, impotence can't help being sexual. So, the best way to persuade a man to see a shrink is to ask him whether he can get it up with his wife. And the best way to persuade a woman to see a psychiatrist is to ask her whether she gets it off with her husband. And if neither do, it's time for therapeutic help.

"The best therapy is simply to choose another life style."

Change the externals of life. Slip off that old snake skin: Take up macramé, jogging, macrobiotics, speed read, eat yogurt, swap spouses, run for Congress, pop greenies, have an affair, read the Great Books, move to California, compose haiku.

It isn't therapy. And it doesn't work to change outwardly if you don't change inwardly. It's why many people love to travel: Movement, they think, means change. But they are simply putting old wine into new bottles. What they want to change is not their environment but themselves. And that's the point of therapy.

Futurists are convinced we must cope with the "change" taking place in our environment. But there is not so much change taking place as motion. And the way to cope with motion is not to look outward at our fast-changing landscape of "life styles," but inward to what is free and real in our own character. That's where therapy helps.

If human behavior today seems fast-changing and "value-free," if everything goes and all conduct is relative, that's not a problem of our culture but of liberty. Liberty is an adventure in self-exploration.

And until we come to terms with our own freedom, we are bound to capitulate to "movement."

An underlying and unconscious force causing this change, something as American as apple pie, and hardly recognizable, is the assumption that *there is no death.* Americans are uncomfortable contemplating death; death is the admission of personal failure. It's un-American.

Coming to terms with our mortality, welcoming rather than fighting the passage of time, and understanding that every dog has his day is co-operating with reality. When we shed our wives and husbands, hop from one job to the next, pick up this year's craze (est and jogging) and lay them down to embrace next trends (bocci ball and lemon yogurt), you can bet your second mortgage you have mislaid the vital center of your life.

Thus, changing a job, divorcing your wife or husband, and moving to a new city, is painfully illusory. We sense we can free ourselves from the past by travel, drugs, new friends, a different career, and sudden celebrity. But it's all a sham and a delusion. Our environment is altered. Our character isn't shed.

Everyone thinks movement changes them. But deep down inside, people realize that while the externals of life might change (more money, another husband, a bigger house, politer children, a better wardrobe) the internals of life (our hidebound character) remain the same. Don't double-cross Mother Nature.

Good fortune drives by and gives us a lift and people go into a purple funk. Whether elected to Congress, a beneficiary of a large inheritance, promoted on the job, a lot of people go to bed with the blahs. Why should good fortune cause unhappiness? Well, our wildest dreams have come true: Our environment has changed but we haven't. No wonder we are in a depression.

Dame Fortune and Mother Nature are the wicked stepmothers of unhappiness. The first gives us a lift; the second gives us a kick in the derriere. Why? *Nothing important has changed.* We still lug around a weak ego, a poor spirit, a fixed character.

The greatest gift God gave men and women was freedom. God is perfect freedom, and "thus God's work is truly our own" (Kennedy). Our job is to use our freedom. St. Paul might have found enlightenment on the road to Damascus. And people today might find instant enlightenment in drugs, born-again Christianity, and primal scream. But true enlightenment is neither instant nor easy nor complete—read the saints and poets.

"God is my therapist."

God is your Creator. But, why, when we talk to God, is it prayer and when God talks to us, it's schizophrenia (Lily Tomlin). If God answers our prayers, that's when our real problems begin!

My point is that we are *free* to be who we want to be. God is freedom. But we can't be free alone. So, if you have a strong belief in God, you might not need therapy. And if you don't, well, you might need a therapist. And if you both believe in God and are in therapy, well, Jesus Christ on Sunday and Sigmund Freud on Thursday afternoon is just the ticket.

"The rocks in his head fill the holes in hers."

The hidden attraction between opposites.

"My wife loves taking care of me, and I like being taken care of."

That's the hidden attraction. But it's not hidden from a therapist. What man didn't like his mother taking care of him? But a man no longer needs a woman to take care of him. Indeed, men might not know it consciously but they feel it subconsciously: They hate being dependent. So, they might unconsciously hate their wives (who take care of them).

Moreover, many women love nurturing men; anatomy is destiny. But working wives grow mighty tired, mighty fast, being depended upon: Wives hate being responsible. Thus, they might unconsciously hate their husbands who need taking care of. But it's not each other they hate: What each hates is the dependency.

Plenty of people marry (and stay married) because the rocks in his head fill the holes in hers. And these marriages "work" so long as neither wants to change. But if she changes, he wakes up ten years later and finds a stranger in his bed. The rocks in his head no longer fill the holes in hers.

"My father's an alcoholic and so's my husband."

A wife whose father was a boozer might marry an alcoholic. Maybe it's momism. "If my mom loved my dad," she thinks, "dad would have stayed on the wagon. I'll show my mom what a woman's love means." So she marries Jake, who laces his scotch with brandy. The rocks in her head fill the holes in his.

Nobody wants to live with a juice head. But therapy helps a woman who is continually drawn to boozing males.

"My mother's a hypochondriac and so's my wife."

What happens when she stops hitting the Geritol bottle and starts hitting the job market? No longer the successful sickie, now she's the successful executive. And what about hubby? Well, he no longer feels needed; he's probably checking out two or three "needy" women this minute.

"Therapy is useful to divorced people who want to try a second time."

And people coming out of traumatic marriages want help. Therapy is useful to everybody at any time unless they are really crazy and don't know they need help. This is the chief reason forty-seven percent of remarriages fail. We change partners, but we don't change the self. Know thyself. Why are you attracted to *this* type of woman and not *that?* Why are you carried forward by a force you can't comprehend? Why are you doomed to repeat the mistakes of the past?

You can't know the self *alone.* So, if you are coming out of one marriage or are about to embark on another, hire a shrink. It doesn't mean you won't marry your intended; it means you will now learn the *reasons* for your *intentions.*

"Therapy will make me hate myself."

Only that part of your character no longer real. Used up.

Continue the list, the list of dirty secrets about the self people have difficulty admitting in themselves, much less confronting in their partners:

 Bellyaching

Boozing
Burping
Crying
Dumb questions
Evasive answers
Hacking
Itching
Procrastinating
Pulling
Snarling
Whining
Worrywarting

The list, taking all marriages in sum, is obviously endless. Un-OK conduct. Unacceptable. Intolerable. Compulsive.

Compulsive actions are what you seemingly can't help doing. You feel forced to do what you do. Helpless. But, as a matter of fact, you have a free will. You can change the self with the help of a therapist.

"I shopped around until I found the help I wanted."

It's important to find the kind of therapist who helps you. And everyone is different: Different strokes for different folks. A list of what to keep in mind when you go shopping for help follows:

(1) *Should my therapist be a man or a woman?*

That's up to you. Gender isn't as important as skill. How effective is this person in helping you change? And who cares if your therapist is a Freudian, Adlerian, or Jungian?

(2) *Should my therapist be married?*

Again, so what? A thrice divorced therapist might be better than another therapist who is married. The point is to find out if this person is interested in saving you or the marriage. The best therapists simply help you save yourself. Avoid "marriage counselors" who have the opposite view.

(3) *Is group therapy recommended?*

It's always educational to see other working couples in the same bind as you. And it's cheaper. Group therapy beats no therapy.

(4) What should I check out?

Does the therapist have the skill to help you? Does this person both listen *and* talk and insist you take responsibility for your own life. Rely on other working couples who have gone into therapy.

(5) How often should I go?

Every day. Every week. Every month. Obviously, the more you go, the more progress you make. Most people don't go enough or long enough. Yes, a *little* therapy helps everybody a *little* bit. But the biggest disappointment for therapists is that everyone wants to be *just a little bit* happier on the job, in bed, and with other people. But really happy? Hardly. Feeling free, really free, scares people.

(6) When should I stop?

Maybe never; maybe next week. Many people go in and out of therapy depending on what they are getting out of life. Nobody graduates from therapy—cured: completely happy.

(7) What should I talk to my therapist about?

Well, start with mom and go on from there.

(8) What about myself?

That's the point of therapy—the self. But plenty of people show enormous resistance to changing themselves. They would much rather change their mothers! The reason we resist personal change is that we hesitate to give up our defenses. Therapy demonstrates that our defenses no longer "work."

(9) Are therapists nothing but surrogate spouses?

No, although the way you act with them often makes them seem so. Therapists show you how you oppress the self. Men don't oppress women; it's their mothers who do. Women don't oppress men; it's their mothers! A good therapist helps you understand your problem might not be your spouse so much as your mother.

(10) Are therapists the parents we never had?

Most people had "good enough" parents. But therapists are the good mother and father we wish we had all of the time. At $65 an hour they should be.

(11) Should both of us go to the same therapist?

If so, go separately at first. Then you might try going together. Otherwise going to different therapists is workable. It depends on what both of you *want*. And which arrangement *works*.

"Therapy is too tough."

Tough, yes. Too tough, no.

Let's examine why:

(1) *"I can't help the way I am!"*

Yes you can.

You can't give up smoking—unless you hate it.

You can't lose weight—unless you hate it.

Feeling that our hateful characteristics are our Character means we need therapy. A compulsive character trait (his need to dominate his wife) or a hateful character trait (her need to be dependent and resentful) is something each wants to change: He doesn't want to dominate his wife; she doesn't want to be dominated. Neither feels free to do otherwise.

A way to start helping ourselves is to start hating characteristics we despise in ourselves. Substitute another action in its place. It's tough. But it's much worse not changing.

(2) *"Therapy is too slow."*

People take three steps forward and slip back two. But to go faster would destroy us. Personal growth wasn't meant to be fast. Enlightenment isn't instant. And it's interminable: Nobody is too free.

(3) *"I don't want to give up the real me."*

Nobody wants to lose his identity. Terrifying.

Giving up habits of mind or action which no longer work causes people to think they are losing their character. What we are giving up is our unreal characteristics. What we find is our real self. Thus, in therapy, we are not giving up our identity so much as finding it.

(4) *"I'm a creature of circumstances."*

We can't give up being the Victim.

To do so, would be to acknowledge our freedom. Feeling miserable, being a victim, means we are not responsible for our happiness. Self-contempt. And our self-hatred is rooted in our refusing to admit our freedom.

Scary, this idea of freedom. "Gee, I could be happy with my husband." But to do so, she needs to give up being happy in her unhappiness. "Gee, I really love my wife." But to do so means he must quit feeling victimized.

Changing our character, means hating certain characteristics we want to change. The process of changing often means you feel free. "Why," we ask ourselves, "don't I always act this way?"

If a working wife goes after an assignment she wants (and lands it), she feels enormous pleasure. And rage. She becomes furious with herself for always putting herself second and pushing other people for promotions and assignments she wanted.

A working man, who learns how to delegate authority, often grows angry with himself for having squandered the best years of his working life trying to oversee everything himself. He feels like the world's biggest dope.

Well, rage when it has nowhere to go except against ourselves becomes depression. The blahs. Another reason why becoming the person we want to be is so tough.

But keep in mind that personal change must be slow. If it happened overnight and not over a lifetime it could cause a rage so intense we would kill ourselves. No fooling. So, therapy is tough (our resistance), slow (otherwise it would destroy us) and interminable (nobody is ever too happy).

Author, an Afterword from the

I do my thing and you do your thing.
I am not in this world to live up to your expectations,
And you are not in the world to live up to mine.
You are you and I am I,
And if by chance we find each other, it's beautiful.
If not, it can't be helped.

FREDERICK S. PERLS

For the duration of our time together, patient reader, I have been a bully: I've told you to change your attitude, ordered you to take responsibility for the *self*(!), commanded you to look inward instead of outward and all the rest. Indeed, I'm in jeopardy of becoming another prescriptive, mother-loving, rule-maker; maybe even an "expert."

There's a difference between writers and readers: Writers always have the last word. But as is evident by now there is no last word on the subject of the self. And it's yourself this book has been about. My main purpose was to start you talking first to the self and then to the person you live with. And neither of you will have the last word!

The intent has been to repeat a few general themes (but always in a different context) using various octaves. One theme was the decline of the traditional and the rise of the money marriage: The old order giveth away and the new order is having trouble finding the zipper to its fly. My hope is that this book has been in touch with the real world of double-digit inflation, serial monogamy, and the painful tradeoffs between tough love/tough jobs. Any working person interrupted in the middle of a crucial meeting by a telephone call telling him that his three-year-old has fallen down the stairs and broken his collar bone or that his fifteen-year-old tried to join the Marines, knows about both.

That's why I saved the good part for last.

The apt quote you read at this chapter's beginning is the signature of the money marriage. But many people forget the last line:

"If not, it can't be helped."

And some things in life can't be helped. Everybody is dealt a few jokers before his term is run; the last card being death itself. Unfair. We may live like men, but we die like dogs (Hemingway):

ITEM: A working couple, neighbors of mine, attended Sunday church service with their two children and returned home to find their home burned to the ground.

ITEM: Another couple, long-time friends indeed, took their ailing eight-year-old to the doctor who diagnosed meningitis.

ITEM: Still another couple, on their way home late one Saturday night, were blindsided in their sedan by a teenager in a panel truck and spent the next six months in and out of hospitals.

Hanging tough.

But the spirit prevaileth.

The first couple has a new house—the community and church pitched in and saw them through the worst. In the second case, thanks to a good doctor and loving care, their eight-year-old is now a vigorous thirteen-year-old. And in the third instance, due to sheer grit, both are ambulatory, working and moving North to new jobs.

My point is that tough love—married love—helped these three couples say "yes" to life when life said "no." Dealt a joker, everyone with a great spirit (and who is married to someone with spirit, too) is going to play with the pain better than other people with weak spirits.

Tough love is the greatest security in the world.

Catastrophes, crises and disappointments strengthen the spirit. Moreover, tough love helps people cope with anxiety, imagined fears and unreality, too. And co-operating with reality—the pleasure and pain—is tough love; an "I" and "Thou" marriage.

What needs repeating is how responsibility, as I define it, contributes to people's happiness: Nobody is responsible for yourself except the self. But what hasn't been said (because I saved the good part for last) is that people who take care of themselves are able to help others do the same. People learn by example.

Ah, but the culture! The culture says, "Let society take care of you." But a person who lets other people take care of him is self-defeating; a person who works for others and not for the self is ineffectual. Impotent.

Impotence is the elimination of the self in love and work and with other people; potency is *willingly* loving and working with other people. A far-seeing social policy takes into account everybody's right to pursue (or not pursue) happiness. But policy makers themselves must give up feeling responsible for people and let everybody become response-able. That's anathema to people educated to take care of others. But it's essentially what ails society. "Let me take care of you," is the motto of government, schools, corporations and movements. But the price is people's self-esteem. Take away people's self-esteem—pride—and society has the people in its power.

Freedom is what everyone wants. The enemy of freedom is a culture which erodes people's ability to be responsible. Society, thus, promotes impotence; other people are made responsible for our happiness. Accordingly, sound social policy promotes everyone taking care of the self. The payoff is pride. And people's pride would revive a love of country which would warm the heart of Nathan Hale.

Finally, I satisfied one goal in writing this book, i.e., never using the word "relationship." People who have no more to say about their relationships never shut up. And the very least people can do who have nothing more to say is to shut up (Lehrer). Well, I've had my say and now it's time for you to do the talking.

Index

DICK IRISH is vice-president and co-founder of TransCentury Corporation, a Washington, D.C.–based management consulting firm and a vice-president of Career Planning Consultants, Inc., in Charlottesville, Virginia. For twelve years he has specialized in international executive search. For the past eight years, he has been on the lecture circuit and conducted clinics for job seekers and employers alike on the whole employment process. Recently, Dick has given workshops on the two-paycheck family. He is the author of *Go Hire Yourself an Employer* and *If Things Don't Improve Soon, I May Ask You To Fire Me!* Dick and his wife, Sally, were Peace Corps Volunteers in the early sixties; afterwards Sally served as social secretary to Ethel Kennedy and then managed a day-care center. Currently, she is self-employed and designs needlepoint canvases. Dick and Sally Irish live in northern Virginia near Middleburg, Virginia.